Tradition and Life in the Church

Tradition and Life in the Church

Essays and Lectures in Church History

HANS VON CAMPENHAUSEN

PROFESSOR OF ECCLESIASTICAL HISTORY
IN THE UNIVERSITY OF HEIDELBERG

Translated by A. V. Littledale

FORTRESS PRESS   PHILADELPHIA

Tradition und Leben—Kräfte der Kirchengeschichte
© Hans Frieherr von Campenhausen
and J. C. B. Mohr (Paul Siebeck), Tübingen 1960

In addition to the essays translated here, the original German edition (see
above) included five further essays:
1 The Reformation Self-consciousness and Historical Consciousness in
Luther 1517-1522
2 God's Judgement and Man's Righteousness in Luther
3 The Problem of Images in the Reformation
4 Karl Jaspers and the Philosophical Critique of Christianity
5 Christian Joy

This edition first published 1968
English translation by A. V. Littledale
© in the English translation by William Collins Sons & Co. Ltd., London
and Fortress Press, Philadelphia 1968

Library of Congress Catalog Card Number 68-27859

Printed in Great Britain
Collins Clear-Type Press, London and Glasgow

Contents

Abbreviations

back quite evidently to the religious ethos of Christianity and its original faith. Here arose nearly all the Western world's fundamental questions relating to the philosophy of history. The philosophy of history is, viewed historically, the offspring of the theology of history, just as much as our modern 'world history' has demonstrably grown up out of Church history. Consequently, it is worth while to investigate here the original form of the problem of tradition and spirit; for it is interesting as a prototype precisely in its earliest Christian form, as opposed to its historical development. Later thorough and intensive theological inquiry took the problem further, and as is generally the case, discovered and prepared the ground for corresponding solutions. However, any attempt to transpose reflections of a theological nature into general philosophical, historical, sociological and psychological considerations would generally serve only to deaden their impact and force, and would result in the loss of the system of relationships and productive ideas, and so blur and truncate the whole.

In this connection further difficulties make themselves felt. It may be asked how far a philosophy of history which rejects the concept of the Christian revelation can possibly reach its goal with theological formulations and concepts, transposed, indeed, but firmly adhered to. On the other hand, it may also be asked how the Christian faith in its authentic form is still capable of dealing with the problems relating to the world and history which arise from a widened intellectual vision. The detailed considerations which follow are not intended to provide an answer. They are proposed as purely exegetical and historical. They are meant to be understood solely as a considered presentation of the early Christian consciousness of history and its aim. This was still exclusively theological. The entire body of political, social, intellectual, and cultural conclusions which were the eventual result of the original religious impulse and which expanded or burst its framework, lies wholly outside the early Christian field of vision. Consequently, the tradition we are concerned with does not have as its function the transposition or renovation of intellectual and social life, but solely the renewal of human existence before and through God. And the spirit through which this is achieved must be understood in this context always as the 'holy' Spirit, who determines the moral life of the faithful from the standpoint of God. History itself is the sphere of the divine action; it is, by its very nature, 'salvation history' and not the realm of immanent human ends and aims, as it was envisaged by unbelievers. But it is made such, not simply through a corresponding religious mode of contemplation, but concretely through the event of divine revelation. This in the narrower sense is thereby limited to quite distinct spheres and lines of development of world history. The whole of world history is articulated and summarized by revelation in its own way in that it is both related to it and split by it. This characteristically theological, archaic view of things must always be borne in mind, if what follows, with its precise definitions, is not to be misconceived from the start.

The problem of tradition and spirit is intrinsically historical. It originates from the passage of time and seeks its solution within time. The present is confronted with the question of its position in regard to past tradition, while opting for a future which the spirit now demands and seizes upon. Those who, because of the defects, injustice, or sinfulness of the present generation, are pessimistic about its capacity to create something new and better, are glad to turn to the past. They seek out and shore up its supposedly 'eternal' values, ideals and norms. These are they who 'hold to tradition'. Those, on the other hand, who see before them new possibilities, duties, and aims, without doubting they can be attained, are prone to lay the blame for the existing imperfect state of things on warped views, false teaching, and worn-out traditions, which one must overcome in order to be freed for the future and enabled to achieve a better future. But those sceptics and pessimists who have no confidence at all in human nature, either in the past or in the present, or who, on the contrary, hold the present state to be more or less adequate and satisfactory, will, resigned or complacent, try to adapt themselves to the present and maintain it as it is. None of these attitudes is specifically Christian, but all three are intermingled in the original eschatological historical consciousness of Christianity and are there present in a higher unity, so that, with the disappearance of this unity, they are separated and set beside each other in opposition. Yet, without an understanding of the genuine unitary view of history, there is no possibility of understanding correctly the Christian faith and its relation to the world where all three, past, present and future, are involved and interrelated.

Christianity is a faith based on a complete definitive revelation for this world, the revelation, in fact, of the truth and justice of God for this world, the revelation given in Christ. It is and remains, therefore, a religion of the past and of a tradition that is always valid and cannot be superseded by anything else. But, in affirming this tradition, the Christian looks also towards the future, to the return of the Lord. With the passage of time Christ's will and Spirit have not yet attained dominion, and, in the world as it is, he will never attain it. Christians, however, have received, not the spirit of this world, but the spirit of the ultimate time, that is, of the kingdom of God, eternal, though still in the future. They live as beings oppressed and persecuted, in expectation of the coming victory, which they can do no more than await until God, in a new act, will bring about the new world and, with it, the 'end of present history'.

In the present, the Christian attitude is, therefore, in a peculiar way, at once pessimistic and optimistic, according to whether it has in view the existing 'world', which remains the world, or the promise, which is no less certain and for the Church is no longer merely future, for she has the spirit already. As the religion of the spirit, Christianity is the religion of the commencing fulfilment and realization of the dominion of Christ and of God in time. It is, therefore, at the same time, the religion of struggle, inasmuch as Christians have positively to fulfil God's will in the world, and the world, for its part, seeks to intervene insidiously, to penetrate into and to work in each individual heart. Thus the present time is one of a dramatic provisional state, which characterizes and demarcates the actual world history wherein the Christian lives and is obliged to live.

Hence there arise the manifold questions, pertinent today, of the relations between the Church and the world, but of which, despite their great importance, we will not now speak. For it is clear that the inquiry into the Christian tradition and its corresponding divine spirit is, as such, a purely intra-Church problem.

The inner meaning of the Christian idea of tradition can be understood only in its demarcation from Judaism; for it is within Judaism and in its separation from it that Christianity arose and, in a certain sense, continues to endure. Judaism also knew a complete, definitive and divine tradition, which was to rule the whole of life from God's standpoint and thereby bring salvation and life. This was the tradition of the law. In the Old Testament it possessed a divine revelation and a corresponding juridical, moral, and religious tradition, vastly different from anything the ancient world knew. It filled the Jews with understandable pride. Jesus also, and Paul and the later Christians—apart from a few offshoots that were soon rejected—acknowledged this divine revelation as such. They knew no other God than the God of Abraham, Isaac and Jacob, and for them too the Old Covenant was a real and authentic revelation of the holy will of this God. The criticism that Jesus levelled against the way it was taught and applied, the criticism of the law by precisely the most devout of its adherents among the Jews, did not in the least affect his fundamental affirmation of this law in itself. But that does not dispose of this other fact, that Jesus himself did not envisage the repentance and salvation of his people from a renewal and revitalizing of the piety and exigencies of the old law, but from an inner conversion, the far more radical effect of looking to the coming kingdom of God proclaimed by him. The way to this beginning was to be found, not in fresh endeavours, but in the unreserved forgiveness that he himself, in his personal 'power', pronounced on men's sins.

The infant Church provided the basic interpretation of this new thing that Jesus both signified and was, and raised the affirmation of it through the Spirit, who was the Spirit of the risen Christ, to the status of the 'new law' dominating her entire being. The old law, it was now stated, had become powerless to renew man and free him from the yoke of sin. Christ alone, through baptism and the spirit, gave his disciples a new being, one not brought about and merited by man, but received in pure faith and realized freely in love. Christ on the Cross satisfied the law once and for all. Henceforth, it belongs to the 'old', invalidated world. Christians are citizens of the coming kingdom of God, and as such may and must live a new, holy life of freedom. In Christ, therefore, a new tradition has been founded, by-passing the old tradition of the law, a tradition which obtains whenever it becomes known to man, and he receives, through this Gospel, the Holy Spirit and eternal salvation.

This brings out for us the enormous significance as well as the special religious quality of the Christian tradition. We come to participate in the new liberating power that Christ bestows only in so far as we hear of it, accept it, and are taken into the community and discipleship of his person. 'So faith comes by what is heard' (Rom. 10.17), and 'He who believes and is baptized will be saved' (Mark 16.16). It is all a matter, therefore, in Protestant but also biblical language, of the 'word', and this word is a genuine historical witness, and so, in a real sense, 'tradition'. It is not to be seen simply as an expression of the feeling and attitude to life present among Christians, so that, taken psychologically as 'mere word', it could be brought into the familiar liberal and romantic antithesis. Nor is it merely the imprinting of an eternal truth known in itself, so that it could then, by being taken in an idealist, philosophical sense, be brought into the equally familiar antithesis between such truth and the mere accidental truths of history. On the contrary, the word stands in an essential relation to an event not to be derived from any other, one determining the future as an act of God. It is precisely the event of the mission, death, and resurrection of Christ, which, by God's ordinance, has laid down and established the new tradition of grace and the Spirit over against the old tradition of the law.

Herein lies the essential difference in meaning of the proclamation and propagation of the Christian tradition from the whole previous tradition of the law. It is not there for the purpose of regulating life according to fixed norms, calling on the religious and moral forces in man, who has then to carry these into effect for his salvation. On the contrary, through Christ, and in Christ, everything has already been effected and fulfilled. Consequently, Christ's message comes to the hearer, not as a demand, but as a gift, which he has now only to assent to and accept, in that he commits himself to it, puts his faith in his being redeemed and sanctified, and, in this faith, receives the holy Spirit of God and lets this work. Through the Gospel that he believes, he is no more concerned with his own doing, but simply taken up, as it were, into the action of Christ that has already been accomplished.

It follows from this that the event of Christ cannot be simply a matter of the past, is not bound to the past like the law of Moses, but continues. It lives on, and works in the living oral proclamation. Christ is himself present in his community through the word, constantly assisting, admonishing, consoling, and forgiving. He is, therefore, in the New Testament, constantly and most strikingly represented by this saving word of his, and the 'Gospel', for its part, becomes a living, active, efficacious power which takes hold of men and potently transforms the world. 'And the name by which he is called is The Word of God' (Rev. 19.13). The bond with the word, which is what faith in the Gospel is, is thus a bond with the living Christ himself, and, just as he has already entered on eternal glory, so Christians also are already, through him, entitled to their heavenly country. The Spirit, whom faith has previously received, is the power bringing consummation at the end of time.

This intermingling of the two 'times' in the Church's life comes out with particular clarity in the ministration of the sacraments, which accompanies the preaching of the Gospel. Thus, in the celebration of the Eucharist, the community 'recalls', in a peculiar manner that renews its efficacy, the reality and the salvific meaning of the past death of Jesus on the Cross. At the same time, it anticipates the eternal feast of joy which awaits the redeemed at the end of time in the glory of the kingdom of God; and those who share in the Eucharist are offered the assurance that the Lord, risen from the dead, is now already directly in the midst of them.

Thus the circle of the times seems to be closed in the community of the faithful. The primal truth of the divine tradition lives in the ever-renewed proclamation of it and determines the faithful in their belief and conduct through the spirit, who is delivered to them along with this tradition, and is joined directly to it in that, in each new situation, he brings a new understanding of the meaning of redemption and sanctification, expounds it and gives it validity. But to take, as the whole reality, such a harmonious picture of the continuance of the Christian tradition and of the freedom of the spirit corresponding to it would be an illusion. The Christian community itself is not only in the world; the world too is active in it, as we have said. A falling away from its origins and a betrayal of them are possibilities that threaten constantly, and, with the invasion of an alien, hostile spirit of the world, the tradition itself is falsified, whenever this spirit gains the upper hand. Consequently, the pure tradition must be upheld against such falsifications, and the spirits active in the community must be continuously tested. And so there develops the inner struggle of the Church's history, in the concrete, of course, one of immense complexity and hardly to be separated from the external struggle with the world; though for the sake of simplicity, we leave it on one side for the moment.

What is the true tradition which proceeds from Christ and is the authorized way of making Christ a living presence to us today? Paul was already confronted with this question by the presence in Corinth of certain fanatics, who wished to sublimate the Resurrection by taking it as a 'purely spiritual' event present to them, and so to deprive the historical resurrection of its significance. In this situation he took the line of what history asserted, the line of tradition, as already in part described to him by the testimony handed down: 'Now I would remind you, brethren, in what terms I preached to you the gospel, which you received, in which you stand, by which you are saved, if you hold it fast . . . For I delivered to you as of first importance what I also received, that Christ died for our sins in accordance with the scriptures, that he was buried, that he was raised on the third day in accordance with the scriptures, and that he appeared to Cephas, then to the twelve. Then he appeared to more than five hundred brethren at one time' etc., until the final encounter, which Paul himself experienced and to which he testified (I Cor. 15.1ff.) In later times, with the increasing remoteness from the events, this contention was more and more strongly emphasized. To counter all the doubts and uncertainties that were bound to creep in, it was necessary to hold firmly to the original, 'apostolic' witness, as it came to be called, καθὼς παρέδοσαν ἡμῖν οἱ ἀπ'ἀρχῆς, αὐτόπται καὶ ὑπηρέται γενόμενοι τοῦ λόγου (Luke 1.2). This development ended with the formation of the canon of the New Testament, established from the middle of the second century.

This dispassionate inquiry into origins is what initiated the historical orientation of Christian thought towards the past, from which, in a long, involved, but necessary process, the whole of theology, as exegesis, dogmatic and Church history, has developed. Two considerations must here be emphasized, to show what is *not* meant by this concern with tradition. Firstly, the true aim of this preservation of tradition has never been, in the strict sense, simply historical. It is not a matter of transmitting the data of the past as such, but a matter, rather, of their reality as divinely-established data in the form in which they are proclaimed and play a decisive salvific role in the lives of the faithful. That already comes out in the brief formula employed by Paul, given by him as the content of the primal 'Gospel', that Christ died 'for our sins'[1]. Consequently, it is a question of the Christ

---

[1]The further addition 'according to the scriptures' represents the retrospective linking of the Christian message with the time of the Old Covenant, based on the 'prophecy'

preached, interpreted, and understood as the actual 'Gospel', of the Christ of the past as the Christ for our present, and the risen Lord of our future. Or expressed in another way, it is a question of the Christ-reality—in itself undoubted and necessary—as a Christ significant for us and determinant of us. It is this that makes for us today the purely factual elucidation of Christian origins so tremendously difficult and, to a certain extent, quite impossible. For we always find in the documents of the New Testament, even in the most ancient strata of the Gospels, a Christ interpreted, applied, and made relevant to the time; and this also accounts for the astonishing variations, often apparently contradictory, in the traditions, which at times have been already prolonged in one direction or another, accentuated, interpreted, expanded, or abbreviated.

This, however, is bound up with the second factor, which is that the evangelical character of the Christ-tradition evinces itself as opposed to any kind of legalistic tradition. It is not a question of individual words and acts of Jesus, which must be followed or imitated as prescriptions and exemplars of a positive law or an ideal norm; it is, rather, a matter of the recognition of what Jesus has done 'for our sins' and for us, so that we may 'believe', that is, understand, accept, and live thereby. This form of affirmation is only possible in freedom, and therefore requires a spirit that understands and assents to the significance of what has been done. In this respect, the Christ-tradition is present only for the Christ-spirit: 'Any one who does not have the Spirit of Christ does not belong to him' (Rom. 8.9). He will also, we may say further, in the sense of the early Christian faith, never be able to understand what Jesus really was. Consequently, alongside the acknowledgement of tradition, goes, with equal warrant and necessity, that of the Christ-spirit. And so, just as the inquiry into tradition impels us to historical investigation, so now the inquiry into the meaning of this tradition impels us to a systematic investigation of its very nature, and must, in the course of time, develop in its whole range as dogmatic theology, ethics, and so on. It is the same function as that described in early Christianity as a simple demand to prove all spirits.

---

of the Old Testament. This feature is of decisive importance for the understanding of Christianity, both in regard to dogma and religious history, though we need not pursue it further here.

Accordingly, the real theological and 'spiritual' office is that of rightly interpreting the word given at the beginning. Holding fast to what has been handed down and interpreting it in a living, understanding fashion must always go hand in hand; there is no genuine preservation of tradition without the freedom and responsibility of the spirit that expounds and judges, and thereby guards the original.

In the Church, however, this is the outcome, not of any universal 'historical law' valid for her also, but of the essence and significance of her evangelical truth. It is inevitable that, once we do away with the spirit and trust solely to the binding force of tradition, this truth is distorted and made into a new law, which makes faith itself a form of legal obedience. This is exemplified in what happened quite early in the strict Judaeo-Christianity which later became heretical. Its whole energy was devoted to preserving tradition from falsification, to its transmission and observance. For this the spirit was no longer needed. Christ was expressly denominated the new Moses. Here Christianity, despite allegiance to a person, became a reformed Judaism, with a new reformed Judaic law apparently prescribed by Jesus Christ.

Where, on the contrary, tradition is set aside and appeal is made to a new spirit superseding Christ and his word, it is not really surprising that the ultimate effect is precisely the same. For there can be no new redemption going beyond the full redemption and remission; either there will be nothing at all or else simply a new set of demands and so a new law. This can be seen, for instance, in the 'new prophecy' of Montanism, which, towards the end of the second century, claimed to be a renewal and a superior form of the original Christian message. It appealed to a new outpouring of the spirit, and the ecstatic enthusiasm with which the movement sought to establish itself exercised a fascination on men's minds, producing a feeling of joy and liberation. But when these psychological phenomena and the eccentric hopes of the prophets evaporated and remained stillborn, all that was left of the new freedom was a collection of new and highly ascetic demands held to be promulgated by the 'Spirit', and under the oppressive weight of this doubled tradition the sect gradually crumbled in the following centuries. In other cases, the legalistic power of such a 'third' revelation endured longer. But the abandonment of the original evangelical attitude, that is to say, the distortion of the real meaning of Christianity, in Manichaeism, Islam, or the 'ecclesia spiritualis' of the extreme

Franciscans, had basically the same outcome, a new legalism, Judaic in all but externals.

It follows, therefore, from the very essence of Christianity, that is, from the evangelical meaning of early Christian teaching about Christ, that spirit and tradition have equal value and are equally basic. They both operate in unison in the Church and on the same footing, and neither can be placed above the other. We cannot say that where tradition is preserved merely externally the spirit is always assuredly present, so certain is it that tradition, understood in faith, brings with it the spirit. Nor can we say that where a religious spirit is at work any testing of tradition can be dispensed with, so certain is it that the genuine tradition lives only in the spirit. On the contrary, the proclamation of the Christ-tradition must be made in the spirit and with its interpretation, and the truth of the spirit must be evinced in that it holds to the tradition of the original witness, and also interprets it in fact.[2] This interrelationship is indispensable and decisive.

Two things, in my opinion, follow directly from this as regards the validity of Christian tradition and the plenary authority of the Holy Spirit.

Firstly, the development and advance that takes place in the Church is never such that the origins in Christ and the original faith of the apostles are fundamentally superseded and eliminated. The Church knows two testaments, two covenants established by God, of which the first has been superseded and abolished by the second; but she knows nothing of a 'third Reich', at least in the world of human history, which is where we stand until the end of the world. Progress and development within the Church's history have always been on the lines of regrasping the original truth, of fresh interpretation, application, making actual what Christ once and for all has done and promised. The movement of Church history is one of continuous reformation, which, however, is no endless revolution, but reformation in the true sense. This claim, therefore, to reform what was given at its origins, is one that needs to be tested. It is not enough merely to claim to have the spirit, nor to claim that tradition is being correctly interpreted.

---

[2]The role that 'sound' reason has to play is already indicated in the New Testament; it is a subordinate, because essentially a formal one.

Secondly, the spirit that holds fast to tradition, comprehends and interprets it, cannot be subjected to any outside criterion, any higher court of appeal, beyond the understanding that comes by hearing. Between the Christ proclaimed, who is God, and the Spirit receiving him, who is also himself God, nothing human can intervene to assure, control, and judge. Consequently, it can never be settled in advance —most inconveniently from the standpoint of the politics of Church and State—who in the Church may be the subject of rights and who may not. Truth must vindicate its right; such vindication cannot be eluded by those who appeal to the truth. But, since they can bring this proof to bear only on those who are themselves desirous of hearing and understanding, and since this desire is by no means prevalent and general outside and inside the organized Church, the truth also, when proved by tradition, will never attain to universal recognition and, in this sense, prevail. The New Testament itself promises nothing of the sort. What is there promised is, rather, the separation of spirits, the mutual understanding of those who belong together in faith, and then, certainly, their impregnability and invincibility over against the world.

What a tradition, assured and yet precarious, and what a spirit, following this tradition in obedience and yet in freedom, can mean for the world, and what it cannot mean—for this would be needed, indeed, a further, practical demonstration, which does not fall within the scope of this theoretical treatment. As I said at the beginning, I do not venture to pursue the involved history of the problems here set out in their progress and continuance in the modern philosophy of history. Nonetheless, it seems to me important that whenever one tries to speak pertinently on the tradition and heritage of the West, the sense of the theological mode of thinking, as it appears in the New Testament, should not be lost sight of altogether. For all Christian Churches, the tradition of the New Testament—understood and interpreted according to its spirit—always remains the standard.

2
Faith and Culture
in the New Testament

FAITH AND CULTURE, believing and knowing, faith and science, reason and revelation, believing and understanding—with these pairs of concepts we touch on an old familiar question. It might well be considered an embarrassing question, in view of the extremely diverse answers it has received, from the assertion of perfect harmony to one of absolute incompatibility of the two, in view, also, of the numerous partly convinced, partly embarrassed, intermediate positions, compromises, and hesitant conclusions. The problem of faith as compatible or not with culture, of culture as compatible or not with the assent of faith, has so often been posed and discussed, without ever being solved. It is evidently one of those ever-recurring problems which, of their very nature, can never be definitely concluded and settled: it is also, from its content, a practically inexhaustible one. To discuss its significance in every aspect would virtually involve surveying the entire history of theology and of the human mind. Here we propose merely to attempt to bring out clearly the initial stages of the problem in the history of Christianity, by examining the earliest records relating to it in the New Testament. The later critical and systematic elaborations do not yet appear there. Instead, we are presented with a wholly practical, yet absolutely fundamental, assessment, which proceeds from the centre of the early Christian faith and covers the varied possible results of man's endeavours in the religious and spiritual spheres. It is the main scope and significance of this that we wish to identify and determine in some degree.

'Faith' means, of course, in this connection, not any general spiritual or religious faculty, but the positive early Christian faith in Jesus Christ as the definitive salvation, historically revealed by God to the world. It is only in this recognized restricted theological sense that the word will be used in what follows. On the other hand, by the word 'culture' we mean primarily only the pre-Christian culture, not yet determined or formed by the Christian faith. In the strict sense, the abstract concept of a culture is completely alien to early Christianity. Consequently, we here understand by 'culture', not some definite ideal whose content is exactly determined, but that spiritual possession, only accessible to thought, by which man does not simply know or understand a variety of objects, but which he affirms and grasps in its entirety, in order to 'cultivate' himself, and to open up higher spiritual potentialities of his being. Thus the range of the observations envisaged by our problem is by no means slight. Yet, in view of the normative significance that the New Testament has always possessed for the Christian faith, and still possesses, it seems reasonable to restrict our consideration accordingly both chronologically and factually.

The first thing, then, that we must bear in mind is that early Christianity had basically no concept of a 'culture' in the sense of classical philosophy or culture and its 'paideia', and, indeed, by reason of its oriental provenance, could not have had one at all. The old Israel, certainly, had its intellectual sphere in the form of knowledge and skills of various kinds, but a human culture in the sense of an ethical function and a special spiritual potentiality—what was called 'wisdom'—was mostly taken quite differently, in the sense of the concrete and actual faith: 'The fear of the Lord is the beginning of wisdom, and the knowledge of the Holy One is insight' (Prov. 9.10). The 'knowledge' man so obtains is not the outcome of intellectual effort and of self-culture. It rests on the obedient acknowledgement of the revelation, through which God has communicated to the people his will and his salvation: 'That will be your wisdom and your understanding in the sight of the peoples, who, when they hear all these statutes, will say, "Surely this great nation is a wise and understanding people".' (Deut. 4.6).

An intellectual formation is given, and this wisdom and understanding acquired, only in that the divine commandments are handed down and their knowledge made obligatory. Accordingly, with the progressive development of Judaism into a religion of a book, the study of the 'law' and of the growing tradition of its interpretation—as later in Islam, but here far more than ever in Christianity—became the unique recognized source of a higher learning, that of the scribes and rabbis, and so, one might say, of 'culture'. At any rate, here alone was developed something like a science methodically and scholastically pursued, though the method in question was far from what Greeks and moderns mean by the word. Instructed in his law, the learned Jew and Pharisee always believed himself to possess the true wisdom, and was confident, in the words of Paul, of being 'a guide to the blind, a light to those who are in darkness, a corrector of the foolish, a teacher of children, having in the law the embodiment of knowledge and truth' (Rom. 2.19). Here, then, 'culture' is co-terminous with the knowledge of the divine law. Knowledge means knowledge of God. In other words, it is a question, not of culture in any sense we recognize but essentially of faith itself, and of the obedience of faith in the presence of the revelation of God, through his ordained law in which salvation and life are comprised.

There is no need for us to follow out this view as developed in early, especially early Palestinian, Christianity. Here it underwent, from the outset, an inner transformation, in that the old Mosaic law was replaced by the new 'law' and the living person of Jesus Christ. Yet this does not of itself as yet involve a 'problem of culture'. Early Christianity, however, was, from the beginning, especially in the Greek-speaking world, formed not only by the Judaic and rabbinical heritage, but also by the spirit of Hellenistic culture and its spiritual ideals, and it is here that our problem arises. We are not concerned mainly with the higher philosophical culture, which affected only the upper reaches of society where early Christianity had little impact, and which, by reason of its more rational and abstract character, gave little occasion for a religious confrontation. This is not what the New Testament writers had in mind when they spoke expressly of 'wisdom' or 'knowledge'. They were concerned, rather, with certain religious ideals and trends which were then beginning to percolate into the whole ancient cultural world from the East, and which, later, precisely in their linking with Christianity (and also, in part, with Judaism), came to exercise an enduring historical influence. Nowadays, we group together the manifold, often anonymous, expressions of this new movement or transformation of the spirit under 'gnosis', the term widely used. For here, although not alone, yet in a truly fundamental sense, is raised the question of a higher religious perception.

The knowledge sought after by the Gnostics was no neutral, secular knowledge of the earth and man; it was, above all, the knowledge of

God and of that other world, which is man's true country, which he hopes to regain, and, through knowledge or the recovery of knowledge, to obtain redemption. Gnostic 'knowledge' was very conscious of being quite apart from all other rational knowledge. It was held to be, not 'natural' knowledge, but a special, grace-given, faculty of the privileged man caught up by the divinity, and so, in this religious sense, a charisma. The way to be followed to attain this end had many different aspects; it led through mysteries and sacraments, traditions and revelations. But, in all cases, there was opened up to the Gnostic a new mode of life and thought, to be fostered and cultivated in order to develop the particular, the only true, being of the 'spiritual' personality. In this respect, the Gnostic, striving after the illuminating vision and knowledge of the divine world, with its multiple ascetic practices and ecstatic experiences, may well claim to be a religious ideal of human culture, however alien to the classical or philosophical ideal it be in its world-renouncing dualism. This is, at all events, the form in which the question of a special culture and spiritual elevation of man confronted the Church for the first time and became a problem. What, then, is the relation of the higher, spiritual life of those who 'have' gnosis to the salvation which, historically, lies enclosed in Christ; and in what relation stands the privileged Gnostic to the simple, in this sense, 'uncultured', member of the community, his neighbour, and to the entirety of the 'body of Christ'?

Paul it was, more than anyone else, who posed the question in this form as regards the Corinthians of gnostic tendency, and gave the fundamental answer in clear-cut terms. No doubt, Paul himself, in view of his general spiritual outlook, may be described, up to a point, as a Gnostic; at any rate, the manner in which he accepts positively and makes use of the concepts of 'wisdom' and 'knowledge' shows that he was far from rejecting in advance the ideal they express. But the Corinthian Gnostics were obviously only too liable to make gnostic knowledge the real foundation of their religious existence, and to melt down and recast the gospel of Christ taught to them as the foundation. And so there arose a whole series of conflicting directives corresponding to the particular conceptions and teachings of individual teachers and religious leaders, which threatened to split the community asunder. Paul, then, in his first epistle to the Corinthians, came out strongly against this with a clear condemnation and a recall to first principles: the reality of the community of God is founded, not on the 'knowledge' or convictions of its teachers, but on the gospel of Christ, or, more pointedly, the one Cross of Christ. This gospel is, of its essence, no universal, self-attesting 'wisdom'. On the contrary, it appears primarily as a folly, which, therefore, only 'faith' can apprehend and then, indeed, experience as the living power of God. (I Cor. I.I0*ff*.). If God offers the world a redeemer crucified, utterly disfigured, a saviour on the gallows, and makes him thereby the true 'wisdom' (I Cor. I.30), he consequently, so far from ratifying all the high expectations of earthly wisdom, crucifies them. 'Where is the wise man? Where is the scribe? Where is the debater of this age?' (I Cor. I.20). God's will was precisely that, when confronted by this symbol, every form both of Jewish and pagan 'culture' should be seen as debased, and that his 'foolishness' should gain the victory. In choosing the weak, the despised, the nullity, he has unmasked, not only the glorying of the strong, the respected and the noble, but also the wisdom of the wise, 'that no flesh should glory in his sight . . . that, as it is written (Jer. 9.23) let him who boasts, boast of the Lord' (I Cor. I.22*ff*.).

We can see that here it is the Old Testament idea of the majesty of God that finds, in belief in the humiliated Christ, a new, extreme pinnacle, and its own realization. The same idea echoes, without the special application to the Corinthians' pride of culture, in the post-Pauline epistles (I Peter 5.5; James 4.6). Above all, we already find it in essence and equal significance in the synoptic tradition: 'I thank thee, Father, Lord of heaven and earth, that thou hast hidden these things from the wise and understanding and revealed them to babes' (Matt. 11.25). 'What is exalted among men is an abomination in the sight of God' (Luke 16.15). We have to be 'converted' and become 'like children' (Matt. 18.3). God 'has scattered the proud in the imagination of their hearts' (Luke 1.51); but to the poor, the poor 'in spirit', belongs the kingdom of heaven (Matt. 5.3).

In practice, this means that the Christian must 'never be conceited' (Rom. 12.16=Is. 5.21). The knowledge, which in God's eyes is decisive for salvation, is not attainable through any higher religious culture or enlightenment. Even the highest conceivable earthly wisdom, that of the demonic lords of the world, was, according to Paul, unable to discern in the servile form of the life and death of Jesus, the real meaning, namely, the hidden triumph of God (1 Cor. 2.8). The 'foolishness' of the preaching about Christ is revealed as wisdom only to the 'simplicity' of faith in Christ (2 Cor. 11.3); this wisdom is the direct gift of the divine Spirit (1 Cor. 2.10*ff.*; *cf.* Mark 16.17). In a certain sense, then, it is harder for the 'wise according to worldly standards' to affirm Christ in faith (1 Cor. 1.26); for they must abandon their extreme pride and privilege, and, becoming fools again in the presence of God, the 'only wise' God (Rom. 16.27), admit the bankruptcy of their wisdom, and that precisely on the one point of real importance. Obviously, however, Paul is not saying that human foolishness as such is more apt to reach this objective or possesses in the eyes of God a moral advantage. Such a perverse conception would be simply to transpose the arrogance of the wise. The whole opposition, in fact, runs not on the plane of such relative, worldly and human value-judgements, represented by the terms 'wisdom' and 'foolishness'; it is between man, pure and simple, and God. Thus it moves, from the outset, in another, the strictly theological, dimension. The popular pietistic idea that Paul and the Bible in general hold secular culture and science as such to be a drawback, and that they warn Christians against them would, then, be at fault, even if our texts were in fact speaking of culture and science in the modern sense.

From these fundamental theological statements on 'wisdom' there follow for Paul certain definite, incisive conclusions as to the place of the Gnostic and teacher of wisdom within the community. The humility required by God makes imperative also an attitude of modesty towards his fellow Christian. Christ is the bearer of the life of all Christians; apart from him there is no wisdom or knowledge. And so even the wise man cannot be more than a 'member' of his 'body'. He has, indeed, received his special 'gift' and function, by whose means he can and must 'edify' the whole community; yet, for all that, he has no exceptional place or superior rank. All members have care and concern for one another in the same fashion, and, in fact, the weakest and 'unhonoured' should have the precedence (1 Cor. 12). Consequently, the schismatic tendency of all 'culture' is ruled out. In the Church, from its inner, fundamental nature as given, there cannot be any 'glorying', not even the glory of wisdom, and divisions arising from theological knowledge and the human person of the teacher clearly indicate that, in such cases, faith has broken down; for the basic proviso that governs all 'wisdom' has been forgotten (1 Cor. 1.11ff.; 3-4). Only Christ, his final judgement and the present witness he gives, are authoritative and decisive; whatever is taught over and above these is 'patchwork' and mere provisional, 'transient' knowledge. The man of 'culture' is in special danger of forgetting this, particularly the man of religious and Christian culture. For this reason, he must always remember that real 'abiding', sustaining, and renewing power does not lie in knowledge and extraordinary religious gifts as such, but in love, which, with faith in and hope for fulfilment in Christ, is what essentially constitutes the new life. 'Knowledge', that is mere self-contained culture and knowledge, 'puffs up, but love builds up' (1 Cor. 8.1).

Throughout we are dealing with ideas not peculiar to Paul, but constantly to be encountered in early Christianity. For the idea behind the warning against putting oneself above others we need go no further than Christ's: 'Whosoever will be greater shall be your minister' (Mark 10.43). But this applies also to spiritual arrogance and religious leadership. There is no absolute authority in the community of the faithful (Heb. 8.11f.), and no one should put himself forward as a teacher (James 3.1). This is most trenchantly expressed by the words of Jesus himself as recorded in the Synoptics: the disciples are not to allow themselves to be called 'rabbi' or any other title of distinction. It would be a misunderstanding of this command to see it merely as a general admonition to humility and fraternity, and not also in its special christological relation which gives it a stricter obligation: 'you are all brethren . . . for you have one master, the Christ' (Matt. 23.8-10). Paul took this motive only at the deepest level, and developed it so as to counter the danger of gnosticism. He further required that the special nature of Christian teaching, and the total cleavage between it and all other possible knowledge, should be clear even in the form of speech. He deliberately renounced the 'persuasive words of human wisdom', that is, all the alluring artifices of rhetorical culture. Any attempt to impress by these means would, if successful, 'make void', instead of reinforcing, the preaching of the Cross (1 Cor. 1.17); that is, it would distort its meaning (1 Cor. 2.1ff.). The treasure of Christ must remain in earthen vessels, 'that the excellency may be of the power of God, and not of us' (2 Cor. 4.7). It is from this point of view that Paul affirms his personal destiny, to be an apostle of the Gospel despite his infirmities, and goes on to expound it in the light of this paradox (2 Cor. 11.30; 12.5ff.).

Once we have assessed the fundamental significance of his explanations, the question arises as to whether Paul, in criticizing a too pretentious wisdom, had only the gnosis in view, or also the whole Greek ideal of higher spiritual culture and knowledge. The question is especially relevant when he seems to lay particular stress on the external brilliance of the mode of speech. There are, in fact, instances which suggest such a transition. When Paul contrasts the 'Greeks,' not only with the Jews, as he does repeatedly, but also occasionally with the 'uncultured' barbarians,[1] it is clear that he intends to designate them not only as 'pagans', but also as bearers of the existing world-culture and civilization. But, taking a general view, it is astonishing how little, apparently, Paul came inwardly in contact with it, and how little he entered directly into the questions agitating it. This is not a question of principle with him. As a missionary, in fact, he strove to 'become all things to all men' (1 Cor. 9.22; cf. Col. 4.5f.), and saw himself as precisely the apostle of the non-Jewish, pagan world. But, as soon as the real religious confrontation begins, the Greeks, who 'seek wisdom' (1 Cor. 1.22), always evince themselves in reality, Gnostics. Even when the classical concept of 'philosophy' emerges, and is repelled as a force that leads men astray (Col. 2.8), it is still a question, not of classical ideas and outlook, but of typical gnostic speculations about angels, of Judaeo-syncretistic character.[2] All this does not only throw light on the spiritual atmosphere in which Paul's missionary work was conducted; it is also significant for Paul himself, showing that general questions of learning and culture interested him only in so far as they had direct relevance to religion. For this reason, in his eyes, judgement had already been finally pronounced also on the 'cultured', much admired, Greeks. They are 'heathens,' that is, idolaters, and so altogether 'without understanding' and degenerate: they have not acknowledged God and have spurned his moral laws. And so, 'claiming to be wise, they became fools' (Rom. 1.21f., 31; 3.11:

---

[1]Rom. 1.14 (cf. 3.11); see H. Windisch, ThW 1 (1933) 549. 'The apposition σοφοῖς τε καὶ ἀνοήτοις shows that Paul is conscious also of a relation to culture.'
[2]Cf. G. Bornkamm, 'Die Häresie des Kolosserbriefs', ThLZ 73 (1948) 11ff. (Das Ende des Gesetzes, 1958, pp. 139ff.)

cf. Eph. 4.18). So then Paul, in dealing with questions of gnosis, always remained, in his verdict on the world of the classical Greek spirit, a true Jew.

In the whole sphere of the New Testament, indeed, there is only one man who sensed the depth and scope of the problem involved in the historical encounter of Christianity and Hellenism.[3] This was Luke, 'the physician', as he is called in Colossians (4.14), and certainly the most 'cultured' writer of the whole of primitive Christianity. In both his works, Luke turns, of set purpose, to the representatives of pagan 'society' and culture, in order to show them, in their own language and fashion, what Christ meant for them. In addition, at one of the climaxes of the Acts, he builds up, in idealized form, the great scene, in which the protagonist of the new faith and the representatives of the ancient Greek wisdom and culture confront each other, the contrast being emphasized to bring out its symbolism: Paul, the elect apostle of the whole Gentile world, goes to Athens, the renowned centre of the ancient culture, there to dispute publicly with the Athenians and their philosophers about the Christian revelation.[4]

The encounter is prepared with much the same care as, later, his no less significant arrivals in Jerusalem and in Rome, and the classical stage of the Areopagus is purposely chosen to provide a hearing for the sole example of a great sermon to the Gentiles that Luke ever gave. The way he makes the apostle begin is itself indicative. Paul had, beforehand, surveyed the city's monuments, and was, it is expressly stated, stirred to indignation at their idolatrous character (Acts 17.16). Nonetheless, far from giving vent to his anger, he tries to establish a positive connection: the 'unknown God', whom certain altars seemed

---

[3] It is very doubtful if the Ἕλληνες who, in John's gospel, desired to see Jesus (12.20), can be really held 'representatives of the Greek world' (so Bultmann, *Das Evangelium des Johannes* [1941], 323). Probably, they were so called simply as representatives of the pagan world in contrast to 'the Jews'; *cf.* W. Bauer, *Das Johannesevangelium* [1933], 161. At any rate, there is no word indicating and specially signifying the Greeks and their culture.

[4] Acts 17. For what follows, see especially M. Dibelius, *Paul on the Areopagus* [=*Studies in the Acts of the Apostles*, 1956, pp. 26ff.]. Against the renewed attempt to preserve the historicity of the speech by W. Schmid, 'Die Rede des Apostels Paulus vor den Philosophen und Areopagisten in Athen', *Philologus* 95 (1942) 79ff.; see W. G. Kümmel, *Man in the New Testament* (rev. ed. 1963), 90-2, n. 101.

to proclaim (17.23), the invisible world-upholder testified to by ancient Greek poets (17.28), is now—the sermon goes—brought close to the Athenians in a 'man', whom God has appointed before the coming judgement to preach repentance, and has raised from the dead (17.31). These preliminaries serve to make more impressive the account of the effect of the sermon, which Luke considers, not of course, as falling short, but as the best possible to such an audience. Paul's success in Athens remained modest; he was almost a failure. The Epicurean and Stoic philosophers,[5] in the consciousness of their intellectual superiority, ignore him as a half-educated 'word-sower' (σπερμολόγος), and the gospel of the Ἀνάστασις, the resurrection, which at first they seemed to envisage as a new divinity and found 'interesting' (17.18), provoked them to 'mockery' (17.32) when they saw its real meaning based on the historical testimony which, for Luke himself, was the core of the whole Christian message. Only a few, 'certain men', in Athens accede to Paul and find faith.

From this it should be evident how basically and extensively Luke agrees with the judgement of Paul, despite his quite different temperament and the different aspect in which he envisaged the problem of culture. For gnostic 'wisdom' Luke had scant regard; but he knew the true spirit of Greek culture far more intimately and vitally than Paul—by reason, it would seem, of a direct personal participation in it. At all events, he was, as is shown by his studied, literary mode of expression, much more capable than Paul of entering personally into the actual cultural needs of the Greeks. What, in this regard, can hardly have been, with Paul, more than a general principle was, with Luke, a method carefully selected to avoid any unnecessary offence to cultured pagans. Yet Luke was no more inclined than Paul to trim the content of the Christian message and to mitigate its 'scandal', in the face of the resistance of an alien 'wisdom'. Even Luke saw clearly the inevitability of a collision between the true Christian Gospel and the speculations of, not, in his case, Gnostics, but philosophers. He emphasized anew, in his own fashion, how the possession of higher culture, far from facilitating the transition to faith, made it more difficult. For him also

---

[5] It is, of course, no accident that precisely these schools are mentioned; only it does not by any means follow that Luke means that the others, for instance the 'more devout' Platonists, were prepared to believe. Anything of the sort would have been stated unequivocally.

there were 'not many wise according to the flesh' who accepted the Christian teaching; once it was understood in its literal sense, it seemed, in the eyes of the 'wise' and philosophically cultured, not wisdom, but rather foolishness and absurdity.

There is no conclusive evidence for any different view of the matter to be drawn from the New Testament. At most, one may adduce the story of the 'wise men from the East', the μάγοι ἀπὸ ἀνατολῶν, in order to detect a positive judgement as to the value of pre-Christian culture (Matt. 2.1-12). Here the reference is neither to gnostic theosophy nor to Greek philosophy, but solely to the astrological learning of the Far East, whether Babylon or Persia. The mysterious astral art of the Magi did, in fact, correctly assign the time and place of the Saviour's birth, and the wise men who practised it set out on the way in order to pay homage to Jesus and witness to him. It is a beautiful legend, but its significance is hardly to be pressed in this context. Apart from this instance, recorded by Matthew alone, magic and its practice is always alluded to in the New Testament and in primitive Christianity in a derogatory sense, as evil sorcery and, so to speak 'black', forbidden magic.[6]

The result, then, of our investigation should be quite clear on its negative side. Throughout primitive Christianity there is no trace of any enthusiasm for culture; learning and culture are, fundamentally, without significance for the faith. In no sense were they held as a prerequisite for its preaching, and the fruits of the latter, far from agreeing with those to be expected from the former, were opposed to them. It is not allowable to tone down this judgement of primitive Christianity by the plea that early Christian communities lived, for the most part, isolated from culture. The fact itself is indeed indisputable; nevertheless, the absence of other solutions favourable to culture is not explicable on the ground that the problem as such did not come within their purview. For, as we have seen, it was in fact envisaged as regards both gnostic and philosophical culture, and the answer that was given was always the same: it followed of necessity from the very nature of the Christian revelation and the Christian faith. These involved inevitably the collapse of all human values and so of all the confident

---

[6]Acts 8.8,11; 13.6,8; Barn. 20.1; Ign. *Eph.* 14.3; Did. 2.2; *cf.* Acts 19.19. This pejorative sense is not necessarily present in non-Christian usage: *cf.* for example Bultmann's instances in *ThW* 1 (1933) 692, Note 14.

claims of the spirit and of culture, since Christ, in his coming, had revealed something beyond all man's capabilities, which alone makes it the real salvation for all men—the salvation, that is, of the real, inaccessible God and his 'wisdom'. This is, in fact, the reason why it is so frequently called a mystery.[7]

It is only when these factors are fully understood and given their due theological emphasis that one can assert with the same assurance a relative *right of culture*, though in a different, less important, sense. Indeed, on account of the definite religious meaning behind the early Christian criticism of culture, and in order to guard against the opposite extreme, it is necessary that this should be done. Certainly, the severe judgement on the 'fleshly' wisdom of this world (2 Cor. 1.12; 1 Cor. 1.20; 2.6; 3.19) strikes culture right at the point of its main preoccupation, namely, its claim and endeavour to give man an absolute 'existential' hold, from which he can assert himself purely and simply, that is, even before God, in the dignity of his human nature. The fundamental impossibility of such an attempt, and the fact that God has judged it for its presumption should be evident from the Cross, if this is acknowledged as our justification, sanctification, and redemption, and as our 'wisdom' (1 Cor. 1.30). Yet a wisdom that, in this sign, recognizes its ultimate helplessness and 'foolishness', which discards its highest religious or rather 'demoniac', pretensions, and is as if disempowered—a purely human wisdom in this sense is not subject to theological condemnation. This is not a conclusion fabricated to accord with modern aspirations. It is to be found in the New Testament itself, in those parts, already noticed by us, which treat of gnostic or Greek wisdom.

Paul, as a missionary to the Gentiles, besides being a debtor both to the 'wise and to the foolish' (Rom. 1.14), knows some who are 'wise' even within the Church, spiritually eminent and cultured personalities who have become Christians (1 Cor. 1.26). It does not matter here that they are, as we have seen, relatively 'not many'; what matters is that, whether few or many, they have remained, in the community, what, 'according to the flesh' (in a human view), they were before, namely, 'wise', just as *in the Church* there still continue to be Jews or

---

[7] Mark 4.11; Rom. 16.25; 1 Cor. 4.11; Col. 1.26f.; 2.2; 4.3; Eph. 1.9; 3.3 ff.; 6.19; 1 Tim. 3.9,16. Very significant is the alternation between μαρτύριον and μυστήριον in the tradition of 1 Cor. 2.1.

Greeks and barbarians. There is no question of any requirement that the 'wise', on entry into the community, should forgo or abandon their knowledge or culture as a disfigurement. That would be as senseless as prohibiting a Christian to be rich, or free, or a man, or a woman, particularly since it is, in fact, stated that, in Christ, these social and natural differences 'are no more' (1 Cor. 12.13; Gal. 3.28; Col. 3.11). That means they exist no longer in the sense of an absolute value or pre-eminence, as something that, before God or the brethren, can carry any weight, and, in this sense also, differences of culture, as we have seen, cease to exist in the Church. Whoever now wants to boast anew of his wisdom thereby denies the folly of the Cross, and in this becomes himself foolish again (1 Cor. 1.31; 3.18; 2 Cor. 10.17; James 1.10). To take, however, such passages as a reason for suppressing and denying all culture would be the same kind of misconception as that of the ancient ascetic who, for the sake of 'perfection', thought it incumbent on men and women to wear the same form of dress, to lead their married lives 'spiritually', and went to the extreme length of castrating himself.

A proper understanding, then, of what Paul says about wisdom brings us to a *dialectical judgement* on culture, one which applies not only to a composite, religiously neutral culture of a general sort, but to the higher gnostic 'wisdom', fostered even in the community of the faithful. This wisdom also has no final, absolute value, and will pass away. But when, aware of this, the wisdom remains wisdom of the Cross, it is itself a 'gift', and Paul himself is ready to foster it 'among the perfect' (1 Cor. 2.6f.; 2 Cor. 11.16); he gladly welcomes the wonderful wealth of knowledge brought into life by the working of the Spirit (Rom. 15.14; 1 Cor. 1.5; 2 Cor. 8.7; Phil. 1.9f.; Col. 1.9; 3.16). But, since this 'wisdom' or 'knowledge' is given after as well as before to certain persons rather than others (1 Cor. 12.8; 13.2), there now again appears in the Church something akin to spiritual teachers and instructors. What continuously matters is simply that the basic proviso governing their work be not forgotten, that they are constantly ready to give up the wisdom of their thinking and hold it for foolishness: 'If any man think that he knoweth any thing, he hath not yet known as he ought to know' (1 Cor. 8.2). But if anyone desires to build further on the 'foundation' of faith in Christ, he may well make the endeavour. It may turn out that the last day will not 'burn' all that he has built, and that he may even 'receive praise' from God. But before the last day, in the world of time, no one is in a position to pass judgement, and it is foolish to cause division in the community on account of such transient matters (1 Cor. 3.10; 4.6). Thus, faith gives free rein to 'knowledge' and the higher religious culture, despite all their dubious qualities; only so can they continue to be significant in their own way and to be of service and profit to the community (Rom. 15.14; 1 Cor. 14.6). They can even 'receive praise', and, in any case, their ultimate doubtfulness is not so significant as their dependent nature or the praise given to human foolishness. What does, however, apply to all without distinction is the admonition not to be childish in understanding, but to be like children only in malice, but adults in understanding (1 Cor. 3.1; 14.20; Rom. 16.19; Eph. 5.16f.; Matt. 10.16).

Perhaps even more important than these direct statements is the fact that the New Testament writers are so prone to take up the existing concepts and ideas of gnosticism and to apply them in a new way. They do so, not only for a tactical purpose, to facilitate 'conversion', but in the setting of the Church itself and to express appropriately its own religious convictions; furthermore, they do so, not just 'inconsiderately' as it were, but often quite evidently of set purpose, and especially when a danger threatens from a faulty understanding of gnostic wisdom. And precisely in this situation they do not, as is often the case later, evade the spiritual danger, regarding it with misgiving and hostility, but endeavour to meet it directly, bringing out its 'true', positive sense, as determined and fixed through Christ. For in Christ 'are hid all the treasures of wisdom and knowledge' (Col. 2.3). That is to say, all that the gnostic culture can rightly offer and promise attains its real and fruitful fulfilment only in accepting Christ. Certain as it is that the gnostic wisdom never of itself reaches the true 'hidden' end of its striving, 'the mystery of God', it is equally certain that this striving is taken hold of by Christ, and through him, paradoxically, appeased. The two ideas belong together; one or other may receive the greater emphasis, but they are not played off against each other. If Paul, in the disunited community of Corinth taught for preference the decisive, unifying folly of the Cross that shatters gnostic pride, the epistle to the Colossians emphasizes, in opposition to the anxious rigidity of Judaising gnostic legalism, the contrasting freedom from all the apparatus of precepts and 'dogmas',[8] which is the freedom of Christ. An analogous approach is adopted by the author of the Epistle to the Hebrews. He sees himself confronted by a gnosticizing practice of angel-worship, and points out that Christ is fundamentally other than the angels whom he rules. This, however, does not exclude a positive evaluation of the angel-world; in fact, its preaching only becomes clear precisely when its importance is scaled down to the correct measure.[9] A similar line of thought seems to lie at the basis of the Christology of the Epistle to the Ephesians,[10] and, at least in intention, to be that of Ignatius of Antioch.[11] But here we must refer, above all, to the Gospel of St. John. The boldness with which he engages with gnostic ideas and brings them into relation with the incarnate Christ, refuting them and, at the same time, giving them a new slant, is unparalleled even in the New Testament.[12] But our intention is not to follow out this whole development as regards its content. We mention it only on account of its significance as being typical of what was to follow, as the earliest example of the manner in which the Christian faith takes to itself a spirituality of its nature hostile or, at any rate, not entirely friendly, in its approach. Christianity, accordingly, never lets itself be incorporated into the existing *Weltanschauung*, but, on the contrary, claims to be itself the fulfilment of all the strivings of the mind. At the same time, it gives free scope to any culture that does not attempt to incorporate Christianity, and, in the presence of the revealed truth of God, recognizes its own limitations and its purely provisional and relative value.

This conclusion is a fundamental one, and so must be valid, not only for the gnosis, but for any form whatever of human intellectual culture. In regard to the special problem of the gnosis, we may add that, in judging theologically the value to be ascribed to theosophical and similar 'spiritual knowledge' and its particular 'cultural potentialities' in the light of the New Testament, one must act with prudence

---

[8]*Cf.* G. Bornkamm, *supra*, note 2; also E. Käsemann, *Leib und Leib Christi* (1933).
[9]*Cf.* E. Käsemann, *Das wandernde Gottesvolk* (1959).
[10]*Cf.* E. Schlier, *Christus und die Kirche im Epheserbrief* (1930).
[11]*Cf.* E. Schlier, *Religionsgeschichtl. Untersuchungen zu den Ignatiusbriefen* (1929); also H. W. Bartsch, *Gnostisches Gut und Gemeindetradition bei Ignatius von Antiochien* (1940).
[12]On this *cf.* in particular R. Bultmann, *Das Evangelium des Johannes* (1941).

and reserve. In general, however, we come somewhat nearer to the question of culture in the modern sense only if we leave the gnosis on one side, and attend closely to the relationship with *philosophy*, that is the rational enlightenment of late antiquity. Certainly, for the Church as a whole, the confrontation with it takes on a profound significance only at a later date, at a time when the standards of judgement prevailing in early Christianity already begin to lose their hold. The literary outcome of this encounter is, on the whole, not to be found in the New Testament; but even the beginnings of this process, which we see alongside the negative judgement, are highly instructive, since they show once again the same dialectic as we have already seen applied to the gnosis and its values. It is self-evident that the significance of a rational philosophy, even when it has ceased to be, in the 'demonic' sense, faith in itself and in its own reason, never penetrates so deeply into the strictly religious sphere as the corresponding affirmation of the gnosis. Its significance lies, above all, in its formal, logical, critical and communicative function. But the duty of discussion, of producing an objectively clear and, in this sense, rational exposition of her own thought, which the Church, precisely as a missionary Church, must insist upon, renders impossible a simple rejection of all philosophical culture.

This much is certainly already clear in the writings of Paul. He holds strongly, for example, that his communities should not give to those outside the impression of a group of madmen (1 Cor. 14.33), and for conversations with pagans he seems to recommend not only a friendly approach, but even an agreeable, pleasing style of utterance.[13] Along with spiritual ecstasy, rational understanding of what the Church is concerned with has its own inalienable rights (1 Cor. 14.14). This shows how we are *not* to interpret the renunciation of the 'learned speech of human wisdom'. The foolishness of Christian preaching is not opposed either to an intelligible mode of expression or to logical argumentation, which Paul himself, especially in his proofs from Scripture, regularly employs, though to us his employment of it seems defective as being too rabbinical a mode of syllogizing. Still more indicative is the frankness with which, on occasion, he appeals to the reason of his readers, and summons them to exercise their calm consideration and purely natural openness in examining the

[13] 1 Col. 4.6. This applies only on the assumption that this epistle is by Paul.

matter.[14] His condescending designation of an imaginary opponent as ἄφρων (I Cor. 15.36) springs, stylistically speaking, directly from the 'diatribe' as a mode of clarification in popular philosophy.[15] This does not make Paul himself a philosopher, but, with all his rationality in general, he never lets his hearers forget that what he brings to them is not ultimately accessible to reason and culture, but only to faith, and yet, for that very reason, is the truth.

The requirement to deliver an answer on the Christian faith to any-one who desires it occurs also elsewhere (I Peter 3.15; Tit. 1.9). The actual difficulties involved here are again felt by Luke more than anyone. He was the first, perhaps, to divine the particular offence which the Christian message must represent precisely to the man of Greek culture and spiritual formation, when the true object of faith is to transcend the sphere where reason and intelligence hold sway. He knew the tendency to elude the exposition of Christianity through rejecting it either as the expression of a lack of culture (Acts 4.13) or alternatively of excessive learning (Acts 26.24).[16] But for that very reason the pagan reader who has 'understanding' and desires a factual approach (Acts 13.7) should not be disappointed. The Christians are not 'mad', but 'speaking the sober truth' (Acts 26.25). And therefore they are always ready to make a rational approach to their critics, as Paul to the Jews and to the philosophers in Athens (Acts 17.17).[17]

Yet a definite approach to the intellectual attitude and terminology of the philosophical enlightenment is found only in the *latest epistles* of the New Testament, that is in the pseudo-Pauline pastoral epistles and the second epistle of Peter. It is true that even here faith is certainly not understood as a matter of culture or of reason. It rests, as pre-viously, on the 'revealed' word of preaching (Tit. 1.3), and its nature as something not simply accessible to reason is, in a manner, even em-

[14]Also I Cor. 6.5, where the 'wisdom' of the community-judge can hardly be meant solely in the sense of a supernatural charisma.

[15]*Cf.* R. Bultmann, *Der Stil der paulinischen Predigt und die kynisch-stoische Diatribe* (1910).

[16]It may be recalled that the account of how Jesus at twelve years old astonished the scribes (Luke 2.46f.) is exclusive to Luke. St. John's Gospel touches on the same problem in a different fashion. 3.9ff.; 7.15; 9.34.

[17]Here also properly belongs the stress laid on the historical evidence of eye-witnesses and on the credibility of the Christian tradition; *cf.* in particular Luke 1.1ff.

phasized by the fresh stress laid on its historical basis in tradition (1 Tim. 16.20; 2 Tim. 1.12, 14; 2 Peter 2.21). Yet, on the other hand, the attempt is evident all through to bring out the character of the Christian teaching as intellectually sound, balanced, far from 'uncultured', and, for this purpose, the author deliberately takes over the terminology of the cultured 'world'. In addition, the polemic is directed not so much to the pagan criticism as against the errors of a 'heretical' (Tit. 3.10; 2 Peter 2.1), 'falsely called' (1 Tim. 6.20) gnosis. It is concerned, as we can see from the depreciatory tone, with uncultured and unstable personalities, who—like 'irrational animals' (2 Peter 2.12)—have gone astray in 'vain discussion' (1 Tim. 1.6; 6.20; 2 Tim. 2.16) about 'cleverly devised myths' (2 Peter 1.16) and 'stupid, senseless controversies' (2 Tim. 2.23). To contend with such poisons was needed a bishop, 'an apt teacher, forbearing' (2 Tim. 2.24), who avoids 'godless and silly myths' (1 Tim. 4.7), and, in dignified and concrete language, can silence adversaries and instruct his hearers (2 Tim. 2.25; Tit. 1.9*ff.*). For the heretics are not only weak in faith, but corrupt in mind (2 Tim. 3.8).

These standards of style are highly informative. For they treat rational and *cultured thought* almost as an *ally* of 'sound' belief (1 Tim. 1.10; 6.3; 2 Tim. 1.13; 4.3; Tit. 1.9; 2.1), and in any case are far from opposing it. 'To the pure all things are pure' (Tit. 1.15). But it does not follow from this that the false teachers attacked were themselves contemptuous of culture. On the contrary, their contentious questions and disputes are far more suggestive of a more or less 'cultured' equipment, even though the actual philosophical culture may at times be quite modest. The situation, then, corresponds exactly to what we know from the latter part of the second century. All Christian groups assert that they teach a wisdom far superior to the world and its wisdom. They all tax their opponents, from time to time, with being dependent on pagan mythologies or philosophies. None, however, on that account can be held to be uncultured or to condemn culture and reason altogether. Only towards the end of the century does this picture begin to change. It is then that, for the first time, appears something like an anti-cultural *reaction* against the confusion of gnostic and 'philosophical' theories and false doctrines, a reaction supported by the *simplices* in the communities, who were dismayed by them: they wanted now to have nothing more to do with theology and intellectual culture.[18] But it is highly significant that they could not make their protests prevail in the Church. All the theologians of note opposed them, and the solution of the problems, so far as it went, took a quite different course. It was only the pagan adversaries of Christianity who gladly seized on narrow-minded expressions of intolerance to reproach the Church, which they were incapable of viewing in a serious light, as uncultured and incapable of culture.

It is important to view and evaluate this development in its broad lines, if we are to envisage rightly the original relationship of Christianity to the question of culture. Otherwise, under the influence of what emerged later and characterized quite a different set of circumstances, it will be fundamentally misconceived. At this point, we need not pursue further the line of historical development, and may leave it. Nor, as we said at the beginning, do we propose to go into the problems of *systematization* which arose in early Christianity. Only two brief observations may be permitted in conclusion, so as to preserve the result attained from the coarsening and distortion to which it is otherwise liable, and to present it in its true and original perspective.

It is clear that the general concept of 'culture' which we have assumed and retained throughout our argument does not occur in this form in the New Testament, and rests on an abstraction. It enables us to bring under a single denomination such different entities as gnostic 'wisdom' and the insights of rational philosophy, and, in addition, it admits other forms of culture not envisaged in the New Testament, for which it is equally appropriate. Such a general application is, in fact, possible and justifiable, because the early Christian verdict on secular knowledge was not reached through an analysis of cultural values and entities, but simply emerged from the doctrine of Christ. It was a 'judgement of faith', that is, the comprehensive knowledge of what Christ signified for the believer, and comprised from the outset, in its exclusiveness, even when undeveloped, a pronouncement on what significance human culture as such can no longer claim and what significance still remains to it. It concerns, therefore, culture in general, and so all individual forms of culture, since they are all, of their very nature, subject to this general verdict. It is only with this general

[18]*Cf.* J. Lebreton, '*Le désaccord de la foi populaire et de la théologie savante dans l'Église chrétienne du 3me siècle,*' *RHE* 19 (1923) 489*ff.*; 20 (1924) 5*ff.*

theological verdict that we have been concerned. But, in fact, we have in the process done no more than outline an extremely general, necessarily abstract framework, into which all concrete questions of a determinate culture must first be fitted. Yet, in practice, it is precisely these which matter. It is obvious that the theological judgement on 'culture' also has a very different aspect and weight according to the particular cultural contents and values under consideration. To some extent, that is evident already within the New Testament: the various 'culture-ideals' of the gnosis and of philosophical rationalism—notwithstanding their 'fundamental' parity of treatment—are differently seen according to their special potentialities and limitations, and differently assessed in their positive significance. A corresponding effect will emerge when the relationship of faith is taken further and applied also to modern cultural ideals, that is, above all, to modern scientific and technological culture and to the artistic cultural ideal of the personality formed on aesthetic lines.[19] Here it is enough to call attention to this. The New Testament contains nothing whatever like a compendium of all possible cultural values, and the openness it shows in the matter should not be taken amiss, but rather welcomed. What the human spirit is and is capable of is ultimately shown only in the movement of the spirit itself, that is to say it must be found directly, verified and expanded in the living cultural work, and admits of no determination by means of an 'encyclopaedia' of the spirit which tries to fix it from the outset and know it all, as it were, beforehand. From the standpoint of faith, we must beware, above all, of the ascetic distortion of the idea of culture, which today in practice tends mainly to suspect as a forbidden luxury any higher activity of the spiritual life that seems of no direct 'usefulness' and, in this barbarous sense, to be not absolutely necessary for the 'neighbour'. This form, too, of hostility to culture is remote from the New Testament. The words it uses of bodily nourishment may well be applied to spiritual, that, 'when received with thanksgiving, it is sanctified by the word of God and prayer' (1 Tim. 4.4f.); for 'every good endowment and every perfect

---

[19]With the modern scientific culture, and calling in particular, the question arises as to the possible 'service' that the man of 'culture' as such can render to his neighbour and the community or society. The New Testament, it is evident, never speaks expressly of this.

gift is from above, coming down from the Father of lights' (James 1.17; *cf.* Phil. 4.8).

The second point is of greater importance, and should not be over-looked. Up to now we have been carrying out a somewhat broad abstraction, doubtful perhaps in its consequences, in speaking simply of culture, wisdom, or philosophy as such—as of certain free-float-ing spiritual potentialities and realities in themselves. The New Testament, however, speaks of the wise, of the gnostic, and so on. It speaks of *persons*, and of spirit and culture considered as the human condition, actual forces bringing fulfilment of life, operative only in particular 'cultured' men. Otherwise, it would not be possible to see in culture, as the New Testament does, a religious and moral question, and to incorporate its workings, not in a cosmos of the spirit, but in one of love, that is, in the community. From this standpoint must be seen what we have said about the opposition as well as the—relative—harmony it is possible to establish between culture and the Christian faith. In either case, it is a question of a personal encounter and a personal decision, which the whole man must make. Ultimately, man does not live, even in his spiritual life, simply on account of the spirit, of abstract, scientific and theoretical potentialities, but because he wants, by their means, to fill a definite place in life, and, above all, to apprehend a definite meaning for his whole existence and to fulfil it. Accordingly, faith also should encounter him, not as a mere sum of various religious and moral convictions and concepts (the idea of a 'Christianity' never once occurs in the New Testament), but only as a concrete utterance that makes demands and promises in a definite 'name', and claims a concrete and personal confession—as a decision in the presence of an equally definite and concrete human society and its history. It is clear that here there can be no gradual, unbroken transition, as is always conceivable with a mere adoption and expansion of certain values and ideals. Culture, in its previous sense as giving significance to life, must, rather, be rejected *in toto*. It must, in the words of Paul, be counted as 'loss', as 'refuse' (Phil. 3.8*f.*), if faith is to begin and if Christ—and, at that, a Christ 'as crucified'[20]—is to appear in the place where culture reigned supreme.

Only if the problem is seen thus, as an existential one involving the

[20] 1 Cor. 2.2; *cf.* Gal. 3.1; 5.11.

whole person, does it make sense to speak of the persistence and further growth of culture for the believer and in the world of faith. In this setting, as we have seen, it is a matter of a culture of only relative significance, robbed, so to speak, by faith, of its absolutist claim. For how could such a claim be possible, without suspending the spiritual life as such? The spirit, of its very nature, cannot desire to limit itself. In the course of its infinite inherent movement it cannot suddenly halt, change its methods, and accept limitation from without. The demand that it should recognize as a *spiritual* potentiality what it can no longer permeate spiritually is absurd and obviously incapable of execution. But the *man* who lives a spiritual life can actually experience such an upheaval in that what he spiritually perfects and masters he can no longer accept as an adequate, meaningful basis for his existence. He can take his culture in this sense as something imperfect, accounting, accordingly, for the limits of the spirit (which he sees clearly from within) and apprehend in faith a new, positive ordinance and promise of God precisely in the Cross and the personal witness of Christ as he comes up against them. In this the laws and potentialities of spiritual knowledge and culture are not absolutely eliminated, modified, or destroyed; but they lose, for the man of culture who takes his stand on faith, their absolutist meaning and their spiritually baseless claim to dominance over the whole man. The meaning and direction of his spiritual work are thereby, in fact, changed. Culture is taken more lightly and, at the same time, more seriously than before, and certainly interpreted and determined differently; which in itself could be precisely termed the product of faith.

What, however, does this transformation mean *spiritually*? Is it possible to go beyond the previous knowledge of the unique historical form, beyond the concrete, responsible decision of each case in turn, and to frame something definite about the interconnection of faith and culture? Are there boundaries, standpoints, guiding principles, universally valid for the culture informed by Christian faith, which create something of a firm, *spiritually* recognizable *connection* between the existence of the believer, as such, and the spiritual work of the intellect that he performs? Here we are confronted once again with the old, recurring question of the true relation between faith and culture—faith, knowledge, and science—with which we started. I do not venture to give a definite answer to it. It cannot be disputed that the Christian faith continuously influences the world of the spirit and of culture, precisely by the subordinate position it imposes on it, as well as in other ways. It is equally evident that even in the world of the objective spirit it does not simply pass by without trace, and the historian again and again recognizes, in the historical forms of Western culture, the eloquent, even though unrepeatable, expression of this connection. Whoever strives for a systematic view of the phenomenon will always tend to go a step further, and to establish between the two entities a firm theological and philosophical bond that transcends time, as was most brilliantly attempted in medieval scholasticism, but certainly not there alone. Yet, in such attempts at bridging the gap in a firm, methodical manner, danger is always apparent; and it ultimately appears doubtful if this can be done at all without impairing, on the one hand, the freedom of the spirit in its indefinitely progressing self-culture, and, on the other, the sovereignty of the unfathomable God and of his revelation. We are, then, left with a pure confession of the Christian faith, which can only be a confession of prayer and hope that the humility and bondage of the believer may be precisely what furthers the freedom of culture, and that the freedom of the tireless spirit may be precisely what furthers the earnestness and single-mindedness of faith.

3
The Events of Easter
and the Empty Tomb

THE EASTER NARRATIVES have, in the past generation, as indeed always, been studied scientifically, and the general progress in the study of primitive Christianity has naturally furthered this work. Yet it seems to me that, with all the various researches into literary history, history of tradition, motive-history and form-history, there has been undue neglect of the inquiry into history pure and simple, that is, the inquiry into the historical core of that to which tradition gives its historical testimony.[1] Interest in these types of approach to the Easter event threatens to smother the event itself. But the philological work that necessarily has the first word in assessing the sources must not lead us to hold as secondary the strictly historical inquiry into what took place, the actual sequence of events and their interconnection, nor to relegate it to the fringe as crude and commonplace. Our legitimately critical attitude, justified as it is, towards a naïve psychologism and historicism has held us back from a direct exploitation and interpretation of the ancient texts. It does not, however, absolve us, on the ground of a better and more promising method, from the task of posing anew and answering the question the historian is bound to face; that is, of deciding how far and with what degree of probability the actual events and their sequence can still be ascertained.

The following study is intended as historical in this sense. Consequently, it will not reproduce in extenso the work of source-criticism achieved up to the present, nor will it wander at large in the ever-broadening field of tradition-history.[2] It will, in fact, be brief, and make

[1]'As soon as it is a question of determining the historical cause of the tradition of the literary data differences of opinion arise', as E. Fascher rightly pointed out as long ago as 1927. *Die Auferstehung Jesu und ihr Verhältnis zur urchristlichen Verkündigung, ZNW* 26 (1927) 4.
[2]The most important of all the earlier studies of this question is that of Ed. Meyers, *Ursprung und Anfänge des Christentums* I (1921), II (1923); but it has the drawback of

use of only the material that, after critical examination, appears useful in reconstructing the exterior happenings after the death of Jesus up to the first Easter encounters, now recognized as decisive for the origin of the Church. I hope to be able to show that such a reconstruction is quite possible in broad outline, that, in any case, there is no occasion to despair, from the outset, of its possibility as regards the essentials. The result, it seems to me, cannot be without its bearing on the theological understanding of the resurrection message; but this aspect I leave wholly out of account in my investigation.

The oldest and most reliable account we have of what the disciples experienced at Easter is that of Paul in the fifteenth chapter of his first Epistle to the Corinthians. This is universally admitted. Any investigation of the subject must start with this. In the historical information it provides it is gratifyingly exact, but disappointingly brief. In fact, it is no more than an enumeration of the more significant appearances of Christ—first to Peter, then to the Twelve, then to five hundred of

depending on an already antiquated method of source criticism, and it confirmed, especially in the minds of theologians who did not always do justice to its merits, a general distrust of this procedure. Em. Hirsch, *Die Auferstehungsgeschichte und der christliche Glaube* (1940), made its appearance under somewhat dubious theological auspices, and this was the main factor in the estimates it received. The following study more or less agrees with its historical conclusions, but aims at giving them a broader and more balanced base. Nowadays the historical, as well as the systematic, discussion of the resurrection problem must start out, above all, from the great work that Hans Grass has devoted to the events of Easter: *Ostergeschehen und Osterberichte* (1956). It is repeatedly at variance with the findings of the present study (in its first edition, 1952), and issues in an essentially negative judgement on the source-value of tradition, particularly of the tomb narratives. Nonetheless, I am glad of the considerable agreement between us in method and even in concrete findings, and my aim is to take into account, as far as possible, his basic critique, even when, as unfortunately is usually the case, it does not wholly convince me. From the older literature, the following still deserve attention: E. von Dobschütz, *Ostern und Pfingsten*, Eine Studie zu 1 Cor. 15 (1903), and, from another aspect, the account of the literature given by H. J. Holtzmann, *Das leere Grab und die gegenwärtigen Verhandlungen über die Auferstehung Jesu*, Theol. Rundschau 9 (1906), 79ff.; 119ff. A comprehensive view of the more recent literature is given, from the Catholic standpoint, by P. de Haes, *La résurrection de Jésus dans l'apologétique des cinquante dernières années* (Rome 1953).

the brethren at once. There follows an appearance to James, then to all the Apostles, and finally one more to Paul himself.

This account meets all the demands of historical reliability that could possibly be made of such a text as things stood. The first Epistle to the Corinthians must have been written at Ephesus in the spring of A.D. 56 or 57. But Paul says that he had himself 'received' the data and 'delivered' them. He had made them the foundation of his missionary preaching, so that they were well known also to the Corinthians. They were recalled only as having been taught earlier, and Paul assumes a corresponding knowledge, wherever Christ had been preached, as a matter of course. It is a case not only of an old, but of a long-formed tradition, formalized and, in that way, preserved. Consequently, we may assume that he himself, at the very beginning of his apostolic activity, had 'received' it—whether in Damascus, or a little later in Antioch or Jerusalem, where the formula presumably originated. Thus, between its creation and the event it conveys, hardly more than a decade could have elapsed, and probably only half of one. Now, it is certainly a matter of dispute how far the actual text of this ancient, originally Aramaic, formula went. The conversion of Paul can, by no means, have formed part of it, and, in the mention of the five hundred brethren, Paul inserts, on his own account, an observation that equally does not belong to it. Probably the old text breaks off at the mention of the Twelve. Nonetheless, there is hardly any reason for holding the rest less reliable or, indeed, purely imaginary and legendary. Paul had personally known not only Peter, but also James, and had visited them in Jerusalem right at the beginning of his career.[2a] He counted himself as one of the Apostles. Even the most sceptical person, who rightly enough should deny to those concerned here a 'purely historical' interest, could hardly hold that they never spoke to one another about those crucial events, which the leading personalities had themselves experienced and used as the main topic of their preaching. Paul, therefore, had received first-hand information on the subject with which he dealt. There is also the fact that Paul, no vague and confused thinker,[3] lays great stress on the reliability of these accounts, explaining that he does not allude to them simply in passing or in the context of quite different questions, but

[2a]Gal. 1.18f.
[3]His concern for exact dates can be seen also in 2 Cor. 11 and Gal. 1f.

that he solemnly emphasizes his complete assurance of their absolute credibility. Finally, it is a matter, not of anything particularly complex, or of theological explanations and detailed texts, where slight modifications and shifts of emphasis could occur unintentionally,[4] but of perfectly simple, important, definite, well-known facts.[5] Anyone who, in spite of this, would doubt their reliability must perforce doubt all the deliverances of the New Testament—and not stop there!

There should never have been any doubt that Paul's account was intended to be chronological.[6] It starts with the death, the burial, and the resurrection of Jesus 'on the third day'. The provenance of this last time indication is doubtful. It itself appeals to the 'scriptures', and this detail must be correct, if only because the datum as such could acquire the 'dogmatic' interest, which enabled it to be taken up into the ancient formula, only through a biblical connection.[7] No other explanation carries any conviction. On the other hand, it is not at all easy to derive it from scripture alone; for here there is—in the texts

---

[4]These might well be suspected, for example, in the Last Supper tradition, a comparable text, as told in 1 Cor 11.23 ff., which, in addition, was influenced by the cult as practised.

[5]For this reason, it seems to me extremely improbable that the visions of James and the Apostles should have originally been at odds with those of Peter and the Twelve, that the different groups of adherents should, therefore, have put out the experience of their leader as the first and crucial one, and the various accounts only 'later'(?) placed in sequence as they appear in Paul. Such is the view repeated in our day by Ulrich Wilckens, *Form- und traditionsgeschichtliche Untersuchung der Missionsreden der Apostelgeschichte* (Heidelberger Habil. Schrift 1958). The formal parallelism of the parts, pointed out by Harnack and others after him, is not sufficient ground for it. Later, James was certainly, in the strict Judaeo-Christian groups, assigned a place at the outset as a chief witness and main authority, as the Gospel according to the Hebrews shows (Jerome, *vir. ill.* 2); but this allows of no conclusion bearing on the first years; cf. H. J. Schoeps, *Theologie und Geschichte des Judenchristentums* (1949) 122ff.

[6]The chronological sense of the successive εἶτα-ἔπειτα-ἔπειτα-εἶτα is sufficiently emphasized by the concluding ἔσχατον (15.8), and perhaps also by the ἔκτρωμα (see below). What Michaelis, *Erscheinungen*, pp. 23 ff., urges against the chronological interpretation may be plausible as regards each separate detail, but to sustain it against the whole tenor of the passage, with its frequent indications of time, is quite arbitrary.

[7]It occurs again and again also after Paul (Mark 8.31 par. ; 9.31 par.; Luke 24.7,46; Acts 10.10, etc.) and is repeated as a formula in countless confessions; F. Kattenbusch, *Das apostolische Symbol* 2 (1900), 642.ff; B. Metzger, 'A suggestion concerning the meaning of 1 Cor. 15.4b', *Journal of Theological Studies*, N.S. 8 (1957) 118ff., removes the phrase κατὰ τὰς γραφάς from the neighbouring τῇ ἡμέρᾳ τῇ τρίτῃ, making it refer solely to the resurrection. But this is certainly wrong.

available to us—hardly a single testimony that must unquestionably be taken in this sense.[8] For this reason, it is also difficult to adduce a proof on this point from later Scripture. The New Testament itself knows only the appeal to the 'three days and nights' which Jonas passed in the fish's belly,[9] and this time indication does not, at least formally, agree wholly with the older resurrection datum 'on the third day', even if the differing computations can be reconciled according to the Jewish manner of reckoning.[10] It must, then, be assumed that 'the third day' was probably somehow already given before it could be discovered in the Old Testament and taken over into the confession. The liturgical explanation of the datum according to the calendar of feasts can, now that we know the age of the underlying formula, no longer be seriously entertained. At the time of its origin there was not yet any Christian celebration of the Sunday, from which, counting backwards to Good Friday, one could determine the time interval. It is more appropriate to see the three days as a typical number which plays a certain role in a number of different historical contexts.[11] In particular, three days became accepted as the time during which the soul dwells in the neighbourhood of the corpse before the latter decays.[12] But all these are derivative factors, extremely indefinite and far from cogent. Thus, at the very least, we must allow the possibility that the statement about the 'third' day was meant to be historical.[13] Of course, this historical datum cannot be found directly

---

[8]On this, most recently, Metzger, pp. 118f.

[9]Matt. 12.40; it is lacking in the parallel places Matt. 16.14 and Luke 11.29f.

[10]G. Delling, Art. ἡμέρα in ThW II (1936) 952f.; cf. Augustine, De consensu evang., III, 66. In any case, this manner of reckoning is still more understandable if we are dealing with a historical statement rather than a purely formal one of traditional use.

[11]Cf. F. Nötscher, 'Zur Auferstehung nach drei Tagen,' Biblica 35 (1954) 313ff., and the literature there cited.

[12]A. Meyer, Die Auferstehung Jesu (1905) 182ff.; C. Clemen, Religionsgeschichtliche Erklärung des Neuen Testaments (1924) 96ff.; J. Leipoldt, Die sterbenden und auferstehenden Götter (1923) 77ff.; ibid. 'Zu den Auferstehungsgeschichten,' ThZ 73 (1948) 737ff. For a contrary view, Metzger, p. 122 and also Schneider, in spite of his purely 'religious-historical' attribution of the resurrection, pp. 85f.: 'It is not from hellenistic material that the three days between the death and resurrection were taken, since Paul already derives them from the Old Testament and Matthew gives the story of Jonas as the source'.

[13]When H. Conzelmann, in his article 'Auferstehung Christi I' in RGG³ 1 (1957) 700, explains that the dating is 'of its nature not a historical, but a "dogmatic" datum'. he

in the resurrection, of which, according to the accounts of all the older canonical Gospels, there was no witness. It must, in the first place, be connected with the process of becoming aware, the 'discovery' of the resurrection that had already happened. Yet this discovery, as I would emphasize precisely here, can hardly have been caused only by the first appearances of the risen Christ. These took place, in all probability, not in Jerusalem, but in Galilee, and, for the journey there from Jerusalem, the time—especially when the sabbath is taken into account—was too short.[14]

That the disciples had their first meeting with the risen Christ in Galilee is expressly stated in St. Mark's Gospel [15]and also in that of St. Matthew;[16] as also later in the Gospel according to St. Peter.[17] An echo of this is contained also in the supplementary chapter of St. John's Gospel, which is otherwise orientated to Jerusalem.[18] Of the older evangelists Luke is the only one to rule out the Galilean tradition and to refer all the events of Easter to Jerusalem or its proximity. The theological reasons prompting this siting will not be

---

sets up, in my opinion, a false antithesis, and fails to resolve the basic difficulty of a purely dogmatic attribution.

[14]L. Brun, *Die Auferstehung Christi in der urchristlichen Überlieferung* (1925) 45, 67, saw this clearly enough, but drew the false conclusion that the first appearance to Peter must have been in Jerusalem; *cf.* against this, though with insufficient foundation, J. Finegan, *Die Überlieferung der Leidens- und Auferstehungsgeschichte Jesu* (1934) 103, n. 5. On general grounds, a meeting with the risen Christ on a journey from Jerusalem to Galilee is not untenable, such as advocated, by analogy with the *Quo Vadis* legend, by F. C. Burkitt in *Christian Beginnings* (1924) 87f. It would, however, contradict the prophecy of the angels, Mark 16.7 par. and be left hanging in the air: Kirsopp Lake, *Beginnings of Christianity*, ed. F. A. Foakes Jackson and K. Lake, I, 5 (1933), Note II, The command not to leave Jerusalem and the 'Galilean tradition', pp. 7ff., esp. p. 13.

[15]Mark 14.28; 16.7.

[16]Matt. 28.16. Here, of course, Matthew follows Mark. But that his own special description of the happenings in Galilee (28.16ff.) must go back to Mark certainly cannot be assumed—contrary to W. Marxsen, *Der Evangelist Markus* (1956) 53.

[17]Ev. Pr. 14.60.

[18]John 21.1. See Bultmann, *Das Evangelium des Johannes* (1941) 546: 'The editor clearly desired to combine the Matt.-Mark tradition of a Galilean appearance of the risen Christ with the Johannine standpoint. In adding now these accounts, after already relating two manifestations of the risen Christ (John 20.19-23; 24-29), he had to correct the tradition, from which he took vv. 1-13, on this point, and to emphasize that here the third "manifestation" is recorded.'

discussed here.[19] That the Jerusalem tradition is secondary may already be deduced from the preponderant evidence of the older witnesses.[20] And a final argument is contained in our text of St. Paul.[21] The appearance, there mentioned, to five hundred brethren (and sisters?) can hardly be situated in Jerusalem; it, therefore, points likewise to Galilee. Even if the round number 'five hundred' may be an exaggeration, the gathering would be too numerous for a private house, and a synagogue—even were it large enough[22]—would hardly have been accorded to the adherents of Jesus in Jerusalem.[23] We cannot consider an open-air service on the Mount of Olives. That only leaves the temple to be considered. But quite apart from the intrinsic improbability of an appearance there and the impossibility of keeping away the unbelievers then as always, such an extraordinary occurrence would never have passed without trace into oblivion, and Luke certainly, with his love for the temple, would have attached great importance to it and gladly recorded it.[24] Thus there only remains for this appearance a gathering in the open somewhere in Galilee,[25] and,

---

[19]On this H. Conzelmann, *The Theology of St. Luke* (1960) pp. 93f., 132ff.; P. Schubert, 'The structure and significance of Luke 24' in *Neutest. Studien für R. Bultmann* (1957)², pp. 165ff., 183ff.

[20]Among these can also be counted the apparent model for the calling of Peter in Luke (5.13-35).

[21]Conzelmann, in *Auferstehung*, col. 700, argues that the probable origin in Jerusalem of the formula is indicative of the place of the appearances; but this seems far from cogent.

[22]In Jerusalem we have no old synagogues left. The buildings we know in Galilee would be mostly too small. On these see H. Kohl–C. Watzinger, *Antike Synagogen in Galiläa* (1916) and C. Watzinger, *Denkmäler Palästinas* (1935) 107ff.

[23]Grass (*op. cit.* n. 2 *supra*) p. 122, argues to the contrary that the primitive community must with time have created space for itself, 'so that even on occasion it could meet to the number of 500 (in the open)'. But here we are at the very beginning of its development; and so this assumption, contestable on other grounds, has all probability against it.

[24]Thus, contrary to Gal. 1.17ff., he makes Paul the recipient of a kind of vision relating to his mission in the temple. Acts 22.17ff.

[25]According to Matt. 28, 16, we could, with Dobschütz (*op. cit.* n. 2 *supra*), p. 33, envisage a mountain as the place of the event. But the widely prevailing fondness for manifestations and revelations on mountains makes this detail suspect; *cf.* the material in H. Riesenfeld, *Jésus transfiguré* (1947) 217ff.; also W. Schmauch, *Orte der Offenbarung und der Offenbarungsort im N.T.* (1956) 67ff. Cf. especially what the 'Sophia Jesu Christi' says (77; 9ff.) about the mountain in Galilee, 'which is called "place of ripeness and joy",' where Jesus, after the resurrection instructed his twelve disciples and seven women— 'Die gnostischen Schriften des Kopt. Papyrus Berolin. 502', edited and produced by W. C. Till (1955) 195f. A total rejection of a symbolic and typological interpretation of the

as regards external circumstances, this is least improbable.[26] Galilee was the old homeland of Jesus, whence his adherents came and where they were strong; and later it had large communities, independent of Jerusalem, which themselves sent out missions.[27]

The appearance to five hundred brethren is, in Paul, the third in the series, and, as we have said, is not perhaps part of the old kerygma. In the beginning the appearance to Peter stood alone. This is, in view of the clear statement in Paul, not open to doubt, and it also accords with the pre-eminent place accorded to Peter in the early Christian tradition. It was on this account that Peter became the rock on which the Church was built. And, therefore, this encounter with Peter was, so it seems, also mentioned by Luke, and in a kerygmatic formula he took over. But, strangely enough, he does not actually relate it. Before alluding to it, he tells the story of the disciples at Emmaus,[28] who did not even belong to the twelve whom the risen Christ met outside Jerusalem. On returning to the city with the great news, they were received with the jubilant cry, 'The Lord has risen in truth and appeared to Simon'.[29] What is so striking is how the report of what is, after all, the main thing, is telescoped, announcing but not describing it; and this has long aroused the suspicion that Luke must have had definite grounds for avoiding any description of the appearance to Peter. Perhaps, in its special features, it could not be ascribed elsewhere than to Galilee, and so it contradicted the Jerusalem tendency

---

mountain, with W. Foersters, *ThW* v (1954) 484f., can hardly be sustained. What Holl, *Preuss, Akad. d. Wissench*, 1921=*Ges. Aufs. z. Kirchengesch* 2 [1928], 46f., adduces against Galilee as the site, and for Jerusalem, is quite without force. If Paul observes that, of the five hundred, 'many' are still alive, and 'some' dead, that by no means supposes that they must all have been in a place where they could have been found at any time. On Holl's objection against such a crowd of disciples in Galilee, see n. 27 below. For further literature on the question, *cf.* Kümmel, *ThR* 18 (1950) 21ff.

[26]I must admit that it is not clear to me why, as Conzelmann, *Auferstehung*, 699f., thinks, a preference should be accorded *traditionsgeschichtlich* to the Jerusalem accounts, and still less why Marxsen, *op. cit.* p. 52, rejects altogether my reasons for Galilee. Other considerations, beside traditio- and form-historical, have their rights.

[27]This seems to me that E. Lohmeyer has fully proved in his otherwise unconvincing book, *Galiläa und Jerusalem* (1936).

[28]Luke 24.13-35.

[29]Here there is probably a correction of the original account: Grass, *op. cit.* pp. 35ff. The reading λέγοντες instead of λέγοντας is certainly not original.

of his narration.[30] However, he could not simply omit it, since it was crucial and formed part of the most ancient tradition. It was, therefore, simply indicated, and all the detailed circumstances and the precise place of the meeting were, strangely enough, left vague.

Nonetheless, a supposition may be ventured that would lend support to what has been said up to now. It is precisely Luke who presents, in contrast to all the other evangelists, a special vocation story of Peter, the legend of the 'miraculous draught of fishes'. In it the Lord takes Peter by surprise among his boats and nets, and makes him his *first* disciple who should, from then on, no longer catch fish, but men.[31] It has often been observed that this latter motive of the mission would be eminently appropriate to an Easter narrative. Have we here, perhaps, transposed in time, a reflex of the first meeting of Peter with the risen Christ? The legend, also, of Peter walking on the water, has been recalled in this context, but the connection is not so obvious.[32] On the other hand, a decisive factor pointing the same way is the resurrection story of the last chapter of John[33] and of the Gospel according to St. Peter,[34] in which the risen Christ again appears to Peter when fishing in the lake of Gennesaret, and the motive of the miraculous draught and of the mission—at any rate in John[35]—once more appears.[36] Any solution can only be hypothetical, but it seems

[30]This is, of course, only a supposition. It was, as I point out later, already expressed, with the same reasoning, by E. Stauffer, *Vor- und Frühgeschichte des Primaus Petri, ZKG* 62 (1943-44), p. 19. 'The missing account told of appearances in Galilee, and the details of this narrative were presumably inseparably bound up with this locality. Luke, however, only wanted to know and report the appearance in Jerusalem'. At any rate, such an explanation seems to me more probable than the assumption that the particular eschatological overtone of this first meeting, its suggestion of the expectation of the Parousia, was the reason for its disappearance.

[31]Luke 5.1-11; *cf.* Matt. 1.17.

[32]Matt. 14.28*ff.* The same may certainly be said of the Transfiguration account and Peter's confession, which Bultmann, *The History of the Synoptic Tradition* (1963) 259*ff.*, suggests were transposed from Easter.

[33]John 21.1*ff.*   [34]Gospel acc. to Peter, 14.60.

[35]The text of the Gospel according to Peter breaks off beforehand. Also in the epist. apost. 11, Jesus appeared, according to one manuscript, when Peter was fishing.

[36]The question cannot be pursued here in detail. For a discussion of it, see Bultmann, *Johannes*, pp. 545*ff.*; Stauffer, *Vor- und Frühgeschichte*, pp. 19*f.*; O Cullmann, *Petrus, Jünger-Apostel-Märtyrer. Das historische und theologische Petrusproblem* (1952), pp. 63*f.*; Grass, *op. cit.* pp. 74*ff.*, and the literature there mentioned. Bultmann himself holds the fish haul and the accompanying meal as merely a pictorial expansion of the original image used in Mark 1.17. *Synopt. Tradition*, pp. 217*f.*, 230.

to me that there is a distinct probability that the first appearance of the risen Christ to Peter was at the fish haul on the lake of Gennesaret in Galilee.[37]

The fact that Matthew says nothing about the first, crucial meeting with Peter seems, at first sight, to be most strange, precisely because he, unlike Luke, keeps all along to the Galilean standpoint of Mark. Matthew, however, altogether simplifies and concentrates the Easter story in a radical fashion. As the conclusion of his Gospel he brings only one single great appearance to all the disciples, who had gone beforehand to a mountain in Galilee, as Jesus had commanded.[38] All the varied particularized accounts of the meetings with the disciples are overwhelmed and absorbed by this monumental closing scene,[39] and so the appearance to Peter, as a separate event, is left out. It is, in a way, included merely in the one, ideal concluding tableau.[40]

At a later date, attempts were made, according to individual tastes and trends, to present other persons as there at the beginning and the subjects of the first resurrection experiences. Thus James or Levi, Mary Magdalen, Nicodemus, or even the mother of Jesus was placed where originally Peter was. These accounts are of no historical value, and so without interest for us.

The appearance to the Twelve, or, strictly speaking, to the eleven apostles, which, according to Paul, followed that to Peter, is vouched for in tradition practically everywhere.[41] This is easily understood when we consider the importance that 'the Apostles' in this regard had for the later Church. If the appearance to Peter and to the five hundred took place in Galilee, so must also that to the Twelve, which

---

[37]Certainly, in the Gospel of John and probably also in that of Peter, Peter is not alone with Jesus on this occasion. But he is right in the foreground, all the same, and is the first, according to John, to reach Jesus, before all the rest. Likewise, in John 20.6, he is the first of the disciples to approach the tomb, and, if we may take the beloved disciple as a symbolical figure, even the first to reach it. The narrative, in this form, is presented in the secondary version, Luke 24.12.

[38]Matt. 28.16ff.

[39]On the meeting with the two women, Matt. 28.9f. (see note 82 below).

[40]Further reasons which could account for the disappearance of the Peter tradition are assembled in Brun, 50ff.

[41]The old Gospel of Mark seems to have said nothing at all about Easter appearances; but that to the Twelve (and probably that to Peter) is, from Mark 16.7, assumed as known.

came between them. If we consider the Last Supper tradition and the connected legends of the multiplication of the loaves, we may venture the supposition that this appearance took place when the Apostles were together at a meal, or else that it culminated in a meal with the risen Lord. The frequent mention of eating and drinking in the Easter narratives could point in this direction, even if the meaning of the action was variously interpreted.[42] But this remains uncertain,[43] and we must be content with the plain fact of this appearance witnessed to by Paul. Paul says nothing about how we must envisage its historical connection with the first appearance to Peter. Peter was himself present at the second, and so there must be some connection. One might suppose, for instance, that Peter, having attained complete certainty through what he had experienced, gathered all the rest together, and that the appearance was then repeated. With the third appearance, a great development has obviously taken place.[44] By now it is already an imposing circle that has assembled round the Apostles; the 'Church' is coming into being, and the formation of a community has been solemnly inaugurated in Galilee.

As to the next two instances given by Paul, we are almost completely in the dark. On the appearance to James all we have is a later, quite unreliable account in the Gospel to the Hebrews.[45] It is possible, though not necessarily the case, that for James himself it meant a conversion;[46] for, in the lifetime of his brother, he seems to have held apart from him.[47] In that case, the appearance must likewise be trans-

---

[42]Luke 24.30*ff.*; John 21. 12*ff.*; Gospel of Hebrews according to Jerome, *vir. ill.* 2; Mark 16.14; *cf.* Acts 1.4 (?); 10.41. An unmistakably anti-Docetic tendency is seen in Luke 24.41*ff.*; also in Ign. Smyrn. 3.3.

[43]On this question see Brun, pp. 72*ff.*; O. Cullman, *Early Christian Worship* (1953) SBT, 10. In any case, the meal, as Brun, p. 66, observes, could well have taken place in the open.

[44]There is no reason to connect it with the Pentecost legend of Acts 2. W. G. Kümmel, *Kirchenbegriff und Geschichtsbewusstsein in der Urgemeinde und bei Jesus* (1943) 8; Jos. Schmitt, *Jésus Ressuscité dans la prédication Apostolique* (1949) pp. 138*ff.*; Grass, *op. cit.* pp. 99*ff.* And, even if this later legend should contain some kind of echo of the event recorded by Paul, one cannot draw any historical inference from it.

[45]Jerome, *vir. ill.* 2.

[46]Dobschütz, *op. cit.* pp. 24*f.* If this be accepted, the sequence of the appearances builds up to a fine, though, of course, unsought climax—from the apostle Peter to the neutral James and the persecutor Paul.

[47]Mark 3.21,31*ff.* par.; 6.3 par.; *cf.* John 7.6,10.

ferred to Galilee; for how could James have been in Jerusalem?[48] At all events, the important place he has from now on in the primitive community must be due to this meeting with Christ. But we know nothing in any detail.

For the appearance to 'all the Apostles' we lack any further sources. It had to do with their being called and sent out; for the Apostles were the earliest missionaries of the Church. They formed a special, not really small, band of persons, to which Peter and, later on, Paul also belonged.[49] But it is doubtful if James also belonged, and, in consequence, all attempts to find a definite connection between his meeting with Christ and the Lord's appearance to 'all the Apostles' remain uncertain. It is conceivable that the appearance to the Apostles was in Jerusalem. But it is equally possible that it was precisely this appearance that caused the leaders of the young community to move off to Jerusalem and there, in the holy centre of Israel, to begin the battle for the people, to which they were called.

The later calling of Paul stands by itself. It was, as he emphasizes, the last appearance, and, in fact, something portentous. Probably in this Paul was not only thinking of how it was imparted to a raging persecutor who, at a stroke, was thrown down and raised up to be an Apostle, but also of the lateness and absolute improbability of this occurrence, when the Church was already established and further appearances were not to be expected. Certainly, in his own view, this election also had a significance for the Church and salvation-history. He saw himself, in fact, not as an Apostle who should simply continue to transmit the message already being preached, but purely as the Apostle of the Gentiles; and, with this universal view of his office, he opened a new epoch.

After that, in the (roughly) two decades which elapsed, Paul was to experience no further manifestations of Christ. To all appearances,

---

[48]We may admit that James, who had come to Jerusalem for the paschal feast, might not at that time have left the city, but then we would come up against chronological difficulties. W. Grundmann, also (*Die Geschichte Jesu Christi* (1957) 369f.) with Albertz, holds that the appearances to the relations of Jesus were originally in Jerusalem. But later they seem more likely 'connected with his homeland'; cf. Lohmeyer, pp. 53 ff.

[49]Campenhausen, '*Der urchristliche Apostelbegriff*', *Stud. theol.* I (1947) 96ff., especially pp. 105 ff.

he holds the series to be closed[50]—ecstatic experiences and whatever 'visions' may have occurred are on quite a different plane. It must be presumed that he meant the account of the appearances of Christ, as he gave them, to be complete; in other words, he mentions here all the reliable testimonies and witnesses that he knows. Of course, the list could still be incomplete. There may have been other Easter encounters of which he knew nothing, either because they formed no part of the standard tradition, or because, at the time of writing, he was not yet aware of them. However, there are no indications that make this at all probable.[51] By far the greater part of the accounts contained, over and above the Pauline tradition, in the canonical and apocryphal Gospels must be considered legendary accretions without any claim to historicity.

IIa

The account given by Paul renders certain the events of Easter in so far as they happened in Galilee. As to the early Jerusalem happenings, it tells us nothing. All that is said is that Jesus died and was buried and rose again the third day. But the conclusion that Paul must have known already of the empty tomb, since he alludes to the burial, is certainly too bold. Possibly Paul held there was a real change and transfiguration of the dead body and so an 'emptying' of the tomb;[52] but for this

---

[50]This follows from the ἔσχατον δὲ πάντων, perhaps also from the disputed concept of the ἔκτρωμα; cf., on the possible interpretations of this, J. Schneider, *ThW* 2 (1935) 463. It seems to me, in all probability, that Paul uses the word in a special and crude meaning ('untimely birth') which is, naturally, not to be found in the literary tradition. Yet today the tendency seems to be to take the word, with G. Björck, *Coniect. Neotest.* 3 (1938) 3*ff.*, as a quite generic term of abuse ('monster from birth').

[51]Cf. also the observation of Brun, p. 39 (and 65) on the extreme simplicity of the old 'schema' into which the resurrection stories were formerly fitted.

[52]This I held fairly definitely in the first edition of this paper; so also, among others, G. Stählin, 'On the third day', *Interpretation* 10 (1956) 282*ff.* This conclusion seems to follow, above all, from the parallelism between the resurrection of Christ and that of all Christians (Rom. 8.29). But Grass, pp. 146*ff.* has now cogently demonstrated that such a conclusion is not unassailable. Particularly in view of 2 Cor. 5.1, it is conceivable, despite Rom. 8.11, that Paul had not yet held there was a reanimation of the dead body of Jesus, and so had no need either to postulate an 'emptying' of the tomb.

he had no need of the support of definite information. 'Dead and buried'—this expression may simply be used to underline the reality and apparent finality of the death itself, and say nothing beyond this.[53] We must, therefore, as to what happened in Jerusalem, rely exclusively on the Gospel tradition, and this, in the form in which we have it, is later than Paul, and was framed in different circumstances, making it historically less reliable.[54] Legendary elements and apologetic tendencies, in part, also liturgical and polemical considerations, connected with Church politics, are already evident. Of all the accounts received, no two agree with one another. The unfavourable impression we get is appreciably mitigated only if we resolve to set aside altogether the demonstrably later accounts, one and all, and to follow exclusively the Marcan tradition, which was used by the other evangelists as their source, and, by them, elaborated and developed. Admittedly, even Mark does not simply offer the account of an 'eye-witness'. Even with him the accounts of the Passion and of Easter already show the inconsistencies of the different traditions, as well as some amplifications and legendary features. But in general the narrative is far from being purely imaginative. Obviously, it has much foundation in older

---

On the other hand, if he really thought on these lines (and so could no longer speak of a *bodily* resurrection of Jesus in the strict sense), he would have run counter to all that we know of the Jewish hope of resurrection, and have approximated to the 'gnostic' ideas precisely where he seems to have most opposed them. Nonetheless, Paul approaches the problem of the body in this connection from a quite different standpoint from that of later orthodox theology; *cf.* J. A. T. Robinson, *The Body; a study in Pauline theology* (1952), SBT, 5, esp. pp. 78*ff.*; also W. C. Robinson, 'The bodily resurrection of Christ,' *ThZ* 13 (1957) 81*ff.*

[53]In support of this we may adduce Acts 2.9; *cf.* 13.36. Behind these texts, J. W. Doeve, *Jewish Hermeneutics in the Synoptic Gospels and Acts* (1954), 168*ff.*, would see Judaeo-Christian midrashim as a pattern(?). E. Lohse, *Märtyrer und Gottesknecht* (1955), 115, draws attention to Jes. 53.9. Perhaps the Pauline formula should be considered as already anti-Docetic; thus J. Schniewind, '*Die Leugner der Auferstehung in Korinth*', in: *Nachgelassene Reden und Aufsätze* (1952), 122. 'No seeming death, no departure of the ἄνω Χριστός from the κάτω Ἰησοῦς before or during the passion. Reality of an actual death . . .'

[54]For what follows I would refer once and for all to the exhaustive motive-historical analysis of the resurrection tradition by Lyder Brun (*supra* n. 14), and the form-historical researches of M. Dibelius, *Die Formgeschichte des Evangeliums* (1959), R. Bultmann (*supra* n. 45), Finegan (*supra* n. 14), and Grass (*supra* n. 12). They have even been given a certain attention in Catholic circles, as shown by the careful presentation of J. Schmitt, Art. '*Auferstehung Christi*' in *Lex. f. Theol. u. Kirche* I (1957), 1028*ff.*

accounts, and the presentation itself is so sober and factual that it is quite inadmissible to rule out its content, *a priori*, as untrustworthy. All the statements, including that about the empty tomb, must be taken and examined one by one.

To start with, it is remarkable that Mark, in contradistinction to the other evangelists, hardly attempts to gloss over the frightful solitude in which Jesus met his end. He celebrated the last supper with the Twelve;[55] at Gethsemane, three of them were still close by him,[56] and, at his arrest, a few pilgrims encamped on the Mount of Olives may have pressed about him.[57] But after that, all left him and fled.[58] Only Peter ventured to follow him at a distance into the court of the high priest, and, even so, left him in the lurch.[59] From then on there was no one of the Apostles in his neighbourhood. On the occasion of Simon of Cyrene's carrying the cross there is mention of his sons, who later may have belonged to the community or were known in another connection, since their names are given.[60] The crucifixion itself was only seen 'from afar off' by some women who had come with Jesus from Galilee.[61] Finally, he was taken down by Joseph of Arimathaea, a member, it seems, of the Jerusalem aristocracy, who sympathized with Jesus and his movement, but was not actually an adherent.[62] That is all.

---

[55]Mark 14.17*ff.*   [56]Mark 14.33.

[57]The young man mentioned in Mark 14.51 can hardly be identified with the disciple named in 14.33, or with any of the Twelve.

[58]Mark 14.50.   [59]Mark 14.53*ff.*

[60]Mark 15.21; see Dibelius, *op. cit.* p. 183*f.*

[61]Mark 15.40*f.*; Finegan remarks, *op. cit.* p. 77: 'The presence of the women with Jesus in Galilee is recorded here (v. 41a), but it cannot have been derived from the accounts of his actions in Galilee, since they are never mentioned in that connection. Only Luke (8.2*f.*) speaks of them as being in Galilee. Ps. 38.11 (οἱ φίλοι μου . . . μακρόθεν ἔστησαν) did, indeed, determine the choice of μακρόθεν, but this passage of the psalm cannot be said to speak only of women. Consequently the appearance of the women here is not to be explained by his tendency for invention. It was a statement of fact, without ulterior motive.'

[62]Mark 15.43. Already Matthew, in 27.57 (ὃς καὶ αὐτὸς ἐμαθητεύθη τῷ Ἰησοῦ) tried to fix more exactly his relationship with Jesus, and Luke, in 25.50*f.*, starts the weaving of the legend: the pious and upright man had not consented to the council of the Jewish hierarchy. In the Gospel according to Peter 2.3, he has become a φίλος Πειλάτου καὶ τοῦ κυρίου. On the other hand, in Acts 13.27 the burial appears as carried out by the enemies of Jesus κατοικοῦντες Ἰερουσαλὴμ καὶ οἱ ἄρχοντες αὐτῶν. Here there is no sign of the transfiguration which Mark

This presentation is wholly credible and trustworthy. For the Apostles, as things turned out since the arrest of Jesus, it was no longer advisable to show themselves in public and to stand by Jesus. One is bound to accept that they kept themselves in hiding.[63] So it was that the community had no other first-hand Christian witness for all that happened later than that of the women, who were also present at the burial.[64] One can see why it was that they were named expressly and their presence underlined.[65] Of course, it is possible to cast doubt on this detail also—precisely on the ground of its deliberate emphasis— and so to hold the account of Jesus's burial to be unhistorical. This, however, in view of the mention of Joseph by name, is quite unwarranted.[66] The way the events are related makes them completely plausible and not open to doubt.

This is what we must be quite clear about when we come to judge the account of Easter morning, in which these women appear in action.[67] Should it be judged basically otherwise than all the rest of

---

began with his favourable description of Joseph; but this is not enough to warrant a search for historical 'traditions' behind the preacher's turn of phrase used by Luke; Grass, pp. 179f.

[63] On this question, see below p. 75f.

[64] Mark 15.47. Since they had stayed near the cross, it may well be thought that they met Joseph of Arimathaea there and followed him to the tomb.

[65] It is striking that in Mark 15.40 several women are named, in 16.1 three, and in 15.47 only two. Yet these very differences may be taken as evidence of his *synoptic* reliability. For it could be a matter of different 'sources' which were not balanced against one another in Mark; *cf.* Bultmann, *Tradition*, pp. 276, 284; Grass, p. 181, and, more definitely, R. Thiel, *Drei Markusevangelien* (1938) 202ff.

[66] The tradition as to the burial itself seems not to be uniform, but it should not, on that account, be held as freely invented; *cf.* M. Goguel, *La foi à la résurrection de Jésus dans le Christianisme primitif* (1933) 121ff.; *La naissance du Christianisme* (1946) 42ff.; E. Lohmeyer, *Das Evangelium des Markus* (1959) 351f. Further literature on the burial-question may be found in H. Lietzmann, *ZNW* 37 (1938) 296f. A very conservative assessment of the material and fantastic explanation of the empty tomb are offered by J. Spencer Kennard, jr., 'The burial of Jesus,' *Journl. Bibl. Lit.* 74 (1935) 227ff. Also a conservative, but very scrupulous consideration and harmonization of all the factors of the burial is that of W. Bulst, S.J., '*Novas in sepulturam Jesu inquisitiones*', *Verbum Domini* 31 (1953) 257ff., 352ff., and '*The Shroud of Turin*,' Milwaukee (1957) 77ff. Grass, pp. 173ff., esp. 184, would at least keep open the possibility that all the accounts of the burial are later legends—which would, of course, facilitate the explanation of the 'empty tomb' as legendary; but he cannot adduce conclusive reasons for this.

[67] Mark 16.1-8.

the concrete historical data to be handed down by Mark? This is the crucial question which now arises.

The last narrative of the Gospel has a different character from the preceding in that it is centred, not only on the empty tomb lying open, but also on a 'youth', that is an angel, who explains this phenomenon and orders the women to go and tell Peter and the Apostles. Jesus, who is risen, he explains, is no longer here; he is already on the way to Galilee[68] where they are to follow him. There they will have sight of him. This is, undoubtedly, a legendary account, which anticipates the events which come later in a miraculous announcement. Also the preceding account of the women going to the tomb is not without strangeness. The desire to anoint, 'on the third day', a dead body already buried and wrapped in linen cloths, is, however it be explained, not in accordance with any custom known to us,[69] and in itself unreasonable in view of the Palestine climate.[70] Furthermore, the assertion that the women only realized when they were already on the way that they would need help to roll away the stone and gain access to the tomb implies a degree of thoughtlessness quite out of the ordinary. Accordingly, the later evangelists all made changes in this place, and tried to help out with omissions, new interpretations or broader

[68]The expression προάγει ὑμᾶς εἰς τὴν Γαλιλαίαν could also be translated transitively. Jesus urges on the apostles to follow him to Galilee. This would accord with general use, only it is ruled out by Mark 14.28, and by the quasi-technical use of the word in the N.T. in the sense of 'discipleship'; cf. K. I. Schmidt, ThW I (1933) 130. A journey to Galilee in the sense of a mission to the 'Galilee of the Gentiles' is suggested by C. F. Evans, 'I will go before you into Galilee', JThS N.S.5 (1954) 3ff. This is possible in a verbal sense, but seems somewhat arbitrary. On Marxsen, see note 127 below.

[69]Luke explains the delay by the Sabbath rest: 23.56b. Against this we cannot adduce the Jewish law of the sabbath 23.5 (cf. Semach. 1.2) which allows anointing a corpse on the sabbath, since, apart from anything else, this applies only to one who has just died at home, not to one already buried, to which it would be necessary to travel.

[70]Yet there is no need to see, in addition, with Clemen, p. 97, and Lohmeyer, Mark, p. 296, a contradiction with the anointing story in Mark 14.8. It is too much to insist that the women knew of the earlier prophetic word of Jesus and must have been directed by it, and, besides, it was already in fact fulfilled, and the anointing not repeated. And that they had not yet known of the anointing by Joseph of Arimathaea and of the watch at the grave is a desperate assumption of Bulst, Inquisitiones, p. 273, by which he tries to save the additions given in the parallel accounts. Similar attempts at harmonization may be found, for example, in K. Bornhäuser, 'Die Kreuzesabnahme und das Begräbnis Jesu', NKZ 42 (1931) pp. 137ff., 147ff., 161ff.

rational explanations.[71] Yet however improbable Mark's account may be, these individual features in it do not betray any kind of tendency to the miraculous or fantastic. They should rather be seen as a mere naïve auxiliary to a somewhat primitive narrative art: the wish to anoint the body serves to give some sort of concrete motive to the journey to the tomb, and the concern about the stone was only brought in 'to prepare the miracle and heighten the effect'.[72] No miracle in the strict sense is related, and what remains over and above this narrator's 'artifice'—a journey to the tomb that is found opened and empty—is something quite simple and not at all incredible. The angel's action also is confined within narrow and modest bounds. Likewise, it should be noticed that Jesus does not himself appear at the grave, and, according to the angel, was not yet to appear openly. This is a striking feature that, apart from Luke, no later account has preserved. A legend put out subsequently to certify and supplement the resurrection-message would certainly have had a different construction; nor can we find in religious history any analogy to the scene that could serve to explain it.[73]

There is one further difficulty not yet touched upon, and which is the main support of the opposing view. It is contained in the last sentence of the narrative, which, rightly enough, has always been found puzzling. After the women had looked at the empty tomb and seen the angel they did not hurry off, as one would expect and as they had been ordered, to the Apostles and other adherents of Jesus, to acquaint them with the matter, but fled from the place and remained silent: 'for trembling and astonishment had come upon them; and they said nothing to any one, for they were afraid' (Mark 16.8). That concludes the account, and, according to the generally accepted view today, the whole of the Gospel—a most extraordinary end.[74] The impression,

---

[71]*Cf.* besides the canonical Gospels the Gospel according to Peter, 12.52*ff.* and the Epist. apost. 9 (20).

[72]Thus rightly Ed. Meyer I, 20 (these attempts one should certainly not call skilful in a literary sense—p. 17); likewise Grass, p. 20.

[73]On a somewhat similar story in Roman literature, see K. Kerényi, '*Die griechische Romanliteratur in religionsgeschichtl.*' '*Beleuchtung*' (1927) 10*f.*; Leipoldt, '*Auferstehungs geschichten*', col. 737*ff.*; C. Schneider, I, 73, 84.

[74]I do not enter further on the question of the conclusion of Mark's Gospel. It has been discussed at length, and is not of major importance in this context; *cf.* W.

hardly intended, that it gives is that the women, after this marvellous occurrence, did not obey the plain command of the angel. We must, therefore, conclude that the clear and emphatically expressed charge failed of its purpose, and it remains obscure why the apostles went to Galilee where Christ was to appear to them. Nonetheless, the complete silence of the women is so emphatically brought out and accounted for that it cannot possibly be passed over.[75] The narrator thows his interest in it; he intends to communicate therein something special. Unmistakably he has some definite intention; but what it is is, at first sight, rather puzzling.

This intention cannot be taken exclusively to be that of bringing out the 'numinous terror' arising from the empty tomb and the angel's word.[76] Such a modern and romantic explanation of the last words is certainly inadequate. Something more concrete must have been meant. Consequently, the critics have taken up a traditional and historical explanation, which first emerged with Wellhausen,[77] and later put forward in very varied forms with basically the same meaning. With this last verse, they say, the delayed emergence of the story of the tomb is, in a way, excused; it is meant to convey that 'this resurrection account of the women only became known subsequently'. In other words, it is clear that the whole tradition of the empty tomb is a later legend, and that the narrator himself suspects this or knows it,

---

Bauer, 'Griechisch-Deutsches Wörterbuch zum N.T.' (1958) 1705f.; cf. 274f. Should there have been a continuation, Mark 16.7 shows the direction it must have taken. It seems that the view that Mark 16.8 is the original ending of the Gospel is gaining ground. In that case Acts 20.23-25 and 21.10-4, would present a very similar narrative technique. The martyrdom of Paul is only announced prophetically, and 'since the Acts of the Apostles does not record the ending of the Apostle's life, this prophecy is of still greater significance'; M. Dibelius, *Studies in the Acts of the Apostles* (1956), 158.

[75]This would also hold good, though in a weakened sense, if, with Thiel., pp. 204f. and E. Hursch, *Frühgeschichte des Evangeliums* (1941) 178, we accepted two sources for the verse.

[76]Thus O. Linton, *'Der vermisste Markusschluss'*, ThBl 8 (1929), 229ff. The emphasis on fear and trembling in the presence of a heavenly apparition and the corresponding 'fear not' has all through a typical character, and 16.8 is also to be understood in this light. One cannot, with F. Scheidweiler, *'Das Schweigen der Frauen* (Mark. 16.8) *und das Osterwunder'*, Die Pforte 6 (1954-55) 152ff., postulate a violation of the grave or some other special reason to explain the fright. The evangelist would certainly not have preserved the echo of such a thing in this fashion.

[77]J. Wellhausen, *Das Evangelium Marci* (1902²), 136.

since he tries to cover himself in advance against any doubt in regard to his account, which was, doubtless, astonishing. The tomb was really empty, this fact is proved; and, if it was not yet known at this stage, that is precisely because the women were silent on the point. This is certainly, in view of the heavenly command, a highly awkward and disturbing piece of information; and besides it at once raises, we feel, a host of discrepancies. However, precisely from an apologetic standpoint, one can make allowances for the strange conduct of the women. 'On the question how, with their silence, the author could have learned anything about it, the believing reader will not trouble his head further'.[78]

This explanation is, as we have said, still widely adopted.[79] I do not believe, however, that it can be sustained. One might well attribute to some medieval legend-spinner the kind of crudely elaborated design with which the doubtful sentence was, according to this explanation, formulated, but it is wholly unexampled within the ancient evangelical tradition. At most we could point, in the New Testament, to the second epistle of Peter as a parallel, but it is quite different in scope and comes from the latter part of the second century. Furthermore the account fails in reality to achieve what it was apparently meant to. One can hardly take the text as meaning to the simple reader, and therefore to the author, anything but that the women *first* kept silent, so that the events which followed took place without any help from them and without any regard to the empty tomb.[80] Their silence may have lasted days, perhaps weeks; but at the last the knowledge of the appearances in Galilee and the birth of the community of believers must have loosened their tongues. An emergence of the story years or, it might have been, decades, later cannot be explained on these lines.[81]

[78]Ed. Meyer, I, 18. Dibelius, *From Tradition to Gospel* (1934) p. 189f., gives the explanation a more ingenious turn in that he supposes that an older legend, grown up without ulterior aim, was only later pressed into the service of apologetics. Still, this makes no change in the interpretation of the decisive verse 16.8.

[79]It has been freshly adopted by V. Taylor, *The Life and Ministry of Jesus* (1955) 223; Grass, pp. 22f., and G. Bornkamm, *Jesus of Nazareth* (1960) 183, without going into my objections.

[80]This supposition is expressly brought out by Luke in an analogous context: the Apostles kept silence on what they had seen at the Transfiguration ἐν ἐκείναις ταῖς ἡμέραις, that is, from then until after the resurrection and up to the final glorification of the Lord (Luke 9.36).

[81]W. Baldensperger, 'Urchristliche Apologie'. *Die älteste Auferstehungskontroverse* (1909)

Consequently, in this aspect, the account has nothing doubtful. But before we turn again to the question of its historical value or otherwise, we must, to confirm what has been said up to now, find some valid explanation of the final words of the Gospel; their strangeness cannot be denied. To that end it is necessary to look further afield, and to consider the other accounts of the empty tomb.

11*b*

The Gospel of St. Matthew, in general and especially in situating in Galilee the resurrection encounters, follows the tradition of Mark. Nonetheless, it appends to the story of the empty tomb a first appearance of Jesus to the women,[82] whereas Luke expressly denies anything of the sort.[82a] A further, lengthier addition bears an apologetic char-

---

36, rightly underlines this. His own interpretation, that 16.8 must explain 'the quite incredible absence of the apostles on Easter morning', springs from modern feeling and has hardly any support in the text. In his later work, *Le tombeau vide. La légende et l'histoire* (Paris 1935) 46*ff*., he goes over to the view, as before him the Holtzmann cousins (*cf.* n. 119 below), and now C. Stange, '*Kreuz und Auferstehung*', *ZSTh* 24 (1955), pp. 379*ff*., 383*ff*., that the supposed legend has a historical core: the women did not know that Joseph of Arimathaea had secretly by night carried to his own grave the corpse that had first been removed by the soldiers and left uncared for.

[82]This is especially understandable here, since, in Matthew, the later appearances in Galilee are taken together in a single great scene, itself dominated by the enthronement in heaven and the sending of the Apostles; *cf.* E. Lohmeyer, '*Mir ist gegeben alle Gewalt*', *In Memoriam Ernst Lohmeyer* (1951) 9*ff*. Thus the moment of seeing again and joyful recognition is realized only in the lyrically told encounter with the women. It cannot be taken, with Brun, p. 34, as a substitute for the encounter with Peter. The task, in fact, with which Jesus, in 28.10, entrusts the women is here an evident doubling of the words of the angel in 28.7. The scene could, therefore, have originated as a substitute for the angel scene, with which now (after Mark's account) it appears in combination. The Gospel of St. John goes one step further in this direction. Christ alone brings about (20.17) the illumination of Mary Magdalen and tells her what to do, and the angels, here two, retained from the older tradition, put (20.3) the same question as he, though they are now really superfluous and have no function.

[82a]Luke 24.24. It is only because of Matthew's account that Paul's silence about the supposed meeting with the women (1 Cor. 15.4) becomes a problem at all. It is one which it has been sought, with a superfluous display of learning, to evade on the ground that women, by Jewish law, were not capable of testifying, and so they were deliberately passed over by Paul with his Jewish schooling (so Hirsch, Kittel, Stauffer, Stählin, etc.).

acter—the account of the guards at the tomb and the fraud of the Jewish hierarchy. The motive of these accounts is given in the Gospel itself, where it says that, after the discovery of the empty tomb had become known, the high priests and elders spread the lie that the corpse had been stolen at night by the disciples, 'and this story has been spread among the Jews to this day'.[83] This invention it was the purpose of the account of the guards to refute, showing that a robbery of the tomb was, in fact, impossible, and that its assertion was due solely to conscious malevolence.

As is generally the case when such a specific intention is dominant, the narrator has chiefly in view his special apologetic aim, and so fails to see the absurdities that follow right and left from his account. Our story abounds with contradictions and impossibilities. The announcement by Jesus of his resurrection must be presumed generally known, for the 'high priests and Pharisees' to act accordingly, and they do so with precision: it is only until the third day, the period foreseen, that the watch is needed, and, for this limited period, it is requested from the governing power.[84] The session at which this was resolved upon must have been on a sabbath—a difficulty Matthew himself seems to have felt, since he evades a direct indication of this day by means of an artificial periphrasis.[85] A further contradiction is that the appearance of the angels from heaven, the opening of the grave, and the speech with the women should take place before pagan witnesses. At the decisive moment, the guards were struck with a divine terror, and 'became like dead men'.[86] Nonetheless, it is not to Pilate, but to the Jewish hierarchy, that they make the necessary report on 'all that had taken place.'[87] And although these rascals only put out and spread their own lies,[88] yet the Christians, as the account says, had a precise knowledge of all the events.[89]

This is not the only place where we can detect, in Matthew, an

---

[83]Matt. 28.15.   [84]Matt. 27.63f.

[85]Matt. 27.62. τῇ δὲ ἐπαύριον, ἥτις ἐστὶν μετὰ τὴν παρασκευήν.

[86]Matt. 28.4. I cannot agree that here—as later in the Gospel of Peter and that according to the Hebrews—unbelieving pagans should have been made 'neutral' witnesses of the 'intimated' event of the resurrection; against Grass, p. 25.

[87]The Gospel of Peter 11.43-49 corrects this impossibility. Pilate is the first to receive the report, and only later, at the insistence of 'all' (the Jewish leaders), orders silence.

[88]Matt. 28.11.   [89]Matt. 28.13f.

apologetic aim against the Jews. A further, more remarkable addition can be explained on the same lines.[90] As opposed to the account in Mark, the grave was not yet opened when the women arrived. It was only at that moment that an angel appeared like lightning from heaven, rolled aside the stone,[91] and summoned them to see for themselves that the tomb was empty.[92] Thus it follows, again probably quite unintentionally, what is strange enough, that Jesus must already have gone out of the closed tomb through the stone.[93] But the desired end is attained. The grave was not only sealed and guarded, but remained untouched to the last moment, when the witnesses were at hand, and no thief could have entered it.

The story of the guards at the tomb was taken up into the apocryphal tradition, in which the guiding apologetic intention comes out even more clearly. In particular, the Gospel of Peter brings together various older accounts;[94] chiefly the securing of the tomb is exaggerated, as compared with Matthew, to a fantastic degree. The stone is sealed not merely once, but sevenfold.[95] In addition, it is so incalculably heavy that not only all the guards, including the centurion, but also the elders and scribes of the Jews and, in fact, all those present had to be yoked together in order to roll it away from the entrance.[96] Yet, at the decisive moment, it moves of itself, and rolls away just when the

[90] Now, of course, the women's visit to the grave can no longer be ascribed to an intention to anoint the body; they come merely θεωρῆσαι τὸν τάφον (28.1), But this is, in fact, an improvement on Mark.

[91] The addition itself could have a history, and, as has often been supposed, it may have been originally an introduction to a description of the resurrection itself. But that does not explain why Matthew placed it in quite a different setting.

[92] Matt. 28.2.

[93] Origen, *Contra Celsum*, V, 58, seems still reluctant to draw this conclusion, and it is only in the High Middle Ages that art decides on a corresponding representation: H. Schrade, *Ikonographie der christlichen Kunst I: Die Auferstehung Christi* (1952) 56ff. For early Christian imagery of the resurrection, see now Jeanne Villette, *La résurrection du Christ dans l'art chrétien du IIe au VIIe siècle* (Paris, 1957).

[94] As the Gospel of Peter makes the women come for the anointing after the retreat of the guards, and, in addition, announce the resurrection themselves, there results a highly artificial coming and going as in a classical drama, in which the three unities must be observed.

[95] Ev. Pt. 8.33.

[96] Ev. Pt. 8.32. With a like intention, the western text of Luke 23.53 adds to the various details, taken from Mark, about the stone rolled to the door of the tomb, the information that twenty men could hardly have moved it from the place: . . . ἐπέθηκεν τῷ μνημείῳ λίθον, ὃν μόγις εἴκοσι ἐκύλιον.

angel is to appear and Jesus to come out from the tomb.[97] What is particularly characteristic is the unmistakable intention to multiply the number of neutral and hostile witnesses. Celsus in the second century was certainly not the first to have said mockingly that the alleged risen God ventured to show himself only to his faithful adherents.[98] And now, for the watch, there is erected a large tent in front of the tomb, and all the people, not only from Jerusalem, but from round about, stream there to inspect the place.[99] Nor does the Gospel of Peter fear to describe the resurrection itself,[100] and, indeed, to make the pagan guards and the Jewish elders also present witnesses of the event.[101] Apologetic concern has completely vanquished the religious aesthetic sense. It only remained for the Gospel according to the Hebrews to venture one more step in this direction. According to it, the first person with whom Jesus communicated after his resurrection was the high priest's servant,[102] one of the guards, to whom he himself handed the linen cloth as palpable proof of his having risen.[103]

In all these accounts we see reflected the disputes of the Christians with their opponents. They show themselves as a factor at work on all sides, forming the old tradition and reframing it more and more.[104] This tendency is at work, not only in Matthew and the apocryphal Gospels, but also in John; only here it has been much less remarked up to now. One thing, indeed, in this regard had already occurred to Chrysostom:[105] the detailed account of how the grave-clothes were

<hr/>

[97]Ev. Pt. 9.37.

[98]Orig. *Cels.* II, 63. Likewise, II, 55, 70, and Porphyry in *Macarius Magnes* II, 14; cf. III, 18. *Per contra*, the real Christian basis is stated expressly in Acts 10.40f.

[99]Ev. Pt. 8.31-9.34. According to Josephus 7, 8, the watch consisted of thirty Romans and a thousand Jews.

[100]Equally the Latin codex k of 4th-5th cent. of Mark 16.3. *subito autem ad horam tertiam tenebrae factae sunt per totum orbem terrae, et descenderunt de caelis angeli et surgent(es?) in claritate vivi Dei simul ascenderunt cum eo, et continuo lux facta est, tunc illae accesserunt ad monumentum . . .*

[101]Ev. Pt. 10.38ff.　　　　　　　　　[102]Dobschütz, p. 30.

[103]Jerome, *vir. ill.* 2. *evangelium quoque quod appellatur secundum Hebraeos . . . post resurrectionem salvatoris refert. 'dominus autem cum dedisset sindonem servo sacerdotis, ivit ad Jacobum et apparuit ei . . .'* The question how Jesus came upon new clothes is here not yet envisaged; but cf. Ps. Justin (=Theodoret or Diodorus?) *Quaest. Orthod.* 116.

[104]Of course, there are other essential motives to be considered in this development, but they are not relevant here.

[105]*Hom. Mt.* 90 (91); *hom. Joh.* 85 (84) 4.

laid, and the napkin, apart by itself and rolled up, is evidently to be taken as proof that the body of Jesus had not been stolen.[106] No one who wanted to steal a dead body would first strip it with care so as to remove it naked.[107] This account, then, follows the line which is carried to extremes, even to absurdity, in the Gospel according to the Hebrews.

John, however, is not content with indications of this sort. He recasts, with the greatest freedom, the Easter narratives, and, in so doing, troubles little about the older traditions. But on the suspicion of robbery of the body he speaks in unmistakable fashion, and contradicts it all the more emphatically. When Mary Magdalen, early on Easter morning, finds the tomb empty, her first thought is 'They have taken the Lord out of the tomb, and we do not know where they have laid him'.[108] She repeats this complaint on seeing the two angels in white sitting, one at the head, the other at the foot of the grave.[109] And finally she says it a third time, when Jesus himself stands before her, and she takes him for the gardener, who, she thinks, is the most likely person to have removed the body: 'Sir, if you have carried him away, tell me where you have laid him, and I will take him away.'[110]

It is astonishing how little attention has been paid to the actual situation as made evident here. The account, as presented by John, is a direct answer to the Jewish objections and the doubts they occasioned. In particular, the figure of the gardener and the suspicion that he might have removed the body of Jesus have their origin here. The gardener is a figure vouched for in tradition, and so the question why Mary Magdalen should have taken him as such is out of place. Later Jewish polemic contains various accounts of how the body of Jesus came to be missing. Far the most frequent form they take is that 'Judah the gardener,' an honest man, had foreseen the likelihood of the deception and so removed the body. Then, when the disciples came forward with their resurrection tale and the Jews were highly embarrassed, it

---

[106]John 20.5-7; likewise the interpolated verse Luke 24.12.
[107]Cf. on this also the Coptic Gospel of the Twelve Apostles, frg. 15, Graffin et Nau, *Patr. or.* II, 2 (1907) 172. Pilate dit: 'O hommes, qui détestez votre propre vie, si on avait pris le corps, (on aurait pris) les bandelettes aussi . . .'
[108]John 20.2.
[109]John 20.13. We need not go into the editorial problems of this chapter.
[110]John 20.15.

was he who was able to bring back the body. This was then dragged publicly through the streets of Jerusalem and the Christian lie exposed.[111]

All this was related with variations of detail with which we are not here concerned. The accounts, as we have them in medieval and modern settings, are all of late date and, in part, of fantastic construction. The core, however, is old, and the story of the gardener removing the body is to be found in quite simple form in Tertullian. At the conclusion of his work on theatrical representations he sketches in glowing colours a picture of the greatest one of all, which Christians will one day enjoy, the Last Judgement. Then will Christ come forth as avenger against all his traducers—and here Tertullian turns, in triumphant scorn, on those, in particular, who formerly 'raged against the Lord', that is, to the Jews:[112] 'There he is . . . the son of the carpenter or of the harlot'—another old Jewish slander—'the violater of the sabbath, the Samaritan, the man who was possessed by a devil! There is the man whom you bought from Judas; he it is who was struck with the reed and the fist, befouled with spittle, given gall and vinegar to drink! There is the man whom his disciples stole away secretly, so that it could be said he had risen, whom the gardener took away so that the crowd of visitors should not damage his lettuces.'[113]

This last, as it were, quite inoffensive explanation of the disappearance of the body is, as far as I know, not to be found anywhere else in antiquity.[114] The early recension of the apologetically oriented legend knows nothing of a purposive removal by Judah the gardener, mean-

---

[111]S. Kraus, *Das Leben Jesu nach jüdischen Quellen* (1902), especially pp. 170ff.; cf. pp. 59, 107ff., 126f.

[112]Contrary to the doubts expressed by Kraus, p. 3, it is perfectly clear that, in what follows, the Jews, not the pagans, are meant; cf. especially: *hic est quem a Juda redemistis* (and note 113).

[113]Tert., *Spect.*, 30 Reifferscheid-Wissowa, 29, 13: *hic est ille, dicam, fabri aut quaestuariae filius, sabbati destructor, Samarites et daemonium habens; his est quem a Juda redemistis, his est ille harundine et colaphis diverberatus, sputamentis dedecoratus, felle et aceto potatus; hic est quem clam discentes subripuerunt, ut surrexisse dicatur, hortulanus detraxit, ne lactucae suae frequentia commeantium adlaederentur.*

[114]Yet Amolo of Lyons (841-852) seems to know it (*Epist. seu liber contra Judaeos ad Carolum regem* 25. Migne, PL CXVI 158), when he alludes to the removal of Jesus in a garden full of cabbages (*in quodam horto caulibus pleno*) as a Jewish tradition.

ing, in reality, Judas Iscariot.[115] Yet it cannot have been first put out as a counter to the Gospel of John[116]—whose Christian solution of the problem is, in this form, not yet contradicted. John, in fact, presupposes a corresponding polemical version, which he, for his part, aims at meeting.[117] We may observe that it is no longer simply a question of a repetition of the malicious slander with which Matthew had to deal. The disciples have not stolen the body, but the supposed miracle is due to quite natural and ordinary circumstances, and the disciples simply failed to see this. Thus, the unlikely view that the leaders of the first community, with their readiness for sacrifice, were common rogues and tricksters, is here abandoned. It did not, indeed, die out altogether,[118] but the rebuttal of the Christian message has, in the new form, far more chance of being taken seriously and accepted. It is, therefore, no accident that, in the later Jewish polemic, it replaces the direct charge against the disciples of being grave-robbers and liars. This second form is still accepted today by a number of Jewish scholars in explaining the empty tomb.[119] The Apostles, and the first Christians then, were not deceivers, but credulous, unthinking fools, who fell victims to a deception. On this level of the dispute, a rebuttal such as Matthew brings is obviously not applicable, and, therefore, the account

[115]S. Kraus, *Neuere Ansichten über 'Tholdoth Jeschu'*, Monatschr. Gesch. und Wissensch. Judant 76 (1932) 595ff.

[116]As supposed by W. Bauer, *Leben Jesu*, p. 483, and Grass, p. 59, also holds possible.

[117]Perhaps his Christian reply also had predecessors. This may be indicated, in particular, by the plural in John 20.2, which does not seem appropriate in the mouth of Mary Magdalen, who, in John, is the only woman to come to the tomb. Yet there are similar instances of this form of speech, which throw doubt on any reconstruction of an older source on this basis; *cf.* Bultmann, *Johannes*, p. 530, n.3.

[118]Justin, *dial.* 108, 2 presupposes it after Matthew, but refers to the Jewish messengers as sent with this account εἰς πᾶσαν τὴν οἰκουμένην. Tertullian also, in the passage referred to, juxtaposes two versions of the charge. The Jew of Celsus in Orig. *Cels.* II, 55 seems to see the disciples not as guilty of the theft of the body, but as victims of deception and, at the same time, as frauds.

[119]For example, Jos. Klausner, *Jesus of Nazareth, His Life, Times and Teaching* (1929) 357. 'We must assume that the owner of the tomb, Joseph of Arimathaea, thought it unfitting that one who had been crucified should remain in his own ancestral tomb.' A similar suggestion had been made by Heinrich-Julius and also by Oskar Holtzmann; *cf.* H. J. Holtzmann, *Kommentar zu den Synoptikern* (1901) 105, etc.; O. Holtzmann, *Das Leben Jesu* (1901) 392f. According to P. Deussen, *Die Philosophie der Bibel* (1913) 226f., 'some or at least one of the disciples' must have known where the body of Jesus really was, and their silence is, therefore, a 'little *pia fraus*, which, it seems, must not be passed over'.

in John appears in a different form, corresponding to the new form of the objection to which it is directed. The argument now is that, in the actual circumstances, there can be no question of any presumed error. The disciples were convinced on the spot that no theft of the corpse could possibly be considered. Obviously, they themselves, and Mary Magdalen in particular, had first, at the sight of the empty tomb, entertained this suspicion; they followed it up, and Mary Magdalen was long reluctant to abandon it.[120] But what they saw with their own eyes, not only the placing of the grave-clothes, but above all the person of the Redeemer himself, appearing to them in the place of the supposed gardener, finally convinced them.

IIc

From this general survey let us turn back once more to the basic account of St. Mark's Gospel. We have seen how the apologetic retort to Jewish suspicions has left behind unmistakable traces in almost all the other Gospels, that is, in Matthew, in the Gospel according to the Hebrews and in the Gospel of Peter, and also in John. Luke is the only evangelist whose presentation is free, or as good as free, from such considerations,[121] and only adduces, all the more impressively, the scriptural proof in support of a faith which, otherwise, rests solely on the resurrection appearances. This being so, should not the general apologetic tendency also have had its part to play in Mark? At all events, this seems quite a legitimate question.

Until the present time, such a possibility has from time to time, been entertained. It is, in a way, striking how the fact of the death of Jesus is stated so emphatically, and, as it were, officially established. Pilate is shown as not believing at first, and being astonished on learning from Joseph of Arimathaea that Jesus is already dead. He summons the centurion personally, questions him, and makes him expressly certify the news, before he hands over to the petitioner the 'corpse'

---

[120]Cf. John Chrysostom, hom. Joh. 85 (84) 4.
[121]I assume here that Luke 24.12 is an interpolation. The arguments to the contrary of R. Leaney's, 'The resurrection narratives in Luke (XXIV, 12-53)', New Test. Stud. 2 (1955-56) 110ff. have by no means convinced me.

(πτῶμα), as it is called so emphatically.[122] One may, of course, say that this account is no more than exactly 'historical'; Joseph could have passed it on, say, to the women, and the evangelist simply received and recorded it. But what interest had it for him? One might understand the account in an anti-docetic sense; and then it would exclude the idea of Jesus being only a spirit, a 'phantom',[123] who could not really die, and so could not have risen in the body. Such an interpretation is not impossible,[124] but, in view of the standpoint of the Gospel elsewhere, highly improbable.[125] As far as we can see, Mark has not yet come up against the Christological speculations of the Gnostics. It is more pertinent in this context to take account of more weighty objections: Jesus was really dead, that is, he was not prematurely, as seeming dead, taken down from the cross,[126] and the later disappearance of his body cannot be explained in this way. Admittedly, we do not know if any such idea had been put about so early.[127] However, in view of the speed with which Jesus died, it is certainly not to be ruled out that this idea had been suggested. In this case, then, we would have to do with a defence against sceptical, purely 'natural' explanations of the supposed resurrection of Jesus, along the same lines as the later Jewish polemic.

But we need not go into this. What is far more important is that the last verse, a difficult one, of the Gospel can perhaps be clarified and understood in the light of this consideration. This verse, in fact, is the real *crux interpretum*, for which a satisfactory explanation is yet to be found. The women discovered the tomb empty. Yet, though they were convinced of the fact beyond all doubt, and a marvellous youth had enlightened them on the meaning of what had happened and had also conveyed to them a definite charge, they were so struck with fear

---

[122]Mark 15.43-45.
[123]Thus the Hebrew Gospel in Ign. Smyrn. 3, 2 (Jerome, *vir. ill.* 16).
[124]See note 53 above.
[125]It would be more plausible, if we supposed here, with Bultmann, *Tradition*, p. 274, a later addition (and so lacking in Matthew and Luke).
[126]Finegan, p. 80; M. Goguel, *Les sources du récit johannique de la passion* (1910) 101*f.*, would interpret correspondingly the theme of the anointing in John 19.40.
[127]Later emerges the question of an apparent death in Theodoret or Diodorus(?) =Ps. Justin, *Quaest. orth.* 64; *cf.* Bauer, *Leben Jesu*, pp. 483*f.* On modern hypotheses to this effect, see A. Meyer, pp. 116*ff.*; R. A. Hofmann, *Das Geheimnis der Auferstehung Jesu* (1921) 65; Goguel, *Foi*, pp. 205*ff.*

and terror that they did nothing about this knowledge, and failed to carry out the heavenly command. Of what they had seen and heard they 'said nothing to any man'. Now this, as we have already emphasized, is utterly improbable. But, in view of the Jewish slanders as we know them from, for instance, St. Matthew, this account has straightway a definite apologetical significance. The disciples, the evangelist means to say, had nothing whatever to do with the empty tomb. Just as before they had no part in the removal, so they were absolutely unconnected with what was now experienced; the news of the empty tomb had not reached them either at once or even subsequently. The threads which could have connected them with the empty tomb were simply severed, and all the suspicions which, in one form or another, had been raised against their integrity, were thus seen to be deliberate and untenable slanders. The empty tomb was an event standing by itself, and the testimony to it by the experiences of the disciples in Galilee only came subsequently. For this reason, it merits a double faith and respect; the disciples themselves had nothing to do with it. Now, also according to Mark, the disciples found themselves on Easter morning still in Jerusalem. The divine messenger delivered direct from the empty tomb the command that they should go off to Galilee, and it seems almost unthinkable that his words, as formulated, were originally spoken merely into the wind. The strange disobedience of the women, which seems to have entailed no further consequences, makes the account in its present form even more contradictory. Yet all this seems to me highly significant. Exactly as in Matthew, the inconsistency of the narrative betrays a secondary, deliberate twist given to the tradition[128] and this is quite understandable.[129] In his anxiety to forestall an obvious objection and

---

[128]Originally, therefore, the account must have had a different conclusion. That Mark 16.7 should have formed a 'pericope conclusion' I neither stated nor meant; and so the criticism of Grass, p. 21, n.3, does not apply to me.

[129]According to this interpretation, the emendation (not of the text, but of the tradition) is confined to 16.8; it is no longer requisite to deem 16.7 an addition, as has often been done. The latter is more than ever indispensable in this place, if 16.8 formed the original conclusion of the old Gospel. These words alone convey a definite indication of the final event in which all the rest are resolved, and which Mark shrinks from recording directly. In any case, the text, as part of Mark's Gospel, is old. Both Matthew and Luke read it there in their time, and its inconsistency with their own account was, on Matthew's part, tolerated, and, on Luke's, solved by emendations; cf. also John 20.2. Undoubtedly, therefore, it is a matter of a portion of an

to counter any possible misgiving, the narrator, as so often happens in like cases, failed to notice the strange consequences his story entailed, as soon as it was followed up in a different direction from the one he envisaged.

The explanation adduced has, as we have said, the advantage of

---

old, for us the oldest, tradition. On the other hand, the corresponding prophecy of Jesus in Mark 14.28 must be taken as a clumsy anticipation of the angelic message, breaking up the sequence of the discourse. Here, certainly, we must recognize, with Marxsen, p. 48, 'the hand of Mark'. Apart from this, Marxsen himself offers a totally different explanation of the pericope 16.1-8. He holds 16.7 to be an insertion of the evangelist, for an ulterior purpose, into the older, closed-in narrative, which, yet, in a different sense—whether according to Wellhausen's or my interpretation—had also an ulterior aim (p. 50). This is wholly in accord with Marxsen's idea of the Galilean orientation of Mark's Gospel, an idea which, it seems to me, is not safeguarded in the least in the previous context. Like Lohmeyer before him and, in a different way, Evans (see n. 68 above), Marxsen takes 'Galilee' as not merely a geographical, but also, and chiefly, a theological, concept. Galilee must 'in a far deeper sense than the merely historical' be understood as the 'homeland' of Jesus; 'it is the place where he was active, where—hidden in the proclamation of the Gospel—he now acts, where he will act in his Parousia' (p. 60). This view is placed in connection with the well-known exodus of the primitive community from Jerusalem in the years 66-70, which, in turn, 'evidently' has an intrinsic connection with the 'Parousia awaited in Galilee'. To this also refer the words of the angel, and Jesus's stay in Galilee is to be related to his 'hidden' presence in the preaching in Galilee, as an 'anticipation of the Parousia'. I confess that I find this combination of mythological and modern theological thought a little strange. In addition, the exegesis on which it rests is as weak as it could be. Marxsen recognizes that Lohmeyer's grammatical explanations in support of the supposed announcement of the Parousia by the angel (Mark 16.7) are unsound (*cf.* n. 174 below), and so has recourse, with Michaelis (who takes the verse as a genuine utterance of Jesus) to the parallel insertion, Mark 14.28. What is significant here is, in contrast to Mark 16.7, that the verse 'contains an indication of time (after my resurrection), which—from the situation of Jesus—points to an event set apart from the resurrection, and later in time. Thus only the Parousia can be meant by this verse' (p. 55). That is a remarkable conclusion. It is not apparent why the circumstance that Jesus will come 'after his resurrection' (when else?) from Jerusalem to Galilee 'can' only signify the Parousia, and not equally, or even better, his meetings at Easter with his disciples. These even Mark, as Marxsen admits, must have known about, and all the rest of the primitive Christian witnesses, beginning with the Apostle Paul, made them the primary foundation of the Easter belief. It is all the more unlikely that Mark ignored them in 16.7 in favour of the supposed Parousia in Galilee, in that the form in which he actually relates the discovery of the tomb suffices, at the very least, to give a wholly valid story of the Easter events. Consequently, there is no occasion whatever to discard the obvious interpretation of 16.7 in favour of such an extraordinary hypothesis. On the other hand, I consider the extreme scepticism which makes J. M. Robinson, *The Problem of History in Mark* (1957) SBT, 21, renounce any definite interpretation of the verse in question likewise inadequate.

agreeing with a tendency elsewhere evident in tradition; it is not dependent, like that of Wellhausen, on the arbitrary assumption of various factors. Furthermore, the silence of the women not only clears the disciples of knowledge of the empty tomb, but also preserves their independence; with their later experiences at Easter they become original witnesses of the resurrection, not prepared beforehand by the women and so forced into the second rank.[130] These are, in a way, but two sides of a single theme envisaging, on the one hand, the problem of the empty tomb and, on the other, the character of the disciples.[131] Nonetheless, this second standpoint is nowhere clearly recognizable in the sources; and so, for my part, I would not wish to put it in the forefront.

Furthermore, none of the other evangelists, it is evident, wished to adopt the violent solution chosen by Mark:[132] in other words, they count on the women having fulfilled their charge to the Apostles.[133] Against the Jews a different line is taken by the apologia, in order to exclude the possibility of deception, deliberate or not. Nonetheless, they kept the other idea that the discovery of the tomb was not sufficient for the Easter faith, and was not, by itself, decisive. This idea was more and more elaborated with the typical, increasing clarification and hardening of the underlying purpose. In Matthew it is still obscure how the account of the women reached the disciples, and how they received it.[134] Luke, on the other hand, says that they thought

---

[130]Thus Brun, p. 11; Nikolaïnen II, 65, and Riesenfeld, pp. 285f.

[131]This is how Grundmann, p. 372, connects the two explanations. On the other hand, I am not happy about the way Grass, p. 22, tries to combine the explanation of the Nordic theologians (see preceding note) with Wellhausen's hypothesis, for they are totally different things, and one has to decide which is valid.

[132]See n. 129 above. The Gospel of Peter gives a quite different solution. It omits altogether the command of the angel, 13.56, and makes the disciples, 14.58f., go back to their work, disappointed and cast down, without the least inkling. But even here there is no express mention that the women had kept silent.

[133]We cannot, then, for a moment agree, with K. Barth, Church Dogmatics IV, 2 (1958) 147, that here again it is a question of 'contradictions in the tradition that, evidently, no one held it necessary to remove'.

[134]They betook themselves to the mountain in Galilee on account of a previous instruction of Jesus, not recorded in the Gospel itself. Matt. 28.16. Also, the unexplained doubt, especially as it is not evidently overcome, recorded in Matt. 28.17 gives an impression of a remnant of a previous tradition suppressed by Matthew; cf. n. 82 above.

their words, first, to be idle tales;[135] the news caused them a certain uneasiness, but did not arouse any faith.[136] In the later, added conclusion of Mark the disciples did not believe in the first meetings with the risen Christ as told to them,[137] and, in a well-known variant appended here, they tried later to give a circumstantial excuse for this.[138] The Easter account of the *Epistola Apostolorum* describes a lengthier interchange between them and the women, whom they were reluctant to believe, until Jesus intervened directly.[139] In all this we see how the apologetic concern gradually swung from the empty tomb and became more general, no longer envisaging definite objections by opponents, but all 'disbelief', including that of weak Christians.[140] Here also, as in John, the apostolic witness seems so reliable precisely because it was not caused by first, dubious impressions and information, but was the outcome of a struggle against initial doubt and scepticism.[141] Everything was put to the test and error excluded. But blessed are those who do not see and yet believe.[142]

Once again, by way of conclusion let us put the decisive question as to the historical credibility of the account delivered in the last pericope of Mark. If our interpretation is correct, and Mark elaborated the account with a definite end in view, this is still older than the Gospel, and the apologetic controversy over the empty tomb, that we shall be able to follow more clearly later, had already begun. Of course, that is no proof that the account is historical. It is conceivable that the legend, if such it was, was first circulated quite innocently, and that the difficulties it involved only came to light afterwards, and then had to

---

[135]Luke 24.11.   [136]Luke 24.22ff.

[137]Mark 16.11. Here, too, the Emmaus disciples do not believe.

[138]The Freer-Logion behind Mark 16.13, and Jerome, *Pelag.* II, 15.

[139]*Ep. ap.* 10 (21).

[140]From this must be distinguished the particular theological problem of doubt about the corporeal nature of the risen Christ, as it comes in Luke 24.37ff., and in the Hebrew Gospel (see n. 123 below).

[141]Cf. Brun, pp. 26f., 49, 70; W. Baldensperger, 'Le tombeau vide', *RHPhR* 13 (1933) 126ff.; Grass, pp. 29f.

[142]John 20.29. Yet in John also it seems that only the beloved disciple came to 'believe', without scriptural proof or any news of appearances, solely on the ground of the empty tomb. John 20.8; cf. H. Strathmann, *Das Evangelium nach Johannes* (1951) 256.

be removed.[143] The narrative, indeed, has, to some extent, an undoubtedly legendary character and the question may be raised whether,
in these circumstances, it is at all feasible to search for an historical
'core' and to try to extract it by a rational process. On the other hand,
we have already brought out that the story as a whole does not give
the least impression of the marvellous or fantastic or of being in any
way incredible. It is only the form of the 'young man', whom we
must take to be an angel, that appears clearly 'legendary', and it can
be dispensed with easily enough.[144] The names of the women, the
dry, concise detail of what they found in the grave and could not at
first explain, by no means point to its being a pure invention, and the
supposed signs of a later origin that some have chosen to discover are,
in our view, to be understood in a different sense. Particularly striking,
as we have pointed out, is the absence of any appearance of Christ at
the tomb; the prospect of an appearance to the disciples and Peter
was reserved for Galilee.[145] In this way, the details fully agree with
the old Pauline catalogue—at least, no contradiction can be proved.
Paul also, who makes no mention of the discovery of the tomb, may
well have known the story in this form and transmitted it accordingly.[146] From this standpoint, too, no objections or doubts can be
alleged.

Nonetheless, the story in its entirety cannot be explained as simply a
legend with an apologetic purpose for then it would not have speci-
fied three women (who, by Jewish law, were not competent to testify)
as the decisive witnesses. In fact, the Jew of Celsus made mock of such
weak support for what was, in his view, a fundamental datum of the
Christian faith in the resurrection.[147] If, on the other hand, the story

---

[143]This is evidently how Dibelius, *From Tradition to Gospel*, p. 189f., sees the development in the sense of Wellhausen's interpretation, rejected by us, with its—therefore
secondary—intent.

[144]Cf. Bultmann, *Tradition*, p. 290. 'The angel has no independent significance, but
only plays the part of the *angelus interpres*'. That, of course, does not justify any kind
of literary device.

[145]Mark 16.7; cf. p. 59 above.

[146]Cf. pp. 54f. above. The opposite assertion is often made, but is quite arbitrary;
cf. for the contrary view F. Loofs, *Die Auferstehungsberichte und ihr Wert* (1908) 14ff.

[147]Orig. Cels. II, 55. τίς τοῦτο εἶδεν; γυνὴ πάροιστρος, ὥς φατε, καὶ εἴ τις
ἄλλος τῶν ἐκ τῆς αὐτῆς γοητείας κτλ.; cf. n. 98 above. The singular γυνή shows that
the 'Jew' here bases himself on the Gospel of John, where Mary Magdalen appears

of the empty tomb is historical, then, in the situation as it was after the execution of Jesus, it is quite understandable, as we have already pointed out,[148] and to say the least, not at all unnatural, that at first only a few women, out of all his adherents, should have ventured as far as the tomb. Equally, the datum of the 'third day' can be explained as historical only from this standpoint, and not from that of the later appearances in Galilee.[149] Yet another factor tells, it seems to me, above all in favour of the credibility of the tradition. The name of Joseph of Arimathaea and, with it, the account of the burial of Jesus must be historical;[150] they cannot be simply discarded. But if the primitive community had any kind of information, based on fact, about the burial of Jesus, the investigations on the subject of the tomb must have begun, certainly, very early. What was actually found and shown was, in all probability, an empty tomb,[151] and, unless we are prepared to explain everything, with the Jews, as a fraud and a subsequent fabrication, it is hard to see why the discovery should not have happened in the way, by the persons and at the time stated by the most ancient tradition. Any other explanation is unverifiable.[152] Anyone who likes to hold that there was a substitution or some kind of mischance can, of

---

alone. Bauer, *Leben Jesu*, pp. 480f.; Goguel, *Foi*, p. 195. Then perhaps the predicate πάροιστρος is supported by Luke 8.2f. Baldensperger, *Urchristl. Apologie*, p. 18, n. 20, would assume, without any clear reason, another old tradition, on which Celsus drew.

[148]*Cf.* p. 57f. above.

[149]*Cf.* p. 45f. above.

[150]*Cf.* p. 56 above.

[151]Whether the tradition as to this survived and the Church of the Sepulchre is situated on the 'correct' place is a different question, which I cannot answer affirmatively with such assurance as J. Jeremias, *Golgotha* (1926) and, in accord with him, A. Parrot, *Der Tempel von Jerusalem, Golgotha und das heilige Grab* (1956) 123ff.; *cf.* Grass, pp. 40ff. At any rate, archaeology does not pronounce definitely on the age and 'genuineness' of the data on which any view must be based.

[152]This applies, to all appearances, also to the inscription, apparently originating in Nazareth, Διάταγμα Καίσαρος, of an edict directed against the violation of graves, if the attempt is made to connect it with the case of Jesus and to evaluate it in regard to our question; *cf.* J. Irmscher, 'Zum Διάταγμα Καίσαρος of Nazareth', *Zeitschr. f. neutest. Wissensch.* 23 (1949) 172ff.; Grass, pp. 139f.; on the contrary, Stauffer, *Jesus*, pp. 163f. Still more questionable would it be to cite the *Shroud of Turin*. It is no question here of a forged painting, but probably of an at least partially 'genuine' imprint of a real corpse; *cf.* Bulst, *Shroud* (n. 66 above) and the bibliography there. But as long as the cloth is kept from scientific investigation, it is hardly possible to reach a certain judgement.

course, let his imagination run as he pleases—anything is possible, in that case, and nothing demonstrable. But this has nothing to do with critical investigation. If we test what is capable of being tested, we cannot, in my opinion, shake the story of the empty tomb and its early discovery. There is much that tells in its favour, and nothing definite or significant against it. It is, therefore, probably historical.

III

Thus, two essential and reliable pieces of data emerge from the confused mass of material handed down to us: a series of indubitable appearances of Christ, which must be placed in Galilee, and the discovery of the empty tomb in Jerusalem. At a very early date attempts were made to align the two accounts as closely as possible, that is to say, to make the first appearances begin at the empty tomb, and then, finally, to shift them all to Jerusalem. But whenever this tradition, especially from the conservative standpoint, is repeated and defended as historical, any solution of the kind becomes impossible, since it contradicts the evidence of the most ancient sources. Yet the opposite attempt, made for the most part by liberal scholars, to base everything solely on the Galilean appearances, and to dismiss entirely the tradition of the empty tomb, seems to me irreconcilable with the sources. Admittedly, Mark's witness is not on a par with that of Paul; but, even so, it is old, in no way contradicts Paul, and cannot simply be ignored. Both pieces of data, therefore, the Galilean appearances and the empty tomb, must be upheld. They form the fixed points of departure, and point the line to be followed, for a consistent account of the events of Easter to be reconstructed.

I know, of course, perfectly well that any kind of reconstruction is bound to be hypothetical, but it is not without its uses. Something results almost of itself, when the data attained are simply juxtaposed. Something further is revealed when the data are combined intelligently, especially if we do not refuse in principle to supplement them by the further details contributed by Luke. He is the only one of the evangelists to show at least an attempt to collect together the older accounts and to work them up 'historically' into a general picture of the first era.[153] In any case, a certain trust in his account seems to me more reasonable than the prevailing tendency to dismiss, without more ado, all that he and the other evangelists offer, and to start with general suppositions and free-ranging combinations which, unsupported by the sources, simply hang in the air.

This applies, above all, to the question of the attitude and frame of mind of the disciples after the arrest of Jesus and his crucifixion. The first thing that is absolutely clear is that we have no direct evidence at all about their actual state just before the decisive events, and that, whatever has been said about it is more or less grounded on supposition. Not only Luke, however, but also Mark and all the evangelists are in accord that the disciples first remained in Jerusalem, and were still there when the tomb was discovered empty. There is not the slightest reason to doubt the correctness of this. It is utterly improbable that the disciples after the nocturnal arrest of Jesus, should have fled away from the place; or even, on the day after, a day of rest according to the traditional chronology, should have returned to Galilee, or indeed on the sabbath itself during the feast. Even Mark, of course, asserts nothing of the sort when he says that all the disciples, in the confusion of the arrest, immediately 'fled away,'[154] that is, they left Jesus in the lurch, and like sheep without a shepherd, were 'dispersed', in fulfilment of the old prophecy.[155] The opposite assumption

---

[153]Precisely because Luke approaches this problem as a theologian and historian at the same time, he is not content with half-solutions. He is entirely against the whole Galilean tradition, as it contradicts his own basic conception of the place of Jerusalem. On the other hand, the Easter stories themselves show, most impressively, how he wanted to discard as little as possible of the material he had. Thus he is the only evangelist to mention the vital first meeting with Peter, in spite of the difficulties it caused him (pp. 49-50 above), and, in the words of the angel which in Mark point to Galilee, he preserves at least the mention of Galilee—a piece of 'literary criticism', strangely enough, with almost a modern flavour. Luke 24.6; *cf.* Acts 13.31(?); *cf.* M. Karnetzki, '*Textgeschichte als Überlieferungsgeschichte*', *ZNW* 47 (1956) 174. In my view, the characteristic quality attributed by Ed. Meyer, I, 33*f.* to Luke's way of working is not so misconceived as many theological critics hold; *cf.* M. Dibelius, *The First Christian Historian* in *Studies in the Acts of the Apostles* (1956), p. 123*ff.*; also Morgenthaler, *Die lukanische Geschichtsschreibung als Zeugnis* 2 (1948) 26*ff.*

[154]Mark 14.50. καὶ ἀφέντες αὐτὸν ἔφυγον πάντες. It is no contradiction of this that Peter again emerged and followed the Lord 'from far off'. And also the unnamed young man, who, in Mark 14.51*f.*, left his garment in the hands of the police, would not have run 'naked' to Galilee.

[155]This is made wholly clear by Matthew, when, announcing the 'dispersion' (Zech.

of an immediate 'flight' to Galilee is no more than a 'legend of the critics',[156] though astonishingly prevalent—which, out of the entire tradition, cannot adduce a single word in its favour.[157] Admittedly, there comes to its support a further legend of the apologists, which already appears, in rudimentary form, in the Gospel of Peter[158] and in Justin Martyr,[159] though, in its full development, it is purely modern, and has no support in the canonical Gospels: the legend that the disciples, after the death of Jesus, lost hope once and for all, turned their backs on all that had gone before, and took up their daily work again. Their hopes had not been fulfilled, and so, apparently, had proved illusory. This dark picture of their resigned state was the appropriate background for the sudden, wonderful, and liberating effect which, as

---

13.7) in Mark 14.27, ὅτι πάντες σκανδαλισθήσεσθε adds, for his part, (26.31) an explanatory ἐν τῇ νυκτὶ ταύτῃ. But neither had Mark in view any longer period of time for the 'dispersion'.

[156]Thus M. Albertz, 'Zur Formgeschichte der Auferstehungsberichte', ZNW 21 (1922) 269; likewise, Marxsen, p. 52; cf. also J. Weiss, Der Erste Korintherbrief (1910) 350, and, earlier, Loofs, pp. 20ff.

[157]At least, no word that would be taken in the sense it has at present; cf. n. 176 below. One could, in support of the flight of the disciples, adduce John 16.32, but wrongly. The right interpretation of the verse is given by Strathmann, p. 229. Should one choose to take εἰς τὸ ἴδιον 'absolutely strictly', it would certainly then mean 'that the disciples would go to Galilee, from where they first came.' But this would be contrary to John's meaning, since, according to him, they were assembled, on Easter day, in Jerusalem (20.19). Consequently, the expression 'to his own' is used in an indeterminate sense, perhaps somewhat belittling: each to his own corner. What it amounts to is that each looks only to his own safety, and Jesus is left alone. J. Jeremias, ThW5 (1954) 705 would take John 16-32 as an already traditional reference to Is. 53.6. Apart from this, even if, with, for instance, Grass, pp. 117ff., one does not accept the following account of the disciples' motives in withdrawing, and continues to hold the empty tomb to be a mere legend, it is still not necessary to have recourse to a flight of the disciples. Some time or other, the pilgrims to Jerusalem had to return to their own part of the country. What needs explanation is, not the return to Galilee, but the repeated journey to Jerusalem.

[158]N. 161 below. Yet here it is assumed, indeed said expressly that the disciples remained at first in Jerusalem till the feast was over: Ev. Pt. 14, 58.

[159]Just. Apol. I, 50, 12: μετὰ οὖν τὸ σταυρωθῆναι αὐτὸν καὶ οἱ γνώριμοι αὐτοῦ πάντες ἀπέστησαν ἀρνησάμενοι αὐτόν; dial 53.5: μετὰ γὰρ τὸ σταυρωθῆναι αὐτὸν οἱ σὺν αὐτῷ ὄντες μαθηταὶ αὐτοῦ διεσκεδάσθησαν, in fulfilment of the prophecy, Zech. 13.7; dial. 106.1; [οἱ ἀπόστολοι] μετὰ τὸ ἀναστῆναι αὐτὸν ἐκ νεκρῶν καὶ πεισθῆναι, ὑπ' αὐτοῦ . . . μετενόησαν ἐπὶ τῷ ἀφίστασθαι αὐτοῦ, ὅτε ἐσταυρώθη . . . Fundamentally, there is nothing here beyond the corresponding passages of the Gospels. All the same, these words are taken, in conjunction with the Emmaus story and John 21, by H. W. Bartsch, 'Parusieerwartung und Osterbotschaft'. EvTh7 (1947-8) 128 as further evidence of the supposed flight of the disciples to Galilee.

was thought, could be brought about only by the meeting with the risen Lord himself, an event simply beyond understanding and utterly unexpected.

But the idea that this was the way things went is, from every point of view, improbable. The death of Jesus cannot have come to overwhelm his nearest companions as something totally unexpected. One can, of course, rule out the prophecies of the passion, later put together, as pure *vaticinia ex eventu*, and grant that the disciples, at the entrance into Jerusalem, had indulged in the wildest apocalyptic hopes, and dreamed of a triumph that was to come any minute. But in the days that followed, when the storm was gathering, they must, one would think, have felt something of what was preparing, have sensed also, perhaps, that Jesus himself did not wish to avoid the catastrophe, but rather—and this is what may well be doubted—went consciously to meet it. At the latest, during the celebration of the Supper, however much in the dark about details, they must have felt what was imminent. This is shown, in a certain way, by the story of Peter's denial, which there is no reason for rejecting.[159a] Peter made an attempt to remain still true to the Master, menaced and apparently ruined, and so did not even then abandon him completely.[160] Can one imagine, in these circumstances, that he and all the other disciples, after the condemnation of Jesus and his death, simply drew a line and, as it were, settled with all the past, and then went back home, 'as if nothing had happened'? This is how, in fact, the Gospel of Peter, in the latter part of the second century, presents the matter.[161] To me, however, it seems that a situation, such as that supposed by Luke, in the Emmaus story, has more probability from the outset. In it, the disciples had not simply scattered, or else they had, after the first fright, in part reassembled. They talked together and tried to fathom the meaning of what was apparently incomprehensible.[162] Their bewilder-

---

[159a]It is, of course, a different question whether it belongs to the old content of the passion tradition, and was not rather added at this point later. Bultmann, *Tradition*, pp. 3264 ff.; Dibelius, *From Tradition to Gospel*, pp. 179f, 183, 214 ff.

[160]Admittedly, one could take this as an act of purely human loyalty, or say that Peter did not wish to give up all as lost till the last moment. But this would be a bold assumption.

[161]Ev. Pet. 14.59f: ἡμεῖς δὲ οἱ δώδεκα μαθηταὶ τοῦ κυρίου ἐκλαίομεν καὶ ἐλυπούμεθα καὶ ἕκαστος λυπούμενος διὰ τὸ συμβὰν ἀπηλλάγη εἰς τὸν οἶκον αὐτοῦ. ἐγὼ δὲ Σίμων Πέτρος καὶ Ἀνδρέας ὁ ἀδελφός μου λαβόντες ἡμῶν τὰ λίνα ἀπήλθαμεν εἰς τὴν θάλασσαν ...

[162]Luke 24.14f.

ment and helplessness was so great that even the news of the empty tomb did not mean anything;[163] yet they were still far from accepting the apparent end of Jesus and their hopes as final. They had not 'finished' with it all, had not yet reconciled themselves to all that had happened.

Of course, such a rendering of their attitude has hardly any reliable and definite 'account' as a foundation, but that does not mean it is necessarily 'false'. In any case, there is no other old version contradicting it. Perhaps Mark and Matthew saw the situation in much the same way as Luke; only they said nothing about it. The crucial point, however, is not the general state of affairs, but the definite information Luke gives about the attitude and conduct of Peter. According to his account, it would follow that Peter had never, even after the crucifixion of Jesus, gone astray in his regard. In spite of all, he had preserved his 'faith', and so finally won over the others. This is what Jesus himself had proclaimed, before he spoke of the denial, in the form of a prophecy.[164] Peter saw the fate that was threatening Jesus, imprisonment and death; it was already present before his eyes,[165] and he swore that, even so, he would not abandon him. Jesus, in foretelling the reverse, at the same time assures him of his prayer which, in the hour of reckoning now coming to the disciples, would keep Peter in his faith; his faith would not 'fail'. What this means is that Peter would, indeed, break down in a human sense, come to a moral collapse, but not to a complete abandonment of his faith in Christ. Once he had repented his lapse, recollected himself, and been 'converted', he would be able to raise up and 'confirm' the others.[166] Accordingly, the very eloquent look with which Jesus renewed contact with Peter after his

---

[163]Luke 24.22ff.

[164]Luke 22.31f. Against Bultmann's strange view (*Tradition*, pp. 287f.) that this had originally nothing to do with the story of the denial, see Finegan, p. 15, n. 2.

[165]The readiness to follow the Lord καὶ εἰς φυλακὴν καὶ εἰς θάνατον, Luke 22.33, has no connection with a martyrdom of Peter: K. Heussi, 'Ist der sogenannte Petrustradition bereits im Lukasevangelium und schon kurz nach dem Jahre 70 bezeugt?' *Wissensch. Zeitschr. d. Friedrich-Schiller-Universit.* Jena 6 (1956-57) 571ff. The expression should not be taken as a general, exaggerated way of speaking; it has a definite meaning corresponding with the actual situation; cf. John 13.37f.

[166]The reading preferred by F. Blass, *Evangelium secundum Lucam* (1897) 99 and by Stauffer, *Vor- und Frühgeschichte*, p. 20, n. 58, σὺ δὲ ἐπίστρεψον καὶ στήρισον instead of καὶ σὺ ποτε ἐπιστρέψας στήρισον brings out less strongly the reference of the command to a later future, but does not alter the basic sense.

denial of him[167] was not only one of sorrow, exciting shame, but signified, in the very moment of the disciple's bitter humiliation and disappointment, the firmness of their inner union, or else its restoration. Peter had lost his pride and self-confidence, his belief in his own loyalty; but he never really lost the Lord himself, whom, in the bitterness of repentance, he found again.

I am far from holding that the picture here drawn is, in every single detail, 'historical'. In his Gospel, Luke reflects the later community's veneration of Peter,[168] and is evidently striving throughout to put the rest of the disciples also in the most favourable and edifying light possible.[169] Nonetheless, the idea that Peter, in the critical days after the external catastrophe, was the only one to remain loyal or, at least, not to have given up everything, perhaps also the first to rekindle hope and to have kept together or regrouped the others, has striking support in tradition. Something similar is already suggested by the Pauline account,[169a] and would generally accord with the leading role ascribed to Peter in the whole ancient tradition. It can hardly be accounted for solely by all his work later in the Church. This has often been felt and underlined;[170] but it is not in the least necessary to make this development begin only with the resurrection meeting,[171] though its decisive significance is obvious. We must go back further, if it was the case that the disciples, in fact, left Jerusalem and went to Galilee under Peter's direction. This, however, is the oldest tradition, one that does not just go back to Luke (who, in accord with his Jerusalem outlook, rather effaces it), but is presupposed by Mark, and is still preserved by Matthew.[172] We must, therefore, follow it.

---

[167]Luke 22.61.

[168]On this, see Goguel, 'Did Peter deny his Lord? A conjecture', *Harv. Theol. Rev.* 25 (1925) 1*ff.*; Strathmann, pp. 229*ff.*

[169]*Cf.*, especially Luke 22.28. The mention of the γνώριμοι (the same expression as in Justin, *Ap.* I, 50, 12, see n. 159 above) leaves the question at least open whether they were still present at the crucifixion.

[169a]See above, p. 49.

[170]Most recently by Cullmann, *Peter*, pp. 25*ff.*, 57*ff.*

[171]The expression ἐπιστρέψας, used by Luke, by no means suggests here a meeting with the risen Christ.

[172]In John's Gospel 20.17 and the Gospel of Peter 13.56 Jesus, or the angel, announces not only the departure of the Lord for Galilee, but also his return to the heavenly Father himself.

The words of the angel at the tomb do not imply, we have said, any kind of precipitate 'flight' of the disciples. They point, rather, to an orderly journey to Galilee to be taken under the leadership of Peter;[173] his name is, at any rate, the only one to be mentioned, and so given prominence.[174] Jesus Christ, the message runs, is already on the way there—the present tense is used—and the disciples are to follow him without delay, in order to see him there.[175] The angelic message is itself, certainly, legendary, but does it not, in spite of this, describe the situation as it really was? Here now, it seems to me, we have reached the stage when the discovery of the empty tomb must be brought in, and its role estimated. For it can hardly be seriously doubted that the news reached the disciples when they were still in Jerusalem. The contrary, biased assertion of Mark is secondary, and, in view of the tenor of the angelic message, as preserved in the other Gospels, merits little consideration.[176]

It is clear that the news, suddenly impinging on these men in their bewildered, despondent condition, must have had a violent effect. Admittedly, there is in our tradition, as we have seen,[177] an increasing tendency, for certain definite reasons, to play down this effect; but it cannot have been absent. Perhaps it was not at first unequivocal. It is perfectly conceivable that the empty tomb was not taken unreservedly as a certain proof of the 'resurrection', and that doubt and uncertainty were also expressed. But the report could also have been understood in the sense conveyed by the words of the angel: 'He is

---

[173]Mark 16.7.

[174]Lohmeyer, *Markus*, p. 312; *Galiläa*, pp. 10*f*. It is sheer arbitrariness for Lohmeyer to see, in a supposedly technical use of ὄψεσθε an allusion to the Parousia. Ὁρᾶν means simply 'to see' and nothing else (in the passive—1 Cor. 15.5*f*.—it could also mean 'appear'). The actual content of this 'seeing' is determined by the context. A special, 'technical' use of the word in the sense of the Parousia cannot possibly be sustained; thus also Michaelis, *Erscheinungen*, p. 138, n. 58; Marxsen, pp. 53*f*. It is conceivable that the hope of the disciples, as they went to Galilee, was directed not only to a reunion, but to the parousia itself. But it seems out of the question that our present tradition, formed on the basis of the first appearances evidently of quite a different orientation, should have kept any trace of this perhaps earlier expectation.

[175]See above, p. 58.

[176]Whoever considers that this message was recorded precisely to cover up the actual flight does so through a preconceived opinion, and not on the ground of the text itself.

[177]See pp. 59*ff*. above.

risen—(for) he is (certainly) not here (any more)!' If one is prepared to accept this interpretation, certain conclusions follow of themselves. Where, then, was Jesus to be found? Jerusalem, the godless capital of his enemies, the city where he had been persecuted and nailed to the cross was no place for his reappearance. He must have gone back to his own country, to Galilee, where he had worked, where he had his adherents, where he and all his disciples were at home,[178] the holy land of their memories and now of their hopes. Peter, in particular, must have seen things in this light and carried the day, in that he reanimated the uncertain, half-doubting minds of the others. It is hardly surprising that the resolve then made came later to be seen as a direct indication from heaven, and was put into the mouth of an angel, who was said to have spoken at the empty tomb. One might also ask if, as tradition asserts,[179] earlier allusions, spoken by Jesus himself, were now recalled to mind, and played a part.[180] On the other hand, we can hardly think that the disciples foresaw from the beginning the entire course of events; this is never implied in the Gospels. The decisive impulse that set everything in motion was the discovery of the empty tomb.[181]

The subsequent development presents hardly any difficulty, and has already been dealt with in the light of Paul's statement.[182] The journey to Galilee was undertaken just as commanded by the angel at the tomb or nearly so. The appearances at the lake of Gennesaret or elsewhere in Galilee brought final confirmation of all that had been believed and hoped, and confuted those who still had doubts.[183] Then it was that the Christian mission and preaching had its beginning. The Easter faith received its foundation, and the return to the holy, yet impious, city of Jerusalem meant the proclamation of the new, universal claims of the risen Lord before 'all the people'.[184] The history of the Christian Church had begun.

---

[178]*Cf.* Mark 14.70 par., and Acts 1.11; 2.7; 13.31.

[179]Mark 14.28=Matt. 26.32, Luke 24.6.

[180]I am quite unable to agree with Nikolaïnen, II, 33*ff.*, that they had such a determinate effect.

[181]In this way, the datum of the 'third day' is explained in the simplest way, as we have said (pp. 46*f.* above); so Grundmann, p. 372, and, in the sense of a working hypothesis, Grass, p. 129 ('Is the tradition of the empty tomb in essence reliable?').

[182]pp. 48*f.* above.   [183]*Cf.* Matt. 28.17; also n. 134 above.

[184]It seems to me not improbable that this took place on the Feast of Weeks, fifty

Now let us briefly rehearse the historical sequence of the events under discussion. In almost every detail it rests upon ancient traditional statements; but the sources themselves are admittedly of unequal value, and both their interpretation and their selection, in particular their combination, must always remain hypothetical. This does not mean that they are left to arbitrary choice. The only part that, in my opinion, admits of no doubt is Paul's account. Mark is, if considered critically, still a valuable source, and even Luke, conscious of writing as an historian, conveys further information and aspects that are not to be neglected. All the other evangelists have a moderate value only in confirming or continuing the older accounts.[185] Accordingly, I take the following as the course of the Easter events:—

1. After the arrest and death of Jesus, the disciples first remained in Jerusalem (all the Gospels), but did not come out into the open any more (Mark and Matthew). We are precisely informed about their state of mind; they were bewildered and downcast, but by no means resigned to what had happened (Luke).

2. Very soon, probably on the 'third day', some women from the adherents of Jesus, discovered that the grave was open and empty (all the evangelists). At this point, there were no appearances of Jesus (Mark, Luke).

3. The news caused unrest among the disciples. In particular, Peter seems to have understood the empty tomb as a pledge that the resurrection had occurred and to have influenced the others accordingly (Luke).

4. Thereupon, the disciples betook themselves to Galilee, under the direction of Peter (Matt., Mark, [Pet.]), in the hope of meeting Jesus there (Mark, Matt.).

5. There followed first an appearance to Peter alone (Paul, Luke), then to the 'Twelve' (Paul, all evangelists),[186] then to the five hundred brethren (Paul), then to James (Paul, Heb.) and then to 'all the Apostles'

---

days after the Pasch, celebrated as the Feast of the Renewal of the Covenant; so G. Kretschmar, 'Himmelfahrt und Pfingsten', ZKG 66 (1954-55, pp. 209ff.) 252f.

[185]This, of course, only applies to the subjects of the present inquiry.

[186]Admittedly, this can be known with certainty only from the Gospels of Mark and Peter. Luke assumes (as perhaps John) a somewhat greater number of persons, Peter probably a smaller.

(Paul). Most likely, these should be thought of as following in rapid succession.[187] It is however, possible that the two latter appearances took place in Jerusalem. At any rate, here we later find Peter, James, 'the Twelve', and a wider circle of Galilean disciples (Paul, Acts).

6. Much later came the last appearance to Paul, which, in every respect, is outside the series (Paul, Acts). It is not impossible that, in the first period, further resurrection encounters took place; but all the accounts of these are, in the highest degree, doubtful.

The only thing in this whole sequence that remains puzzling is what started it off—the problem of the whereabouts of the dead body. There is no reliable testimony at first hand as to how the tomb was opened and how the body disappeared. On the Christian side, all we have is the confession of the resurrection, which rests on the basis of the subsequent appearances. On the Jewish side, there is a series of tendentious accounts, providing other and contrary explanations, but they never give the impression of being derived from definite observations and statements of real antiquity. The matter, therefore, remains, from an historical standpoint, obscure. This, obviously, does not mean that it can be explained only by a 'miracle'. One could, as has been said, entertain the idea of a subsequent removal or shifting of the gravestone, of a theft of the body (only *not* by the disciples), of some malicious procedure on the part of the enemies of Jesus, or of some kind of accident. In addition, one could if so disposed, enlist hypotheses drawn from natural science and theosophy; here, in the absence of any available information, the imagination has the field to itself, as wide as it is barren. Anyone, who prefers instead to accept the bodily resurrection, abandons the sphere of what can be analogically understood and, with it, any discussion in historical terms. This, however, will not alarm anyone who believes in the bodily resurrection of Jesus. Here we are dealing with an event unique in every sense, with which the new 'aeon' begins and in which therefore, the old world with its laws definitely ends. Consequently, from the nature of the case, such an event is not to be assented to as merely 'probable'; it must be seen as necessary and theologically 'natural', as it were. The position is difficult only for those who would take the resurrection faith seriously,

---

[187]n. 184 above.

yet hold the bodily resurrection superfluous or unacceptable. For them there remains only the somewhat awkward expedient of following the old Christians in their confession of the risen Lord. but the Jews in what occasioned this confession.

IV

A further systematically theological treatment of this problem does not come within the scope of the present investigation. We may, however, be allowed, by way of conclusion, to touch on the question as to the sense in which the historical events here established may, as such, deserve to be regarded as fundamental. It goes without saying that the bare historical data we have been able to provide can in no way be considered to be an adequate reproduction of what the primitive Christian message was at the time, as regards its meaning and content. This message cannot be understood except through an adequate interpretation of these events, apart also from an unfolding of the power directly speaking in them, a power they possessed in being so regarded. Thus the bare data in the New Testament are never met with in this methodically prepared nakedness and secular setting. 'Faith comes from what is heard' (Rom. 10.17), and so through preaching, which grasps and presents the fact and its interpretation as fundamentally an indissoluble and actual unity. The credibility of the message rests not on bare historical proofs, but, on the one hand, on its existential ratification in the spirit and through 'signs that follow', and, on the other, on the character of the events as fulfilments in salvation-history, or, dogmatically speaking, on the 'proof from scripture'. This, however, does not mean that the history can be treated as unimportant. It belongs, in fact, of necessity to the witness, which, apart from it, would lose its meaning. Notwithstanding its actual, life-giving sense, the resurrection remains a real event of the historical past, and is the object of tradition, preaching and faith. Its preaching, therefore, cannot evade the historical problem, nor can it, by any means, be exempted from historical examination.[188] Already the evangelists

[188]Even when, as is the case today, this can be methodically executed only by the difficult, but unavoidable process of abstracting from the sources all they try to convey in the way of interpretation. It can be readily seen that such an attempt applied to the

conducted themselves on these lines in their accounts of Easter. With all their *naïveté* and awkwardness they faced the 'critical' doubts which showed themselves, and, as well as they could, refuted them 'historically'. Even Paul did so, though for him faith itself did not simply rest on an 'historical' basis.

With the emergence of scientific history in the modern age, the nature of apologetics has changed considerably from what it was originally, and the old method of countering historical doubts has been replaced by a wholly different one. The simple appeal to alleged miracles and to legends that assume variable and contradictory forms is seen to be useless; in fact, it is this that now provokes criticism and doubt. It is hopeless, then, to reiterate this mode of proof or to attempt, in a would-be critical fashion, to bring 'scientific' considerations to its support. It would be better to make a *sacrificium intellectus*, if one were prepared to do so. Accordingly, Protestant apologetics during the nineteenth century was often driven, in order to meet historical doubts, to find a psychological and apparently rational basis for the resurrection, combining it with an appeal to the fact of the Easter faith. The sudden reversal, it was said, in the state of mind of the disciples would be quite inexplicable apart from a corresponding real event to produce it. We have already seen what the answer to this would be from the historian's standpoint. Psychologically, this argument is not convincing, in the first place, and it is astonishing how much favour it still enjoys. Nowadays, however, a different form of apologetic is prominent, which accords somewhat better with the existing state of research. The present trend is to underline and exaggerate the inadequacy and confused character of the received accounts, and to make out that the actual story of the resurrection completely eludes the methods of historical criticism. All that remains is simply the biblical witness as such, the kerygma, which demands faith, and to which,

---

resurrection tradition very soon comes up against insurmountable barriers (pp. 86*f.* above). But it is sufficient to see and respect these. To forbid in principle any inquiry beyond the texts themselves, and to pose critically the problem of the events lying behind them, would infringe, from the outset, the rights and duties of the historian, and, in my opinion, would thereby be fatal theologically. On this I would take a decided stand against Karl Barth's Notes in his *Dogmatik*, IV, 2, pp. 166*f.* Cf. on this problem also C. H. Ratschow, *Der angefochtene Glaube, Anfangs- und Grundprobleme der Dogmatik* (1957) 55*f.*, 309*f.*

therefore, one has to submit in faith. But this solution also is too simple. The covenant thus concluded between an allegedly radical faith and historical scepticism in reality serves only to withdraw it altogether from the particular assault of history and historical reason.

In opposition to this, one of the concerns of the present study has been to show that, from an historical standpoint, there is no justification for such sweeping scepticism in regard to the traditional accounts. Yet, this does not of itself remove all the difficulties. In fact, what is really disturbing about an historical reconstruction of the Easter events is that it makes everything seem so simple and fit in so perfectly. The things that have been brought to light for us are neither absolutely miraculous nor completely unrecognizable. Everything may very well be either interpreted purely 'naturally' or misinterpreted.[189] Faith is, therefore, by no means, rendered immune from attack when it is referred to the witness of the resurrection as the unique, miraculous, salvific act of God that makes it 'free' from the world. In fact, this state of exposure alone is proper to it and brings out all its gravity; and this is precisely what has to be recognized without any reserve, in view of the historical possibilities. The act of God never takes place in a sphere set apart for it, as a neutral and indubitable reality. It remains 'invisible', and reveals itself as what it is only to faith. And when God speaks down from heaven, to the people standing by, it will seem no more than a clap of 'thunder' (John 12.28f.).

Consequently, a theology of the resurrection must abandon the old and foolish attempt to restrict reason to such an extent that the only way out is, apparently, to believe. It must also, for its part, be ready to forego doubtful 'proofs', used by a reason supposedly historical in its working, or a psychological, logical, or even sceptical reason, to facilitate faith in the resurrection and to make the truth of God somewhat more 'probable'. No reason is capable of it, and faith has no need of so perilous an assistance. It must welcome, however, any clarification that human reason can achieve.

---

[189]This is exactly true also of the decisive events of Christ's appearances, which one could very well understand as pure 'visions' in the sense of hallucinations. This is what critics have done times without number, for the most part quite unaware where their interpretations were leading them.

4
Early Christian Asceticism

I

'IF YOU WOULD be perfect, go, sell what you possess and give to the poor, and you will have treasure in heaven; and come, follow me'.[1] These words of Jesus to the 'rich young man'[2] were to point out to the 'first monk', Antony the Egyptian, at a decisive moment, the way of life for him. As he listened to the words being read in the church, they seemed 'meant precisely for him'. He went away, sold and distributed all he had, and began, in obedience to the summons heard, a new, ascetic mode of life.[3] Countless numbers followed him. These words, and the many related ones which were handed down from Jesus, seemed, as it were, the motto of the monastic ideal. For centuries hardly anyone doubted that this was their correct interpretation.

Was it, however, really the intention of Jesus that riches as such should be abandoned? Do they not come from God? Cannot they be used according to his will, and has not poverty its moral dangers? These questions were put, a century before Antony, by Clement of Alexandria, who came to the conclusion that the words to the rich young man were not to be taken literally. In his opinion, property is morally neutral, not necessarily dangerous, even useful. Jesus was concerned with setting the heart free and with a renewal of the interior disposition. His desire was that we should not put our trust in external possessions and cling to riches; but property itself, and a moderate and good use of its advantages, are in no way prohibited.[4]

We are here confronted with two opposed interpretations, which we may briefly designate as the *ascetic* and the *liberal*. They have to do, not only with the understanding of this one passage, not only with the

Matt. 19.21 par.
[2]He appears so only in Matt. 19.20. We have here an interpretation or a misunderstanding of the expression used in Mark 10.20, ταῦτα πάντα ἐφυλαξάμην ἐκ νεότητός μου.
[3]Athan., *Vit. Ant.* 2.
[4]Clemens Alex., *Quis dives salvetur*, esp. secs. 11-19, 26.

conception of riches and property, but with two fundamental ways in which it is possible to accept and appropriate the early Christian teaching, and the 'law of Jesus' in general. They are always recurring when men try to determine what is meant by Christian ethics, the Christian life, or practical Christianity. Perhaps they are not completely reconcilable. The entire history of Christianity can be viewed as an attempt to mediate between these two extreme standpoints and to bring them into some sort of equipoise. But the important question at the outset is not their relation to each other, but the original meaning of the Gospel teaching, and the extent to which they accord with its true intent. Let us look once again, from this point of view, at the story of the 'rich young man'.

It is told by all three evangelists in essentially the same terms.[5] As presented by them, it, first of all, undoubtedly concerns an event in the life of Jesus in his travelling and teaching on earth, and the rich man who comes to him is a definite person—Luke calls him a ruler—driven to him by an inward need. He turns to Jesus as a religious authority, a 'master', to advise and help him: 'Teacher, what good deed must I do, to have eternal life?' At first Jesus answers almost as if rebuffing him: 'Why do you ask me about what is good? One there is who is good.'; and simply reminds him of the plain purport of the divine commandments,[6] in particular those of the so-called 'second table', which regulate man's relations with his neighbour. Their fulfilment is presented as, in every case, right and sufficient; but it was precisely this way that no longer sufficed the rich man. He had followed it 'from his youth',[7] yet feels that something is 'wanting'.[8] Now there is offered him a really personal answer, one that touches him directly and is all-embracing. Jesus turns, as we are told, to the man with love,[9] and calls him simply to his following. He is to leave all he had and possessed till then, and share instead the poor, blessed,

---

[5]Matt. 19.16-22; Mark 10.27-22; Luke 18.18-23.

[6]Cf. Luke 10.26; D. Bonhoeffer, Cost of Discipleship (1959) p. 52.

[7]This is undoubtedly the meaning of our evangelists; the Gospel of the Hebrews is different (Preuschen, Antilegomena III, 5 p. 6). et dixit ad eum dominus: quomodo dicis: legem feci et prophetas? quoniam scriptum est in lege: diliges proximum tuum sicut teipsum; et ecce multi fratres tui, filii Abrahae, amicti sunt stercore, morientes prae fame et domus tua plena est multis bonis, et non egreditur omnino aliquid ex ea ad eos.

[8]Mark 10.21; Luke 18.22.

[9]Mark 10.21. ἐμβλέψας αὐτῷ ἠγάπησεν αὐτόν.

wandering life of the Master. 'Come, follow me'—the same, short, sovereign words with which Jesus once 'called' his disciples.[10] And then comes the sudden change. The rich ruler cannot bring himself to do what the other disciples had done; he is too rich. This way to 'perfection' is too hard, and the 'treasure in heaven' does not outweigh for him his treasure on earth. He goes away 'sorrowful', we are expressly told, and so feeling in himself that his decision, or rather lack of decision, means failure and final surrender. But this did not alter the decision taken; the choice here of a disciple miscarried. It is not unreasonable to try and determine the historical significance of the scene after this fashion. There were other young men also whom Jesus called, who, as the evangelists intimate, did not follow him immediately. Whether it was attachment to parents or friends,[11] or, it may be, fear of public opinion or the allurements of the 'world'[12] that caused the failure in those cases, here it was precisely wealth that held the young man back and wrecked his life.

If we look at the story in its original context and as standing alone, there can, of course, be no doubt that the demand to sell and give everything away was meant literally. St. Antony, therefore, was right, in so far as he understood the command of Jesus, not in any figurative sense, but strictly according to the letter. The sacrifice of home, family and possessions resulted of itself from the way of life which Jesus, homeless and poor, called his disciples to share.[13]

It would be absurd to think that Jesus only wanted to put the rich man to the test, to find out his real state of mind, and did not demand the actual sacrifice. But another thing is equally clear. If we look upon the story as concerning only a particular person whom Jesus, at the time and in circumstances that never recurred, wished to make his disciple, then the words addressed to him cannot be made a universal rule to be followed by all men at all times. In that case, there is no

---

[10]*Cf.* E. Klostermann, *Das Markusevangelium* (1950) 103. 'In view of the conclusion δεῦρο ἀκολούθει μοι addressed solely to a disciple in the strict sense, these words cannot well be meant as a corrective to the preceding answer, v. 19, and a supreme demand of general application'.

[11]Luke 9.59-62 par.   [12]*Cf.* Mark 4.15 *ff.* par.

[13]Luke 14.33; Matt. 10.9 and especially, in connection with the story of the rich young man, Mark 10.28*ff.* par.

question of foregoing wealth as such, and in all circumstances, but for the direct following of Jesus, to which by no means everyone was called in this manner in the lifetime of the Lord.[14]

The real problem of interpretation then, arises from the difficulty of drawing correctly out of a single occurrence and saying, in a past situation, what is permanently applicable and obligatory for every Christian. This is what both the ascetic and the liberal interpretations are engaged upon, each in its own way, and it is quite justifiable to take the story as not simply 'historical' but of actual relevance, and to treat as binding what it may have to 'teach'. This, in fact, corresponds to the intentions of the evangelists themselves. The words and acts of Jesus were never considered merely as history, and handed down 'for their own sake'. They were, from the very beginning, conceived as addressed to the hearer, instructing him and holding out promises. This they continue to be, and only from this standpoint can we understand the form in which they were moulded and the further development and reshaping they underwent. This is particularly clear in the case of the concept of 'following'. Already in its presentation in the Gospel tradition it has, in part, ceased to designate a real activity or form of life, as such, and, therefore, the literal moving along with and behind Jesus of his disciples, the meaning which would be implied in the rabbinical schools.[15] It has become more of an image to show forth the inner bond and common destiny with Jesus which every Christian possesses.[16] It is in this sense that it is now used quite generally; 'He that followeth me not is not worthy of me',[17] or 'cannot be my disciple',[18] that is, a real Christian. In this context, therefore, the story of the rich young man must also be placed.

What, then, does the 'following' of Jesus mean here and elsewhere, if it is to be understood as a general obligation and a promise for every Christian? It is certainly inadequate to take it only as an inner community with Christ and being assimilated to him, as Clement of Alexandria was the first to do. The true follower is something other than an admirer or mystical friend of Jesus; he is the man who is obedient

[14]*Cf.* especially Mark 5.18*f.* (Luke 8.38*f.*).
[15]*Cf.* G. Kittel, Art. ἀκολουθέω, *ThW* (1933) 213-215.
[16]G. Bornkamm, '*Die Sturmstillung im Matthäus-Evangelium*' in: *Jahrb. d. Theol. Schule Bethel* 1948, pp. 49-54.
[17]Matt. 10.38.
[18]Luke 14.27.

to his Lord and 'confesses' him before men.[19]   And, as the world is always the same, it follows above all that he must share the destiny of his master, for his sake be hated and persecuted; it means he must take up his cross and thus 'follow' Jesus.[20]   The pale image of a merely 'inward' conflict misconceives the historical and realistic sense of the word of Jesus, spoken and impinging on the world and to be preserved in the world.   The 'many tribulations'[21] through which one must enter into glory, are meant quite realistically. On the other hand, this suffering cannot simply be taken in an ascetic sense. The disciple of Jesus is not required to renounce of himself the peace and goods of this world. He is 'called' to the following, and must go where the Lord leads him. He is left in no doubt that the way to eternal life passes 'under the cross', and that it will be no better in the world for the disciple than for the master. This, however, does not mean that he has to copy, of his own initiative, the privations and renunciations of the life of the first disciples and of Jesus himself. The follower is not an imitator of a pattern, nor does he simply observe a 'law' which is valid for all time.

In the light of this, we see how the liberal and the ascetic interpretations both come up against the same danger. Since they both look for a universally valid norm of Christian conduct and try to realize it, whether 'inwardly' as a frame of mind, or 'outwardly' through asceticism, they overlook what is precisely the crucial point, namely, unconditional, personal adhesion to the Lord, accepted in faith, and the resultant openness to every concrete form of demand and 'vocation'. It is faith in this sense and no general law, however framed, that constitutes the starting-point of the Christian way of life and morality. Obviously, however, this is not to deny that the concrete decisions entailed by the following of Christ may, in fact, always lead to 'ascetic' ones, and that 'asceticism', in the sense of actual renunciation of this kind, may be a permanent, even perhaps a distinctive form of the Christian life, and therefore to be commended. In what follows we will try to set out, from this standpoint, the meaning of the ascetic life in early Christianity. The subject, considered from an external standpoint, can be divided according to the three main directions taken by the ascetic impulse: the abandonment of property, abstinence from

[19]Matt. 10.32f. par. (Mark 8.38 par.).
[20]Matt. 10.38 par.   [21]Acts 14.22.

food, and renunciation of marriage and sexuality. The matter to be dealt with is interesting enough from the standpoint of religious history and of psychology, and that alone makes it worthy of a comprehensive survey. But, for us, the decisive question is not that of how and in what form asceticism was recommended or practised in primitive Christianity, but the meaning and spirit behind it, and the significance belonging to asceticism in relation to early Christian teaching as a special form and implementation of the 'following' of Jesus.

II

We start with the problem first prompted by the story of the rich young man—that of the ascetic renunciation of property and the justice or injustice of property in general.

It is well known that early Christianity had nothing to do with social demands and programmes, that, in particular, it pronounced no condemnation of private property. There is no need to show this in detail. Jesus himself, who 'had not where to lay his head',[22] appeared as the guest of rich people without reproaching them,[23] and allowed himself to be supported by wealthy adherents.[24]

In sending his disciples out into the world without external protection, poor and destitute, to preach the Gospel,[25] he implied no condemnation of property as such. The 'Apostle', through his office and work, was subject to a special law.[26] Admittedly, in the close community of love of the small primitive community in Jerusalem, private property virtually ceased to be, at all events it played no part.[27]

[22]Matt. 8.20 par.
[23]Mark 2.15 par.; Luke 7.36; 10.38; 11.37; 14.1; 19.5-7. These data, presented in schematic form (R. Bultmann, *The History of the Synoptic Tradition*—1963—334f.) are to be found in Luke, for whom the relations between rich and poor was a special problem; see pp. 98f. below.
[24]Luke 8.3. According to John 12.6; 13.29, Judas was even in charge of a common purse to be used for the poor. Perhaps we have here a reflection, as in Acts 4.37, of a need later felt in the Church; so Bultmann, *Das Evangelium des Johannes* (1956) 318, n. 2.
[25]Matt. 10.9f. par.
[26]This is also clear from the relation in which Paul stood to his communities; cf. for example 1 Cor. 4.8-16.
[27]Acts 2.44f.; 4.32-35; cf. p. 100 below.

But apart from the fact that this account is legendary and evidently exaggerates the so-called 'communism' of this earliest time,[28] it expressly confirms the right of the individual to keep his property if he wished.[29] Private property was, therefore, allowed. What was required of every Christian without exception was, not renunciation of possessions, but good works, almsgiving and compassion for the 'poor', especially those of the community.[30] Covetousness, therefore is seen as the 'root of all evils',[31] since it refuses to help and to share with others. This insistence on practical help and readiness for sacrifice is nothing new or original. It was part of the tradition of contemporary Judaism and its synagogue communities,[32] and was simply reinforced by Jesus's commandment of love and the strong feeling of brotherhood in the new community. But it is probably not the case that this kind of exhortation was specially prominent in the original teaching of Jesus himself.

Nonetheless, it is precisely there that we find a warning against riches, delivered with special, inexorable force and utterly without compromise. But the idea of its 'dangerousness' is not based on general human considerations of regard for the poor and their need and the evil of a loveless mentality. Its standpoint is, rather, the great catastrophe of the coming divine judgement, the prelude to salvation, for which we must prepare ourselves. It is this we have to confront; for it alone we must be ready, with no reservation. Herein lies the power of 'riches', which, perhaps more than any other power here below, gets in our way, impeding and confining. This is precisely shown, with exemplary clarity, in the decision of the rich young man. So it is that to this story is subjoined a discourse of Jesus to the disciples, pointing the conclusion of what had just happened: 'How hard it will be for those who have riches to enter the kingdom of God! . . . It is easier for a camel to go through the eye of a needle than for a rich

[28]Otherwise, the act of Joseph Barnabas, Acts 4.36, would not have been related as something extraordinary; *cf.* also 12.12.
[29]Acts 5.4.
[30]Matt. 6.2; Rom. 12.13; 2 Cor. 8.14*f*.; Gal. 6.10; Heb. 13.2; 1 Tim. 6.18*f*.; 1 John 3.17*f*., etc.
[31]1 Tim. 6.10; Pol. Phil. 4.1; *cf.* Luke 12.15; Eph. 5.3; Col. 3.5; 2 Pet. 2.14; Did. 4.5-8; Herm. Sim. 1.8.
[32]*Cf.* H. Bolkestein, *Wohltätigkeit und Armenpflege im vorchristlichen Altertum* (1939) 34.*ff.*

man to enter the kingdom of God'.[33] The salvation of a rich man thus seems quite impossible, and this interpretation is expressly confirmed in what follows. Humanly speaking it is, in fact, impossible; there is only one consolation—here as everywhere else—that 'all things are possible with God'.[34]

This judgement was, as we have said, evidently not intended to have a social or general moral application. To have great wealth is—as is shown precisely by the rich young man[35]—of itself neither unjust nor sinful. But wealth is harmful to its possessor at the decisive moment, because he himself is possessed by it, that is, it takes from him the freedom to choose aright. It fills the man's heart, all his being and will, and never loses its hold, so that he is unable to follow the call of Jesus that demands all. No man can serve two masters,[36] and Mammon is a deceptive tyrant who promises security and enjoyment, just where there is no assurance, and death will rob him of everything 'overnight'.[37] Admittedly, the freedom of the heart can be undermined not only by a false sense of security, but also by a wrongful concern for the necessities of life.[38] The step from poverty into the freedom of God is the only one presented as easy and short,[39] compared with the frightful danger in which the rich are placed, as instanced by the prosperous corn-grower.[40] 'Do not lay up for yourselves treasures on earth'.[41] 'The cares of the world and the deceitfulness of riches choke the word'.[42]

In view of sayings such as these, we may wonder how it was that primitive Christianity did not recommend to everyone the way of renunciation of possessions and, in this sense, the way of asceticism. Certainly, there is no room for a 'liberal' estimate of property and its advantages or for an outright defence of its moral innocuousness.

---

[33]Mark 10.23, 25 par.

[34]Mark 10.27 par. The sequence of the discourse, certainly, seems somewhat confused. According to Klostermann (n. 10 above) 117, the possible miracle relates not to the salvation of a rich man despite his wealth, but to his conversion from wealth itself. The text alone does not suggest such an interpretation, and, apart from this instance, there is no tendency in Matthew or Mark so emphatically hostile to possessions or so markedly ascetic.

[35]Especially in view of 'social' emphasis of the Gospel to the Hebrews, n. 7 above.

[36]Matt. 6.24 par. [37]Luke 12.20; 12.33f. par.; Matt. 6.19.

[38]Matt. 6.25-34 par.; 10.19 par.; 13.22 par.; Luke 10.41; 21.34.

[39]Luke 6.20, see below p. 99. [40]Luke 12.13-21.

[41]Matt. 6.19. [42]Matt. 13.22 par.; cf. 12.5 par.

The glory of this world is the gift of the devil, to bind men to him.[43] In general, however, the Church was content, as with all the other 'temptations' of the world, to counter it with repeated warnings of the gravity of the situation and the greatness of the salvation promised, with the call, that is, to watchfulness, not to asceticism. Nonetheless, the ascetic solution is sometimes given, in fact, by the evangelist who, as a man of the world and of culture, would seem least likely to take this view, namely Luke. In his special contribution (not found in the other evangelists) he hands on the tradition of certain Palestinian groups who stressed their poverty and taught the blessedness of the 'poor' as such.[44] Not only did he impart their ideas, but, to a great extent, made them his own.[45] This is shown in numerous small alterations and additions which his Gospel contains, all pointing in the same direction, and equally by the continuance of the same trend in the 'second part' of his work, the Acts.

In this connection, what is most obvious is the well-known difference in the Beatitudes as described by Matthew and Luke.[46] Matthew held blessed only the poor 'in spirit', and not simply the 'hungry and thirsty', but those who hunger and thirst 'after justice'. His main concern here as elsewhere is to keep the new justice which Jesus brings manifestly free from what is merely external, from all affectation of holiness and false security, even that of the devout Christian in his poverty. Luke, on the other hand, regards the possible misunderstanding with equanimity. He pronounces blessed, without qualification, the poor, the hungry, the reviled, and the persecuted; for theirs is 'the kingdom of heaven'. They, the seemingly disinherited, are the ones to be consoled, heartened, and given joy without end, by the saving grace of God. This, of course, does not mean that Luke sides with the poor in the sense of the 'proletariat', as a social class;[47]

---

[43]Luke 4.6.
[44]See M. Dibelius, *Der Brief des Jacobus* (1959) 39-41; A. Kuschke, '*Arm und Reich im Alten Testament mit besonderer Berücksichtigung der nachexilischen Zeit*', *ZAW* 57 (1939) 31-57; N. A. Dahl, *Das Volk Gottes* (1941) 186*ff*.
[45]This is insufficiently noticed by Chr. Rogge, *Der irdische Besitz im N.T. Seine Beurteilung und Wertschätzung durch Christus und die Apostel* (1897) 14*ff*.
[46]Matt. 5.3*ff*.; Luke 6.20*ff*.
[47]It is wrong, therefore, to call him the 'socialist among the evangelists', as does H. Holtzmann, *Protest. Kirchenz.* 1894, col. 1057. In this he is followed by Rogge (n. 45 above).

he too speaks of those who are reproached and cast out 'for the Son of man's sake',[48] those who, in humility, wait for God's redemption.[49] These, however, the ones who hear and wait, are, for the most part, the poor, the beggars, and the cripples,[50] and, according to the very words of Jesus, the rich as a rule do not lay themselves open to the kingdom of God.[51] Therefore, 'woe' to the rich, to those that are filled, to those that now laugh. Heavenly retribution will not be long delayed. The most forthright expression of this idea of the curse of riches is the story of the rich man and Lazarus. It is startling how riches are presented here as self-evidently sinful, or, at any rate, something that clearly must be punished in the after life with terrible pains, while the poor man, also self-evidently, is compensated with heavenly joy.[52]

Against this background the repeated insistence on alsmgiving gains heightened significance.[53] To those who practise it diligently it can bring salvation at the last day.[54] Terrible is the fate of those who lay up 'treasures' to themselves, and are not rich before God.[55] Hereby the rich are not as such condemned as lost;[56] still the most certain way is evidently to renounce,[57] like Jesus, one's own possessions, and to observe his counsel to the rich young man,[58] his warning to every one of 'his disciples'.[59] 'Sell what you have and give alms!'[60] This is for

[48]Luke 6.22.
[49]Luke 2.38; the whole atmosphere of the first two chapters is significant in this regard.
[50]Luke 14.21. 'The poor and maimed and blind and lame', as opposed to 'the good and the bad' in Matt. 22.10; cf. also Luke 14.13f.
[51]And if they do, they no longer cleave to their riches. Luke 19.8.
[52]Luke 16.19-31.
[53]Luke 11.41; 12.33; 16.9; 19.8; Matt. 26.11=Mark 14.7=John 12.8 is omitted in Luke.
[54]Luke 16.9. Whether this is intended as a direct plea for almsgiving, which most modern commentaries doubt, may remain open; Enoch 39.5 is presupposed as similar. Cf. also Luke 14.14; Matt. 25.34ff., and the rich young man in the Gospel to the Hebrews, n. 7 above; likewise 1 Tim. 6.19. The message which the rich man in the story of Lazarus wished to send to his brothers, Luke 16.27f. could only have been advice to give their wealth to the poor.
[55]Luke 12.21.   [56]Cf. n. 23 above.
[57]Luke 8.3.   [58]Luke 18.22.
[59]Luke 14.33; cf. 22.36.
[60]Luke 14.33; cf. 19.8. On the other hand, in Matt. 13.44f., the selling of possessions in the parables of the treasure in the field and the pearl of great price is purely symbolic.

Luke the way which the first, perfect community of the Christians in Jerusalem evidently followed under the guidance of the Apostles. No one among them suffered want.[61] Whoever possessed land or house sold it and put the money at the disposition of the Apostles.[62] Certainly, Luke, in these statements, accords with certain ideals of Greek philosophy;[63] but they must mainly be understood as the direct fulfilment of what is recommended in the Gospel and should, therefore, be natural to the true disciples of Jesus. Admittedly, Luke refuses to make the ideal community life, as it existed in Jerusalem, a law for all, and so deprive it of its voluntary character.[64] Clearly he does not count on its continuation later in the Church.[65] It cannot, however, be denied that the so-called 'communism of love' in Jerusalem does, in fact, represent his ideal, one which has a fundamentally ascetic character.[66]

In the light of this, it is easy to understand that the situation of the well-to-do Christian in the Church during the whole of the following century was a difficult one. There were not wanting expressions of social disapproval in his regard,[67] and all attempts to justify the property of the 'rich' are manifestly hesitant and inconclusive.[68] From this situation originated the 'liberal' solution put forward by Clement

---

[61]*Cf.* on this Luke 22.35; also 12.15. Later also the Apostles possessed nothing in the way of wealth; Acts 3.6.

[62]Acts 2.44*f.*; 4.32-37; 5.1*f.*

[63]*Cf.* H. v. Schubert, *Der Kommunismus der Wiedertäufer und seine Quellen* (1919) 35-38.

[64]Acts 5.4.

[65]Otherwise, he would not have tacitly implied its limitation to Jerusalem.

[66]H. Sahlin, '*Die Früchte der Umkehr*', *StTh.* 1 (1948) 63 rightly denies that Acts 2. 44*ff*; 4.42*ff.* implies compulsory communism; but would recognize as the only positive duty of private property to be 'an expression of a good community spirit, of the ethic of Christian solidarity'. At the opposite extreme, E. Benz, 'Der urchristliche Kommunismus. Ananias und Sapphira', *Der Kirchenfreund* 82 (1948) 241-247; 273-277, interprets the text, in spite of Acts 5.4, to mean that property is theft (p. 247), and Christianity means Communism (p. 273).

[67]James 1.10*f.*; 2.1-9; 5.1-6.

[68]The adjustment put forward in James 1.9*f.* is not reckoned satisfactory even by the author himself; see previous note. Hermas also tries, in *Sim.* II, to make salvation less remote through almsgiving and the prayers of the poor for the rich, but wealth still remains a detriment. *Vis.* II, 3, 1; III, 6, 5-7. Iren. *haer.* LV, 30 takes it for granted that Christians must participate in the pagan *mammon iniquitatis* (though here the question is treated differently).

of Alexandria, which is far from being merely facile or regardless of religion, but is actuated expressly by the pastoral obligation of protecting the rich from despair, which is no less corrosive of faith than is a false sense of security.[69] Even a rich man can be 'blessed', for it is not riches as such that are condemned, but only the heart and mind enslaved to them. The interpretation Clement gives of the story of the rich young man can hardly be objected to from the standpoint of the original Gospel account. Yet the way in which he sets about supporting his thesis in detail, with ideas and distinctions drawn from the Stoic philosophy, is absolutely fatal. For this confines all moral questions to the sphere of man's 'inner life', and wealth appears only as a basically harmless and neutral thing pertaining to the 'external world'. The world itself, in this view, becomes the 'external' and 'natural' world, and the conflict with it, which the Gospel represents as inevitable, is now only possible, even if probable; it is, at all events, only the 'worst' contingency. The enlightened neutrality which views life objectively tends inevitably to weaken or obscure the sense of how the devil exploits the danger of riches and of the radical demands of discipleship. In this respect, the 'ascetic' interpretation is superior to the 'liberal', when it counsels casting off the bonds of wealth and the voluntary sacrifice of the world's peace. And, for that reason, it can never, in the long run, be supplanted or defeated by any considerations on the lines of Clement. Yet it is significant that the extreme ascetic solution of the question of property was never considered either by Clement or any other second century writer.[70] Up to the time of the first essays in monasticism, it was never envisaged.

III

If we go on to the second form of asceticism, *abstinence from food and drink*, it becomes abundantly clear how little Christianity was, origin-

---

[69] Clem. Al., *Quis dives salvetur* 2, 2f.

[70] Admittedly, Eusebius, *Hist. eccl.* III, 37, 2 relates of the missionaries of the post-apostolic period that they often ἐνδεέσιν νέμοντες τὰς οὐσίας, εἶτα δὲ ἀποδημίας στελλόμενοι ἔργον ἐπετέλουν εὐαγγελιστῶν. But he is here describing an ideal, the heroic sacrifice made to the special tasks of the new form of vocation; it does not purport to solve the problem of property as such.

ally, an ascetical movement. In this respect, Jesus was no ascetic.[71] It is true that his words—again, however, only in Luke—contain a warning against 'dissipation and drunkenness,' inasmuch as these deprive the heart of freedom and watchfulness for the coming of God.[72] But this has nothing to do with asceticism. In fact, the absence of any ascetical element in the character of Jesus caused surprise and offence; his enemies called him 'a glutton and a drunkard'.[73] It is, also, striking how often the evangelists portray him at a meal, as host or as guest.[74] This is no accident. These joyful occasions not only renewed the old Israelite openness to the natural pleasures of life, but also directed attention to the joy of the time of fulfilment, already begun with his coming. In the kingdom of God, also, the just will sit down with Abraham, Isaac, and Jacob[75] to drink wine[76] and eat,[77] and, therefore, the disciples cannot fast as long as the bridegroom is with them.[78]

In the traditional form of this statement there is an allusion to the later fasting practice adopted, after the death of Jesus, by the communities.[79] It cannot be urged that Jesus opposed the Jewish fasting customs altogether. Nor, indeed, did he oppose the sacrificial service, sabbath healing, and the like; and the Sermon on the Mount even gives directions for the true kind of fast that is acceptable to God.[80] The Acts also records a preparatory fast, joined with prayer, before a solemn sending on a mission or an ordination,[81] and, already in the second century, a fixed weekly fast-day was customary in the Church.[82] There is no need here to go into details of this development.

[71]The forty days' fast at the beginning of his ministry, told in connection with the temptation legend in Matt. 4.2 and Luke 4.2 was a solitary instance, and served to provide a reason for his hunger. *Cf.* E. Lohmeyer, '*Die Versuchung Jesu*', *ZSTh.* 14 (1937) 627*f.*

[72]Luke 21.34; *cf.* 12.45 par. The warnings against excess addressed to the young mission communities may also be cited here, even though they were not meant in an ascetic sense: Rom. 13.13; 1 Cor. 6.10; Gal.5.21; Eph. 5.18; 1 Pet. 4.3; *cf.* also n. 103 below.

[73]Matt. 11.19 par.

[74]*Cf.* E. Lohmeyer, '*Das Abendmahl in der Urgemeinde*', Jour. of Bibl. Lit. 56 (1937) 218*ff.*; also '*Kultus und Evangelium*' (1942) 89*ff.*; '*The Lord's Prayer*' (1965) pp. 149*ff.*

[75]Matt. 8.11; (Luke 13.29; *cf.* Apoc. 19.9.)

[76]Luke 22.18. [77]Luke 14.15.

[78]Mark 2.18*f.* par.; *cf.* John 2.1*ff.*

[79]Mark 2.20 par. [80]Matt. 6.16-18.

[81]Acts 13.2*f*; 14.23.

[82]Did. 8.1. The choice of the days shows a deliberate opposition to Judaism.

A regular fast, or a fast on special occasions and for giving added force to prayer,[83] was a widespread practice, especially in Judaism.[84] It was a pious practice, but not the expression of an actual ascetic intention. The further question, how far the practice of fasting in the beginnings of the Church had an additional significance as a declaration against Judaism and its laws, we may leave on one side. In general, the whole question hardly plays any part in early Christian writings. Paul never mentions fasting at all.[85] Luke depicts John the Baptist and Anna, the prophetess, as given to severe fasting,[86] but only does so to complete the picture of these pre-Christian saints as 'devout' in every respect. Never is any theological significance attached to these ascetic characteristics.

The question of food only became really crucial in connection with the new outlook on asceticism in the Hellenistic world, that is, with the dualistic standpoint of the so-called 'gnosis'. This made many devout persons feel it absolutely incumbent on the 'spiritual' man to abstain entirely from certain things, notably meat and wine, or, at least, to do without them on certain days, on the ground that he was obliged to protect and free himself from the devil's assaults through the senses and the world of sense. This they considered to be enjoined as a necessary consequence of the redemption wrought by Christ.

The beginnings of these ascetic practices can already be seen reflected in the epistles of St. Paul. He takes them as a sign of spiritual 'infirmity'; for 'the earth is the Lord's, and everything in it',[87] and nothing in the world has of itself the power to make men impure.[88] Jesus himself had spoken in a similar way against the bondage of his Jewish adversaries to cult observances.[89] Paul, however, was well aware that the moral problem of ascetic 'superstition' was not solved simply by this negative approach. Anyone who is convinced in con-

---

[83] In the same way, fasting is often mentioned in the New Testament as something additional. Matt. 17.21; Mark 9.29; Acts 10.30; 1 Cor. 7.5.

[84] H. Strathmann, 'Geschichte der Frühchriste'. Askese in der Umgebung des werdenden Christentums I (1914), and 'Reallexikon für Antike und Christentum' I (1943) 749ff.; J. Behm, Art. 'νῆστις', ThW 4. (1942) 926-932.

[85] The νηστεῖαι of which 2 Cor. 6.5 and 11.27 speaks, are not voluntary ascetic practices, but privations he was exposed to in his vocation.

[86] Luke 1.15; 2.37.

[87] 1 Cor. 10.26.   [88] Rom. 14.20.

[89] Mark 7.14-23 par.

science that certain foods are polluting is, in fact, polluted if he acts against it.[90] Consequently, the 'strong' must bear in mind the weakness of their brothers, and not bask in their own enlightenment.[91] They can do so without harm, since they act freely without sacrifice of their own convictions,[92] and because the 'kingdom of God does not mean food and drink',[93] that is, salvation is not ultimately gained or lost either by asceticism or by a profession of freedom in this sphere. 'Therefore, if food is a cause of my brother's falling I will never eat meat.'[94]

This approach, of course, cannot be sustained when the 'weak' themselves go over to the offensive and try to elevate asceticism to a law, making of it something of absolute religious obligation.[95] In this situation the epistle to the Colossians takes a strong line against the abstinence, on the ground of law, of the gnosticizing ascetics, attacking it as a betrayal of the freedom of Christ to the earthly and fleshly commandments of men.[96] Later sects went so far as to correct the Gospel tradition itself in an ascetic sense, for instance, by expurgating references to the paschal lamb and to Jesus eating meat,[97] and even to John the Baptist eating locusts.[98] Against this background should be understood the attacks of the pseudo-Pauline pastoral epistles against certain heretics, who insisted on 'abstinence from foods'.[99] More strongly even than Paul, their author appeals to the general conception of creation; every creature of God is good, and nothing is to be rejected, but is sanctified for use by thanksgiving.[100] To the pure all things are pure.[101] Bodily chastisement as such is of little use.[102] Timothy should not hesitate to use a little wine for his health's sake.[103]

---

[90]Rom. 14.14; cf. I Cor. 10.29.
[91]Rom. 15.1.   [92]I Cor. 10.29f.
[93]Rom. 14.17.   [94]I Cor. 8.13.
[95]For the whole problem see R. Bultmann, *Theologie des N.T.* (1958) 29, pp. 336-340.
[96]Col. 2.21-23. The interpretation in detail is difficult and controversial; cf. M. Dibelius, *An die Kolosser, Epheser, etc.* (1953) 27f.
[97]Fragment of the Ebionite Gospel in E. Preusschen, *Antilegomena* (1905) IV, 8 p.12.
[98]Ibid. IV, 2 p.11 (Epiphan., *haer.* 30.13).
[99]I Tim. 4.3.   [100]I Tim. 4.4f.
[101]Tit. 1.15.   [102]I Tim. 4.8.
[103]I Tim. 3.22f.; against immoderation in drink, on the other hand, I Tim. 3.8; Tit. 2.3. Herm. *Vis.* III 10. 7 speaks as follows to the prophet who fasts and prays. βλέπε μήποτε πολλὰ αἰτούμενος βλάψῃς σου τὴν σάρκα.

Thus we see in the New Testament, from Jesus to Paul and beyond him, an increasingly clear rejection of any form of asceticism in regard to food, asceticism, that is, of an essentially religious nature, either recommended or commanded as a means of salvation or purification. This, as we have seen, did not rule out occasional fasting or fasting as a Church custom. Basically, however, the early Christian attitude in this regard was not ascetic; in fact, it was censorious of extreme ascetic ideas on this subject, and, when necessary, rejected them outright.

IV

Whenever asceticism is practised, renunciation of the sexual life forms a part of it; and so, quite early in Christianity, this came to the fore. This problem finds its fullest development in all its ramifications in the utterances of the New Testament. There also, consequently, its fundamental significance is most clearly discernible.

The old Israelite piety, at its origin, was not in the least ascetically inclined as regards sexual matters; but by the time of Jesus things had changed to some extent, and sporadically ascetic ideas had penetrated into Judaism.[104] At the beginning of the Gospel we see the figure of John the Baptist, who, though he did not preach asceticism, certainly practised it in all its forms. The beginnings of Jesus's ministry link up with the group of John's disciples; nevertheless, in his general way of life he did not follow John. His disciples 'do not fast',[105] and he himself, as we have seen, openly disavows the attitude of the preacher of penance who came 'neither eating nor drinking'.[106] Yet Jesus also was unmarried, and the disciples, in following him, cut themselves off from their families and relatives.[107] The only question is whether this sacrifice, which went of necessity with the life of a travelling preacher and his 'followers', can be designated 'ascetic'. At all events, women as such are not envisaged in this renunciation. They simply form a part of those with whom the disciples of Jesus must break all connection

[104]See note 84 above.   [105]Mark 2.18 par.
[106]Matt. 11.18 par.
[107]Luke 14.20. In the parallel place, Matt. 10.37, the wife is not mentioned in most mss. Whether she was omitted by Matthew for the sake of brevity, or added by Luke in his regard for completeness, there is no question of any ascetic intention, or one unfavourable to marriage.

and 'hate',[108] that is, no longer love as they love their Lord.[109] The new obedience and the new community that the following of Jesus creates permit of no limitation or exception in this regard.[110] It does not, however, follow that Christians must keep away from women and condemn the sexual life as such. Jesus himself does not hesitate to associate with the women who 'serve' him,[111] and his first disciples returned later to their wives, even, like Peter, taking them, at times, on their missionary journeys.[112] Here, therefore, there was no 'asceticism'.

All this accords with the words of Jesus as they have been transmitted to us. Not a single one is against the sexual instinct as such. The only sin Jesus seems to recognize in this sphere is adultery, and his conception of this is, admittedly, incomparably stricter and graver than any previously held.[113] No general 'moralistic' polemic against sexual sin in general is to be found in his utterances.[114] This, however, is characteristic of his whole moral teaching. It presupposes the validity and the knowledge of the old commandments of God,[115] and the announcement of the coming great turn of events does not serve merely to intensify their observance or to prescribe anything new, but goes much further in demanding a complete revolution and a wholly new outlook: 'For I tell you, unless your righteousness exceeds that of the scribes and Pharisees, you will never enter the kingdom of heaven.'[116] The time, however, which brings with it this demand is the time of the presence of Jesus, which means that it stands under the sign of unconditional forgiveness. Moral condemnation of the 'sinner' is the affair

---

[108]Luke 14.26.
[109]Matt. 10.37.
[110]Mark 3.31-35 par.; 10.29f.; Matt. 23.8.
[111]Mark 16.41 par.; see J. Leipoldt, *Jesus und die Frauen, Bilder aus der Sittengeschichte der alten Welt* (1921) 16ff.; H. Greeven, *Das Hauptproblem der Sozialethik in der neueren Stoa und im Urchristentum* (1934) 123ff.
[112]1 Cor. 9.5.
[113]Matt. 5.28. The passage 5.31f. has lately been treated afresh by several writers, and its detail interpreted in very different ways. K. Staab, *Festschr. Ed. Eichmann* (1940) 435-452, in agreement with the strict Catholic view, interprets it as saying nothing at all about the case of adultery (παρεκτὸς λόγου πορνείας); A. Fridrichsen, *SEÄ* 9 (1944) sees it in relation to those in the entourage of Jesus; likewise also B. K. Diderichsen, *Festkr.* J. Nörregaard (1947) 40, whose interpretation of the term μοιχεία as unchastity and concupiscence seems hardly tenable.
[114]Preaching to the pagans first made it necessary to enter on these matters and set up fixed rules. (See n. 138 below.)
[115]Mark 10.9 par.; Luke 10.26.   [116]Matt. 5.20.

of those who are 'well', who feel themselves to be without sin.[117]
The 'holy one of God',[118] which he really is, receives precisely the
lost, and lives in the company of publicans and harlots; for it is these
who are ready to come to him and hear him.[119] 'Faith' has brought
them to salvation. Thus Jesus dismisses even the adulteress with the
simple counsel: 'Go, and do not sin again'.[120]

We have, however, in the Gospels one isolated statement of the
Lord touching the question of voluntary 'virginity' and, in this sense
of asceticism. If only by reason of its form, it can hardly be considered
as coming originally from the Lord, but we can leave this question
aside. The statement about the 'eunuchs' is given only by Matthew.[121]
It says that there are eunuchs who are such by nature, others who have
been made so by men, and others also who have made themselves such
—for the kingdom of heaven. 'He that can take it let him take it!'
The introduction and the conclusion designate this pronouncement as
something mysterious,[122] understanding of which is not given to
everyone. Obviously, therefore, we have here an analogy, and the
literal understanding of the passage as a call to self-mutilation, which,
in a few instances, it was taken to mean in the ancient Church,[123]
is undoubtedly mistaken.[124] The introductory question of the disciples
was whether it was expedient to marry,[125] and the answer would mean,
symbolically, that, in fact—exceptionally, and only for those who could
understand it—there was a voluntary, religious renunciation of
marriage. But what is meant by saying that it is made 'for the kingdom
of heaven'?

It is hardly enough to take it in, so to speak, a 'protestant' sense, as
applying to certain external circumstances which might impel the

[117]Mark 2.17 par.   [118]Mark 1.24 par.
[119]Mark 2.15 par.; Matt. 21.31f.   [120]John 8.11.
[121]Matt. 19.10-12.
[122]Λόγος (=דבר) here does not mean only the allegory itself, but the understanding of the ascetical way. Leipoldt (see n. 111 above) 162n. 606 is mistaken in
taking 'this word' as the preceding judgement of Jesus on marriage.
[123]O. Zückler, Askese und Mönchtum 2 (1898) 359f.
[124]This applies at least to the existing tradition of the statement as we have it in St.
Matthew. That there was an earlier version of the statement, to be taken literally, as
K. Heussi, Der Ursprung des Mönchtums (1936) 27f. n. 1, thinks, seems to me very
improbable.
[125]What they say is a rather clumsy outcome of the preceding talk about divorce.

Christian, in his service of Christ, to make a personal renunciation of marriage; to do, that is, what the first disciples did, at least for a time, and what later 'apostolic' missionaries, in many cases, decided upon.[126] This, of course, might occur in many different forms, but in the passage under consideration there is nothing that refers to external circumstances or tasks; it would seem to have in view purely the individual and his free resolve. Besides this, the mysterious form of the statement is best understood if we take it as quite generally applying to a definite personal decision made in view of the eternal goal. Accordingly, there is a spiritual will and decision for perpetual celibacy as a 'charisma', we might say, a special gift of God 'given' only to few. The obscure mode of expression makes evident the awareness that here is being shown an extraordinary way, far outstripping the normal capabilities of the Christian. But, if taken in this sense, it would be perfectly in accord with the tenor of early Christian piety.

It is true that, as we have seen, asceticism in the sexual sphere plays no part at all in the older stratum of revelation common to all the evangelists. We can only fall back once again on Luke, who describes outstanding personalities in this respect also as ascetics.[127] In my view, the four virgin daughters of Philip in Caesarea probably owed their gift of prophecy to their virginity.[128] Philip was one of the 'seven' and so a Greek. With him, therefore, we leave Palestine and enter the Greek world. Here the question of asceticism, from the outset, plays a far more extensive part. The man who, to our knowledge,

---

[126]See in particular the pseudo-Clementine letter *de virginitate;* also A. Harnack, *Sitzungsber. d. pr. Akad.* 1891, pp. 361ff. *Cf.* also n. 70 above.

[127]*Cf.* the traits brought out in the picture of John the Baptist (Luke 1.15,80) and Anna (2.36f.). B. K. Diderichsen goes still further in his interesting essay on '*Efterfolge og Aegteskab i Lukasevangeliet*', *Festkr.* J. Nörregaard (1947) 31–50. According to him, the dissolution of the bond of marriage, which Matthew and Mark await in the future aeon when we shall be as angels, is transposed by Luke 20.35 into the present, and made a condition for future sharing in the kingdom of God. This interpretation of the present tense is, however, improbable, in view of Luke 20.36 (οὔτε γὰρ ἀποθανεῖν ἔτι δύνανται) and a corresponding exegesis of 16.18, as attempted by Diderichsen, pp. 33f., would be in complete contradiction with the normal relations of dependence between the evangelists.

[128]Acts 21.9; *cf.* the Book of Enoch 83.2; 'Two faces I looked upon before I took a wife'; on this, see G. Beer in E. Kautzsch, *Die Apokryphen und Pseudepigraphen des Alten Testaments* 2 (1900) 288. According to the older tradition, some of the daughters of Philip married later. Eus. *Hist .eccl.* III 30.1; *cf.* 31.3=V, 24.2.

first grasped it in its full and fundamental significance was himself a Greek and ascetic. This was the apostle Paul.

Paul does not develop his ideas on the subject on his own initiative; what he has to say about unchastity, marriage, and celibacy emerges in the course of dealing with the urgent questions, anxieties, and desires of his community at Corinth. It is a restless community, rent by discord and party strife. Even in regard to the practical conduct of life, 'gnostic' ideals of a superhuman asceticism rub shoulders with remains of pagan immorality, as yet unvanquished. Rigorism and laxity, scrupulousness and fantasy alternate and mingle. Paul, in virtue of being the founder and final authority of the community, is asked for his opinion. But he cannot simply advocate what he personally considers best and most desirable. He must bear in mind the confused outlook, the moral and religious immaturity of his children, lay down what is essential and indispensable in practice, leaving aside the rest, and be satisfied if the meaning and demands of 'his Gospel' are in the main not obscured or confused, but given their full force.

What he sees as the first and most pressing danger is that of open and unbridled lust,[129] a fundamental libertinism which justifies itself by appealing to the new 'liberty' proclaimed by Paul himself. 'All things are lawful for me'[130]—this slogan is used to permit all kinds of sexual excesses. These belong equally, with eating and drinking, to the inferior, superficial province of humanity; they cannot reach the special spiritual being of the Christian, and, therefore, cannot pollute it. In countering this, Paul must make clear not only the true meaning of Christian liberty, but also the body-soul unity and responsibility of the whole human personality. This he does by pointing to the future resurrection and judgement, which the Corinthian spirituals evidently do not take seriously.[131] Paul fully endorses their thesis as regards eating and drinking. In contrast with the expectation of Jesus and his kingdom, even for him these sense-activities of man are empty external things that will pass away with the world, unimportant and morally 'free': 'Food is meant for the stomach and the stomach for food—and God will destroy both one and the other'.[132] But the 'body'

---

[129]See also I Cor. 5.1ff.; I Thess. 4.3-5.
[130]I Cor. 6.12; 20.23.
[131]I Cor. 6.14; 15.12.
[132]I Cor. 6.13; 10.31 does not gainsay this.

does not belong to the things that pass, that do not fundamentally concern man. It is, in fact, what will one day rise,[133] and what the body does man himself does.[134] The body of the Christian has become the vessel of the Holy Spirit; it belongs no more to man to do with as he pleases, but to Christ who has bought it.[135] Impurity takes from Christ the members belonging to him, and makes them one with the harlot. 'Do you not know that he who joins himself to a prostitute becomes one body with her? For, as it is written, "The two shall become one".'[136]

This way of viewing the theological basis is highly significant. Paul has no hesitation in citing, as regards unchaste unity in the flesh, the same Old Testament passage as Jesus used to prove that God originally intended marriage to be indissoluble.[137] He sees Christ and the harlot as though they were competitors in one and the same sphere. It is an idea that involves ascetical consequences. Paul has no need, in this connection, to refer to marriage, when he impugns undisciplined sexual living. In fact, strictly speaking, he cannot do so in this context; for, as we shall see, the idea of community with Christ as he understands it militates against any sexual union, against marriage no less than against unchastity.

Paul, of course, recognizes marriage, and also that its indissolubility is an undoubted ordinance. He welcomes the opportunity to appeal casuistically to a statement of Jesus forbidding divorce.[138] Adduced as a norm governing the order of the Christian community, it imperceptibly acquires a fresh overtone contrary to the original meaning, and certain accretions and restrictions have to be introduced.[139] The wife of a pagan husband is not obliged to oppose him, if he wishes to dissolve the marriage.[140] In such a case, it must be presumed that Paul's meaning is that the divorced wife should forgo any fresh marriage.[141] On the other hand, a widow has the fundamental right to marry again—only it should be in the Lord,[142] that is in the Christian fashion and so, at least in most cases, with one who is also a Christian.

In these directives, Paul speaks as the practical organizer and re-

[133]I Cor. 6.14; 2 Cor. 5.10.
[135]I Cor. 6.15, 18-20.
[137]Mark 10.8. par.
[139]Thus, significantly, I Cor. 7.11.
[141]I Cor. 7.11.

[134]I Cor. 6.18.
[136]I Cor. 6.13, 15f.
[138]I Cor. 7.10f.
[140]I Cor. 7.15f.
[142]I Cor. 7.39.

sponsible leader of his communities. To get to know his own personal
view of the marriage question we must attend, chiefly, to what he has
to say in answer to the opposing group, the enthusiasts for asceticism,
in the community. The difficulty with them is, rather, whether a
Christian may marry at all, or even whether in marriages already
concluded or to be concluded sexual union should be foregone. It is
clear how strong is Paul's leaning to this conception. His answer
signifies, one might say, a basic No to marriage and a Yes to asceticism
in sex, if not precisely in regard to an already existing marriage.[143]
On this basis, he starts his discussion of the whole question with the
monumental pronouncement: 'It is well for a man not to touch a
woman'.[144] It would be 'well'—the 'untheological', not specifically
Christian, turn of phrase is significant[145]—if all men were as he, that is
could remain unmarried,[146] and his counsel is no different for virgins
and widows.[147] But, in contrast to the unhesitating radicalism of the
Corinthian ascetics, Paul is at once conscious of the dangers, indeed of
the impossibility, of a universal rule of this kind. All men are not alike;
some have the gift of continence, others not.[148] Compulsory abstinence
would only foster and aggravate the force of the passions suppressed.
In such cases, therefore, it is better to marry,[149] and the partners should
not deprive one another, or only for a short time and by mutual con-
sent, when they wish to give themselves to prayer.[150] Accordingly,
there is no question that, in principle, marriage and the married life
are permitted; that it is 'no sin' to marry is stated emphatically by
Paul.[151] But this is all. Fundamentally, marriage, in this view, is no

---

[143]The much-discussed question whether Paul assumes the existence of *subintroductae*
in Corinth need not be treated here. *Cf.* G. Delling, *Paulus Stellung zu Frau und Ehe*
(1931) 86-91, who affirms it: and, against, P. Ketter, *Syneisakten in Korinth?* On
I Cor. 7.36-38, *TThZ* 56 (1947) 175-182.

[144]I Cor. 7.1.

[145]*Cf.* J. Weiss, *Der erster Korintherbrief* (1910) 170.

[146]I Cor. 7.7. The fruitless question whether Paul married as an ordained rabbi, and
had become a widower when he wrote this, should never have been raised. *Cf.* on
this J. Jeremias, *ZNW* 25 (1926) 310ff.; 28 (1929) 321ff.; E. Fascher, *ibid.* 28 (1929)
62ff. and G. Delling (n. 143 above) 141ff.

[147]I Cor. 7.8, 26.   [148]I Cor. 7.7.

[149]I Cor. 7.9.

[150]I Cor. 7.3-5; *cf.* G. Harder, *Paulus und das Gebet* (1936) 20-24.

[151]I Cor. 7.28,36. I Thess. 4.3-5 is precisely a commendation of rightly ordered
marriage as against pagan licence. The praise of married love in the epistle to the

more than a concession to human weakness. Paul says so quite frankly; 'For fear of fornication let each man have his own wife, and let every woman have her own husband'.[152] 'Lest Satan tempt you through lack of self-control',[153] the married life must be continued with. 'To give in marriage' a virgin is, therefore, good, but 'he who refrains . . . will do better'.[154] There can be no doubt at all what Paul personally wishes, recommends, and considers best.

Certainly, one should not take his position to be that the 'concession' of marriage is merely something inevitable in practice, of which he takes account in dealing with his communities. Paul, as a believing Jew naturally holds marriage to be an undoubted right, conferred by God, that he is obliged to recognize. But if his desire to foster asceticism—over and above the requirements of practical necessity —is curbed, indeed, as it were, thwarted and in principle abandoned, it is owing, not to this factor, but definitely to what is new and central in his own Christian faith. Paul believes in salvation in Christ, a salvation that can only be believed here, but believed here without any reserve. For this reason, he proclaims 'freedom' from all 'human' laws, ordinances and judgements which would counteract, supplement or restrict this way of salvation. 'For Christ is the end of the law, that everyone who has faith may be justified'.[155] Certainly, this 'freedom' is no free indulgence accorded to passion or selfish lust. It is, however, freedom from any obligation to a particular order or form of life, as if this would bring anyone embracing it nearer to salvation or were of special value for faith, or indeed, indispensable. The salvation of the Christian is absolutely independent of any external 'state' in which he may be. It does not matter whether one is Jew or Greek, slave or free, man or woman, when called;[156] and this must

---

Ephesians 5.22-33 is, admittedly, not by Paul. Equally, Paul—as distinct from the pseudo-Paul of the pastoral epistles (1 Tim. 2.15)—hardly pays any attention to the importance of the education of children and so to the significance of the family as such. This appears—assuming the authenticity of the epistle—only in Col. 3.20f., referring to the traditional domestic rules, but 'restricted to the bare necessities'. M. Dibelius (n. 96 above); cf. K. Weidinger, *Die Haustafeln. Ein Stück urchristlicher Paränese* (1928) 50-52; 59ff.

[152]1 Cor. 7.2.   [153]1 Cor. 7.5.
[154]1 Cor. 7.38.   [155]Rom. 10.4.
[156]Gal. 3.28; (1 Cor. 12.13; Col. 3.13).

apply equally to whether one is married or not. Thus, Paul comes—almost reluctantly, one might say—to his final decision and doctrine of 'freedom' also as regards marriage. Certainly, in this as in other questions of the external mode of life, it does not seem right for a Christian to seek any alteration, as if, in these matters, anything essential were laid down. Let each one remain in the situation in which he was called.[157] And so, 'Are you bound to a wife? Do not seek to be free. Are you free from a wife? Do not seek marriage'.[158] Here, also, however, there is ultimately freedom. All Paul can do is advise, warn, and give his opinion.[159] He counts, indeed, on this not being neglected, but heeded,[160] for 'I think that I have the spirit of God'.[161] Paul, however, is not himself 'the Lord', and he is concerned to make a clear-cut distinction between what he can put forward, as it were, officially as the Lord's command, and what only personally as his own considered conviction.[162] For he has no desire to exercise compulsion on the Corinthians, but only to advise them as to what is best.[163]

What, then, does he see as the real foundation of the advice to remain unmarried, which he restrains so characteristically and yet imparts with such urgency? He is far from entertaining, at least, directly any sort of outright hostility to the body. Certainly, as an apostle, he must 'chastise' his body and bring it into subjection, and, as an athlete does, abstain in every way;[163a] but utterances like these are made in view of the special demands of the apostolic life. Applied to Christians in general they are simply figurative expressions of the discipline necessary for the future life and for the moral struggle of the Christian life as such.[164] Paul is no dualist in the gnostic sense, and when he speaks of 'flesh' and 'spirit' as the great opposites dominating life, he means something very different from the natural physical opposition of sensible and spiritual substance within man.[165] The basic reason he

---

[157] I Cor. 7.17,24.
[158] I Cor. 7.27.
[159] I Cor. 7.6,28,40.
[160] I Cor. 7.25.
[161] I Cor. 7.40.
[162] I Cor. 7.12.
[163] I Cor. 7.35.
[163a] I Cor. 9.25-27.
[164] Cf. E. Stauffer, Art. 'ἀγών', ThW I (1939) 134ff.
[165] Cf. R. Bultmann, Theology of the N.T. (1955) pp. 232ff.; W. G. Kümmel, Das Bild des Menschen im N.T. (1958) 22ff. Delling (see n. 143) in interpreting psychologically the ideas intended in a theological sense, obtains a far too uniform and one-sided ascetic picture of Paul's attitude.

gives is more of an historical and personal nature, and has in view, on the one hand Christ himself, and on the other the approaching end of the world. We may say, therefore, that the foundation for his view is at once eschatological and christological.

In pointing to the rapidly approaching end of all things, Paul associates himself with the oldest theme of all Christian preaching; 'The kingdom of heaven is at hand'.[166] It is only the use he makes of it, in not simply calling men to penance, that is at variance with its original application. Paul's meaning is that, in view of the imminence of the last, troubled age, there is no longer any meaning in marrying and burdening oneself with the bodily cares of marriage; he wishes, as he says, to 'spare his children' these.[167] This is a new note. Certainly, we find in the Gospels also 'woe to those who are with child and that give suck in the afflictions of the last age';[168] but this does not imply any warning against marrying on that account.[169] Only an ascetic could speak in that way, as Paul does here, as one for whom marriage, as part of the order of creation, had lost all positive value.

At all events, we may ask what else Paul had in mind in so strongly emphasizing these ideas, besides his aim of convincing his hearers.[170] The most profound, the specifically Pauline basis comes out clearly only in a second, christological set of ideas, whose main thesis had already been stated: 'The unmarried man is anxious about the affairs of the Lord . . . but the married man is anxious about worldly affairs, how to please his wife'.[171] The same 'worldly' passion that bound the libertine to the harlot binds also the husband to his wife and the wife to her husband. It fills the heart with useless cares, leaving it no longer free for the one necessary care, which is, in fact, the true freedom from care. 'I want you to be free from anxieties'.[172] This inverts the order of ideas, making community with Christ the central point; it is, as we have said, peculiar to Paul and so new. Yet we can see how it brings out forcibly one of the basic demands of the Gospel idea of following Christ: 'If any one comes to me and does not hate his own

---

[166]Matt. 3.2; 4.7 par.; 10.7 par.   [167]I Cor. 7.26,28.
[168]Mark 13.17 par.
[169]Thus also Leipoldt (n. 111 above) 92f.
[170]Also according to Fr. Büchsel, *ThBl.* 21 (1942) 120, *Die Ehe im Urchristentum*, he does not adduce the crucial point.
[171]I Cor. 7.32f.   [172]I Cor. 7.32.

father and mother and wife and children and brothers and sisters, yes, and even his own life, he cannot be my disciple'.[173] Paul gives this an ascetical meaning, so to speak, just as Luke later does to the question of 'riches' in corresponding fashion. But Paul goes beyond Luke in his clear awareness of giving to the original demand and promise that governs the whole Christian life—Jesus's call to free oneself for absolute obedience, and thus free oneself from this world's ties and cares—a definite interpretation which does not coincide with what Jesus actually said and promised. Paul does not only know that; in line with what was said about eunuchs, the way of asceticism as regards the sex instinct must always be closed to many. He even emphasizes, as against his own ideal, that the basic aim of the Christian relationship with the world is not an ascetic one, but 'freedom'—the freedom of those who have given up 'their own life', or, in Paul's words, have already 'died' to the world.[174] This attitude goes beyond the opposition of marriage and virginity, and, when it is realized fully, makes the special ascetic renunciation unnecessary. And thus Paul describes it in the very chapter devoted to the questions and the possibilities of Christian asceticism: 'It remaineth that they who have wives let them be as if they had none,[175] and they that weep as though they wept not, and they that rejoice as if they rejoiced not, and they that buy as though they possessed not, and they that use this world as if they used it not. For the fashion of this world passeth away'.[176]

The radical ascetic endeavour aiming at a 'celibacy of all the baptized',[177] on which Paul in Corinth imposed a certain restraint, was not

[173]Luke 14.26.
[174]R. Bultmann, Art. 'θάνατος' ThW III (1938) 18ff.
[175]Delling (n. 143 above) 64 adduces this passage in all seriousness as evidence that, according to Paul, we ought 'more and more to lose the desires of sense'. Leipoldt (n. 111 above) 167, n. 754 recalls, in connection with 1 Cor. 9.25, the 'fact well known to the Greeks and Paul' that 'abstinence lends strength'! Cf. on the contrary Bultmann in the following note.
[176]1 Cor. 7.29-31; on which see Bultmann, Primitive Christianity (1960) 244. 'This inner detachment is depicted in Paul's declaration that he knows "how to be full and to be hungry, to abound and to suffer need" (Phil. 4.11-13). And when he exhorts to "rejoice with them that rejoice, weep with them that weep," (Rom. 12.15), he naturally supposes a participation of the believers in the life of the world.'
[177]On the history of this ideal see K. Müller, 'Die Forderung der Ehelosigkeit für alle Getauften in der alten Kirche' (1927), reprinted in Aus der akademischen Arbeit. Vorträge und Aufsätze (1930) 63-79.

overcome thereby.[178] It accompanied the Church in its course through the whole of antiquity, and comes out clearly in much of the apocryphal tradition of the second and third centuries. What is particularly interesting in this connection is a declaration of the Lord of which the sole source is Clement of Alexandria,[179] which runs: 'Let not the married man put away (his wife), and the unmarried not enter into marriage'. This is exactly the same advice Paul gave to the Corinthians,[180] only now it is put into the mouth of Jesus himself. The reservation under which Paul gave it has simply disappeared; even so, there is no question of an absolute obligation.[181] A gnostic Gospel, however, does not hesitate to go further in this direction.[182] In it Jesus declares he has come 'to undo the works of woman'[183]—it is typical how it is the woman who is made the actual carrier of sensuality and of the world's ensnaring by the senses.[184] Death, it goes on to say, will be dominant as long as women go on giving birth;[185] the end of the world will come when believers 'have trampled down the garment of shame', that is when they no longer feel any sexual impulse and so no sense of shame.[186] Then the great division of the world will be overcome, and out of two will once more be made one.[187] In eternity

---

[178]His epistles were corrected by Marcion in this sense. Significant also is the widely adopted reading of Gal. 5.28 which places ἁγνεία alongside ἐγκράτεια.

[179]Strom. II, 15, 97, in Preuschen, *Antilegomena* (1905) XIII, 18, p. 28.

[180]1 Cor. 7.27.

[181]This is shown in the continuation, which refers to the special case of the binding vow: ὁ κατὰ πρόθεσιν εὐνουχίας ὁμολογήσας μὴ γῆμαι, ἄγαμος διαμενέτω.

[182]Perhaps here also should be recalled the Marcionite understanding of Luke 23.2, as in Harnack, *Marcion, Das Evangelium vom fremden Gott* (1924) 235: τοῦτον εὕρομεν ... κελεύοντα φόρους μὴ δοῦναι καὶ ἀποστρέφοντα τὰς γυναῖκας καὶ τὰ τέκνα ...

[183]*Fragm. des Ägypterevangeliums*, Preuschen II, 2, p.3.

[184]With Paul, on the contrary, both sexes are treated alike, practically and morally, in their mutual relationships (1 Cor. 7.4; 11.12); cf. Greeven (n. 111 above). The fact that Paul makes the husband the image of Christ and places him above the wife (1 Cor. 11.7) belongs to a quite different context, and besides is 'an idea whose exact meaning remains quite unclear': W. G. Kümmel (see n. 165 above) 39 n. After Paul's time, the subordination of woman develops increasingly; cf. H. Preisker, *Christentum und Ehe in den ersten drei Jahrhunderten* (1927) 151ff.; 169.

[185]*Fragm. des Ägypterevangeliums*, Preuschen II, 1 a, d, e, pp. 2f.

[186]Thus in the correct interpretation of 2 Clem. 12.4.

[187]*Fragm. des Ägypterevangeliums*, Preuschen II, 1 c, p. 2.

there will no longer be husband and wife.[188] Jesus, it is true, had spoken in similar terms;[189] only what he had said in quite a different sense of the future, angelic existence after the resurrection, is now simply applied to the present, and presented as a moral imperative to all Christians.

However, the prevalence of ascetic tendencies in the early Christian period should not be overestimated. All the testimonies to their existence are of a later date. In the New Testament, and even in the majority of the extra-canonical writings of the early age, there is nothing corresponding.[190] Even the diluted asceticism, as represented by Paul, hardly finds any adherents. The moral instructions of the later epistolary documents do not take up his ideas on this point. What is especially striking is that even in the genealogical narratives in Matthew and Luke[191] nothing in the way of asceticism can be discerned, although the idea of a 'virgin birth' would give an opening. It cannot be maintained that Mary remained always a virgin; for Jesus is the first-born, who was followed by many brothers.[192] That he was conceived without man's co-operation is presented, primarily, as a 'sign' of his miraculous, divinely wrought origin and coming into

---

[188]*Ibid.* V I, p. 12.   [189]Mark 12.25 par.

[190]On this, *cf.*, along with K. Müller (see n. 176 above) and the survey in K. Heussi (see n. 124 above), especially H. Preisker (see n. 184) 143*ff.*, who, however, over-emphasizes the strength of the ascetic tendencies. I was not able to obtain A. Baudrillart, *Moeurs païennes, moeurs chrétiennes* 1: *La famille dans l'antiquité et aux premiers siècles du christianisme* (1929).

  1 Clem. 35.2 praises ἐγκράτεια as a gift of God. Did. 11.11 seems to refer to the 'spiritual marriages' of the prophets, which, however, are only touched upon and not recommended generally. Hermas also, Sim. IX 10.6; 11.8, is aware of 'spiritual marriage', and seems to have wished his own to be such, like the *pneumatikoi* in Corinth; *Vis.* II, 2.3; *cf.* 3.2. For him, however, more important is the struggle against temptations of sense (*Vis.* I) and for virtuous family life: *Vis.* I, 2.4; 3.1*f*; II, 2.1; III, 7.3; *Sim.* I. V 3.9; VII. The same may be said of Ignatius, Pol. 5; *cf.* Pol. Phil. 4.2. Ignatius knows a state of life in the community consisting of 'virgins', who—as in the Pastoral Letters (p. 120 below) may also be called 'widows': Smyrn. 13.1. He knows also free ascetics, who are expressly warned against coming out in public: Pol. 5.2. For the correct interpretation of these passages, see A. d'Alès, *Rech. Sc. rel.* 25 (1935) 489-492. A more explicit recommendation of asceticism occurs only in 2 Clem. 14.3; 15.1, where appeal is made to the Gospel of the Egyptians.

[191]Matt. 1.18-25; Luke 1.26-56; 2.1-20.

[192]Mark 3.31*ff.* par.; 6.3 par.; Acts 1.14; John 2.12; 7.3,5,10; *cf.* on 'the relatives of Jesus' A. Meyer in E. Hennecke, *Neutestamentliche Apokryphen* (1924) 103*ff.*

the world, comparable, rather, to the related Old Testament birth-narratives, especially in their late Jewish form.[193]

The only one of the New Testament writings which seems to glorify asceticism in the sphere of sex is the Apocalypse of St. John. In it the seer beholds in heaven the 144,000 perfect men who 'follow' the Lamb everywhere he goes, and have not 'defiled themselves with women'.[194] If this passage be taken by itself, it seems evident that it refers to ascetics, who seem bound to Christ more closely than all others. But this interpretation can hardly be upheld. The enormous number itself of ascetics —at the end of the first century!—is hard to understand and should give us pause. And if we adduce the numerous related passages in which the seer appears to speak of sexual transgressions, it is clear that these texts must be taken figuratively.[195] The horrible excesses which they recount[196] cannot have occurred literally in the Christian communities and been openly tolerated. John speaks, rather, of temptations to idolatry and apostasy,[197] often described in the Old Testament as idolatry and wantonness, by which the people of God were untrue to the God of the Covenant. Certainly, the theme of a virginal, as opposed to a marriage, bond is new and, as such, significant, but it is still only an image.[198] With the demand for fidelity the seer reaches the theme

---

[193]M. Dibelius, *Jungfrauensohn und Krippenkind. Untersuchungen zur Geburtsgeschichte Jesu im Lukas-Evangelium* (1932) 27ff. (=*Botschaft und Geschichte* I, 1953, 1ff.). According to this, the emphasis on virginity is quite secondary and is of Hellenistic (Egyptian) origin.

[194]Apoc. 14.1-5.

[195]Apoc. 2.14, 20-23; 3.18; 17.2, 4; 18.3, 9; 19.2. This, admittedly, contradicts the traditional ascetic interpretation, in support of which W. Bousset, *Die Offenbarung Johannis* (1918) 381, comes down decisively. It is impossible to take it, with W. Hadorn, *Die Offenbarung des Johannes* (1928) 150, so that the παρθένοι are not ascetics, yet that the passage is an exhortation to sexual purity. Lohmeyer himself, *Die Offenbarung Johannis* (1953), who takes Apoc. 14.4f. to show the penetration of 'ascetical tendencies', feels the contradiction it involves with the undoubted figurative sense of the parallel passages; *cf.* in particular his correct interpretation of Nikolaitismus p. 29; also M. Goguel, *Rev. de l'hist. des rel.* 115 (1937) 7f. Perhaps R. H. Charles, *A critical and exegetical commentary on the Revelation of St. John* II (1920) 7-10, is right in seeing 14.4 as a later interpolation by someone of monastic and ascetic opinions.

[196]*Cf.* especially Apoc. 2.20ff.

[19] *Cf.* also the conclusion of 1 John 4.21.

[198]The change in sex is due to the fact that it is no longer the people as a whole that is personified, but the individual (male) confessor is envisaged.

which dominates the whole of the Apocalypse. There it is never a question of morality and 'ecclesial chastity'; the whole interest is focused on the great and decisive choice between confession and denial, martyrdom and apostasy, life and eternal death, the choice involved in the final struggles and persecutions. The 144,000 'undefiled'[199] followers of the Lamb are, therefore, the members of the perfected Church who have remained true. As such they were already depicted in an earlier chapter[200]—without any reference to a supposed sexual asceticism—and here the explanation is given of their number. Twelve thousand out of each 'tribe' receive the 'seal of the living God'.[201] It is 'the number of completeness in salvation-history —twelve—multiplied by the highest possible factor',[202] the entirety of the 'true Israel' in its perfected state. In any case, all the other Johannine writings are not in the least concerned with asceticism and related questions.[203] This is all the more remarkable in that the theology of the Gospel of St. John and of his epistles comes closer, in other respects, to gnostic thought than does any other part of the New Testament.

On the other hand, the pastoral epistles—under the name of Paul[204] —deliver an explicit and unreserved condemnation of the gnostic rejection of marriage, and, in so doing, complete the picture, already conveyed in the food question, of a very clear-cut attitude. The prohibition of marriage on the part of certain hypocritical, deluding spirits is a misleading doctrine brought in by devils;[205] but an orderly marriage blest with children is the sound order of life, willed by God,

---

[199]Apoc. 3.4; see Charles (n. 194 above) 1.72.

[200]Apoc. 7.4ff.

[201]In contrast with the sign of the beast. Apoc. 16.2; 19.20.

[202]J. Behm. *Die Offenbarung des Johannes* (1935) 45.

[203]Only once is the duty of beneficence mentioned (1 John 3.17); apart from this, the statement in the text applies also to the question of property. 'The very fact that words such as θησαυρός, θησαυρίζειν, πλούσιος, πλουτεῖν, πλουτίζειν, πλοῦτος, πένης, πτωχεία, πτωχεύειν, πτωχός (apart from John 12.5, 6; 13.29 [*cf*. n. 24 above]) occur not at all in John's Gospel and not even in his epistles, is significant': Rogge (n. 45 above) 9. For John's attitude to the State see my essay, 'Zum Verständnis von Johan. 19.11', *ThLZ* 73 (1948) 387–392.

[204]Clement of Alexandria, Strom. III, 53, cites Phil. 4.3 as evidence that Paul was equally anti-gnostic and anti-ascetic, and even himself a married man!

[205]1 Tim. 4.1-3.

in the Christian community.[206] The 'widows', who form a special class like a kind of community-sisterhood, certainly remain unmarried; but for this very reason young widows should not be admitted, but were better married.[207] Above all, a bishop and, indeed, everyone of the clergy should be married, 'the husband of one wife' and know how to rule his household.[208] The expression 'husband of one (only one) wife'[209] is somewhat surprising. Probably it is used only to bring out the necessity of a pure, monogamous morality, and, if so, is not so superfluous as some have thought.[210] The prohibition of a second marriage, in the sense of later canonical ordinances,[211] is not otherwise found in the pastoral epistles; the only time second marriages are mentioned they are, in fact, recommended.[212] Had the author wished to lay down something unfavourable, his mode of expression would be obscure, to say the least, and, in any case, would have toned down the otherwise clear import of his words. Nevertheless, the solution of this particular problem is of no great importance for us any more.

V

We have now come to an end of our survey of the early Christian literature. The question of asceticism has come up in many different connections, and has not received the same answer each time. To the question of property, of 'riches', the answer is quite imperative; here the problem at least admits of a radical solution. In the food question the rejection of the ascetical prohibition is enunciated in the clearest possible terms, as compared with the others, whereas the answer to the problem of marriage and celibacy allows every variety of

[206]1 Tim. 5.10, 14f.; Tit. 1.6; cf. 1 Tim. 2.15; Heb. 13.4.
[207]1 Tim. 5.10, 14. The mocking description of the consequences that would otherwise follow is not very ascetic in tone.
[208]1 Tim. 3.2, 12; Tit. 1.6.
[209]The corresponding requirement for widows also is stated in 1 Tim. 5.9.
[210]Cf. the highly judicious account of the issue by Dibelius, Die Pastoralbriefe (1953) 33. The most recent, thorough examination of the question by B. Kötting, Die Beurteilung der zweiten Ehe im heidnischen und christlichen Altertum, pronounces for a prohibition of second marriages.
[211]Cf. Herm. mand. IV, 4, 2; Athen. suppl. 33.
[212]1 Tim. 5.14.

decision. Throughout, it is a matter of genuine historical developments and opposing considerations. There is no one abstract principle that can settle it all; in fact, there is no unitary concept corresponding to what we mean nowadays by the word 'asceticism'.²¹³ Nonetheless, seen as a whole, the various factors are interconnected and have an inner essential unity. This is grounded in the original call made by Jesus, by which the claims of the 'world' and man's will and desire in all their forms are breached and put in their rightful place. No longer is their validity unquestioned, and so no longer can secular goods and values be upheld in the liberal sense simply for their own sake, still less made obligatory. Only 'one thing is necessary',²¹⁴ and this must be held to solely in all circumstances and whatever the cost.

Asceticism can also be looked upon as a means to achieve this. Nor does this apply only in cases where renunciation is enjoined from the beginning on account of the compulsion of circumstances and duties to be performed, and is, therefore, of moral obligation. Renunciation can be freely undertaken apart from any such external indications, since the temptations of this world might become, without such a decision, too great and perilous,²¹⁵ or because a definite inward call or gift points in this direction.²¹⁶ Yet in such cases 'freedom' still remains of decisive importance—not on the ground of personal preference, but on account of the gravity of the following of Christ and of the bond with him, which is something different from, indeed going beyond, the acceptance of any kind of ascetic way of life or of any law whatever prescribed by man. The New Testament, therefore, knows nothing of any self-imposed obligation under vow,²¹⁷ and, above all, rejects any 'gnostic' confusion of Christian obedience with ascetic renunciation of earthly possessions and resources, of whatever kind, on the ground of their supposed taintedness or impurity. Quite apart from the bond with Christ, this may be countered by the Old Testament

---

²¹³The nearest approach, perhaps, is the guarded ἀφειδία σώματος of Col. 2.23.
²¹⁴Luke 10.42. The variant ὀλίγων χρεία ἢ ἑνός seems intended to give the passage an 'ascetic' meaning, restricting the number of dishes.
²¹⁵Matt. 5.29f.; 18.8f. par. may also be taken in this sense.
²¹⁶Matt. 19.11; 1 Cor. 7.7.
²¹⁷Vows are first mentioned by Ignatius, Pol. 5.2; cf. n. 181 above. With the emergence of vows, which increasingly determined the later development of the problem of asceticism, their significance underwent a radical change.

doctrine of creation with its faith that receives gratefully all the gifts of natural life from the hands of God.

Yet it is clear that the New Testament can give no such answer to the question whether asceticism is right or wrong in itself; for it considers man and his life on earth, not in any timeless 'in and for himself', but solely as with and for Christ, in whom God's absolute will has become, for all time, a person and is here and now present to every man. This will and nothing else is the measure of faith, and this is the meaning of that 'following' which sacrifices and 'hates' all else. It is from this standpoint that certain definite 'ascetic' renunciations may become necessary again and again. Nonetheless, taken 'in and for themselves' they are meaningless, and when taken as significant and necessary as such can only be condemned and rejected. 'For there is nothing from without a man that can defile him';[218] and as there is nothing in the world 'unclean in itself',[219] so there is nothing holy or sanctifying for man outside perfect obedience in the following of the obedient and merciful Christ. Obedience and mercy are 'better than sacrifice'.[220]

[218]Mark 7.15.
[219]Rom. 14.14.
[220]I Kings 5.22; Hos. 6.6; Matt. 9.13; 12.7; Mark 12.32-34.

5

The Problem of Order
in Early Christianity and the
Ancient Church

I

THE CONCEPT OF order, *taxis*, is extremely rare in the initial period
of the Church. It occurs and is stressed on only one occasion in the
entire New Testament. That is when Paul tries to regulate the dis-
turbance in the assemblies of the Corinthian community, in which
ambitious ecstatics begin to give themselves airs, with their incomprehensible utterances. Paul attempts to ward off the dangers thus
threatening, proclaims basic principles and practical rules designed to
obviate confusion and the impulsiveness of the devout, and concludes,
by way of summary, with the following admonition: 'So, my brethren, earnestly desire to prophesy and do not forbid speaking in tongues;
but all things should be done decently and in order' (1 Cor. 14.39-40).
Thus a decorous, orderly mode of divine worship and of conduct
generally is presented as the obvious form in which the spiritual life
within a community should develop, always provided that liberty in
the stirring of their faith and action be not suppressed, the Spirit not
'quenched' (1 Thess. 5.19). These terse utterances of Paul should not
be taken to mean that he wished to convey to his spiritual sons some
surprising novelty; it was far more a matter of a 'recalling' to mind,
which would be immediately understood. In these words on the subject of order Paul is not referring to any central element of Christian
teaching, nor to the source from which the community derives the
power to frame its common action. This is evident from a few verses
previously, where he expressly inveighs against 'disorder' as something
far from consistent with the nature and will of God. 'God', he says,
'is not a God of confusion' (1 Cor. 14.33). But the positive, opposed
concept that he goes on to adduce is not the formal one of mere
'order', but goes much deeper: 'God is not the God of disorder, but of

peace'. Peace with God and the peace that comes from God—this is what designates the true essence and power of the new thing that determines from within the Church in the process of its building up and in the joint action of all its members; it is the power of love and the working of the Holy Spirit who is given by Christ and has taken possession of Christians in their wills and their being. This unique and determining element must be, above all, the main issue in the Church and in preaching to those outside. All the rest becomes manifest of itself, when viewed, and only when viewed, from this standpoint.

This indicates the point from which our problem must be viewed once and for all, from which alone it can be rightly grasped and discussed. The Church does not originate through order nor live by right order, but solely in the Spirit of Christ. If, however, it lives spiritually, then it is in order and attains to order, then, through the Spirit of peace, it also sets right order in its midst, without becoming a slave to this order. In the practical sphere we have here something very similar to the situation regarding faith and knowledge in faith as compared with reason, of which, likewise, not much is said in early Christianity. Faith, indeed, does not come out of reason, and the truth we apprehend in Christ far transcends reason. Yet we do not, on this account, assert the irrationality of our thinking, any more than the disorder of our joint activity; on the contrary, faith works objectively and, to that extent, rationally. God is, we might say by way of analogy, not the God of unreason, but of truth.

From this standpoint we can see that it is no accident that, not only in Paul, but, as we have said, in the whole of early Christianity, so little is said about order as such or even about order for its own sake—in fact, apart from a single letter of Clement of Rome, we may confidently assert that no mention is made of it at all. There were more important, more imperative subjects of preaching, and it was realized that the preaching of Christ was the actual determinant factor. Accordingly, questions of Church order only gradually, as the occasion demanded, and in a quite secondary manner, claimed any considerable attention.

This does not mean that the primitive Church had no desire for order or no order at all. The abhorrence felt by many of the older scholars at recognizing even from afar the presence of any kind of

'Church law' element in early Christianity has become to us today almost incomprehensible. Such elements occur, so to speak, all along the line. That the communities had to provide for the support of the missionaries, that marriages could not be dissolved, that a definite way had to be established to deal with complaints and grievances—all these, and much more besides, were matters of definite regulations, which had force and validity in the Church, ordinances to which, as such, juridical character cannot possibly be denied. Their meaning is, admittedly, a simple one and evident at first sight. They stood the test and so were held to firmly, without there being any need for a definite theory of Church law or any detailed 'theology of order'.

Owing to this and to the very varied circumstances of the primitive Church, these regulations differed considerably in the beginning in the several regions and missionary lands. There was, at first, no uniform constitution, no agreed canon, no one formula of confession. For a long time, variations in the form of worship and in the liturgy continued. But with the intercommunication due to the common struggle against persecutors and heretics, with the organized action of the great ecclesiastical provinces, and, above all, with the unifying effect of Conciliar and State legislation within the one State Church, the differences became fewer. In connection with this there arose the originators of an ecclesiastical jurisprudence, who aimed at promoting uniformity of practice by bringing together and harmonizing the older decisions. It would of course, be quite perverse to judge this very reasonable development a kind of decadence or a regrettable indication of a 'secularization', inevitable or not, of the Church. Indeed, it is of the essence of any order to experience changes and admit exceptions according to the variety of relationships and circumstances, but, on the whole, it strives for unity, which must naturally grow with the size and complexity of the Church and its relationships and can never simply disappear. A theological assessment is concerned not with the degree and extent of the order imposed (although, of course, excess or deficiency in legal organization is always possible, and generally both are even present at the same time), but with the fundamental significance and the place attributed to considerations of order in the Church as a whole and its spiritual life.

The main thing is that the Church lives by the word, the Spirit and the peace of God, and from thence—as Paul claims—it derives and determines its order. Further, either of itself or with the help also of conscious, calm and objective reflection, it continues in order or arrives at it. The constant danger of a Catholic, or near-Catholic, approach to the question of order is that of making this an absolute over against the spiritual source of life and even against the ordered life of the Church, of viewing 'right' order itself as an essential thing to hold on to, and of making it, independently, part of the teaching. This produces the opposed danger of a distorted Protestantism, which thinks to serve the Spirit by minimizing order, seeing it as a matter of indifference, or even destroying it. The consequence of such a negative approach is, ultimately, a like state of dependence on a human conception of order, to which far too much weight is attached, and which is fatal to the Church. There is only one power from which the Church draws its vitality, namely the preaching of the word and of the truth, which brings forth faith and, through faith, the will to right action; and this in turn comprises right order. Order, like good works, always comes in the second place, and can be rightly achieved only when what is first, the unique thing (and in this sense also isolated) is asserted and willed above all else. This is the fundamental principle of the Gospel, which must work itself out in life as well as in doctrine, and ensures that order is neither idolized nor rejected.

This principle of the Gospel was not known, as such, to the ancient Church, and even in the New Testament is hardly to be found in this form; it is, in fact, the fundamental principle of interpretation, which the Reformation first expressly applied to our problem. It is evident that the chief danger threatening the ancient Church is to be found in the lack of such a clear distinction, the 'catholic' danger of unconsciously setting salvation, faith, and justification on the same level as order, the danger of a self-sufficient ecclesiasticism. Order was no longer taken rigorously as a dependent function of faith, but apprehended jointly with it, and seen, more or less, as one with it, the result being that the crucial and paramount significance of the act of Christ and the reality of grace-given salvation became for Christians obscured and diminished. Yet this confused state and its accompanying danger did not yet mean a decline from the Gospel principle, still less its express denial, such as, after its formulation by the Reformation, undoubtedly infiltrated widely into later Catholicism. The ancient Church was, not only in its doctrine, but also in its understanding of order in practice, much more strongly evangelical than people are often ready to admit. I want to emphasize this expressly against a certain unhistorical, highly suspicious, ultra-Protestant criticism, which, wherever it fails to find its reformation formulas, and wherever it meets with a naïve, uncritical commendation of order, readily sees there a betrayal of Christ and his Gospel. It includes in its resultant concept of 'early Catholicism', and brands them accordingly, not only all the Fathers including Augustine, but considerable sections of the New Testament, especially the writings of Luke; nor does it always stop at Paul. Perhaps the most pernicious effect of this pseudo-Protestant contentiousness is the disgust and antipathy due to the immoderation of the alleged Reformation criticism. This, in turn, leads to a distrust and an uncritical rejection of the whole Reformation position on account of its supposed one-sidedness and hostility to order, so that one takes up again, without any serious reservation, the idea of a *consensus quinquesaecularis* and a sacred 'credo ecclesiam'. And so all that the Reformation has taught us definitively about the relative character of order and externals in the Church is only too likely to be jettisoned or, at least, not seriously defended.

I propose now, with the necessary simplification, to present the complex situation in the ancient Church so as to bring out, first, certain positive prescriptions relating to order already effective in early Christianity and observed, in essence, in the ancient Church. Then, in a further section, I shall show how trust in the sanctity of ecclesiastical order threatened to endanger the preaching and appropriation of salvation in the evangelical sense, and, in fact, undermined it. Let us then, first, inquire into the positive characteristics of the aims of the early Church in regard to order, without forgetting that the whole question, as we have said, was at first only peripheral, only emerged as occasion required, and was decided in each individual case that arose. It must also be realized that the general concept of 'order', though always related to the whole and special life of the Church, had a very varied import, and comprised a number of different tendencies and shades of meaning, whether we are dealing with the order of worship and of charitable works, the order of the constitution and of offices, the order of morals and discipline, or, finally, the order of doctrine and belief. We shall not, however, speak of all this *in extenso*.

II

Our discussion of the fundamentals of the question started out from a passage of St. Paul, the *locus classicus*, as it were, of the right relationship between order in the Church and its real, spiritual life. One cannot ignore the fact that this life is something laid down beforehand. The Church is by no means a group that arises out of its members' adoption of a particular way of life and constitution. It is an historical entity, which has received, from the outset, a definite spirit and a definite interior order of love, and already lives wholly by it. It can only, therefore, give itself certain ordinances and institutions—because, fundamentally, it is already ordered and constituted—through the Holy Spirit, who is poured forth in preaching, in the original witness to Christ, and on whose reception in faith and through baptism the reality of the Church rests. In this respect, we can find in the word of God the 'basic order', so to speak, of the Church, and this as such admits of no discussion. All proclamations and admonitions, as well as all concrete order, of the Church always stand in relation to this primordial reality and its explicit acceptance. There is no exception at all to this rule. So it is that Paul always refers his particular instructions and decisions to what he preached in the beginning, and to the marvellous new life of the Christian community. And not only Paul; we can see the same thing in Matthew, when he subsumes the rules to be followed with an erring brother under the words which treat of the shepherd seeking the lost sheep and of the divine forgiveness obliging us to act likewise. In the same way, the pastoral epistles link their rules for domestic life and for the service of the Church with the recollection of the original apostolic preaching, of which no adulteration can be tolerated; and the Didache, our earliest 'Church orders', begins with a description of the way of life as contrasted with that of death. In this it is followed, in part, by later Church orders, or else they precede their statements of the law with a confession of faith. The so-called canons of the apostles conclude with a list of the books of scripture. 'Above all else', begin the *Canones Hippolyti*, 'we must be of the holy salutary faith which relates to our Lord Jesus Christ, the Son of the living God ... By the power of God we are

enwrapped by a firm bond of unity, and separated from those who
... do not stand with us, who are disciples of scripture.'

The individual ordinances and regulations on, for example, the mode
of election, festivals, or the distribution of alms, are not, of course, held
to be derived directly from scripture or the Christian faith—not even
when described, in a broad sense, as 'apostolic'. Yet they must be in
accordance with the original teaching and not opposed to it in any
respect, in that they build up and protect the body of the Church, as
the apostles had earlier prescribed. In every case, it is the ecclesiastical,
apostolic, conciliar, or episcopal authority which lays down the
ordinances, and, guided by the Holy Spirit, makes the decisions as
need arises. There is no such thing as a law standing by itself, outside
the Christian context, which is taken over as such and merely applied
to the Church. I want to emphasize this clearly, precisely because, in
the nature of things, it is often a question, materially, of influences
and borrowings from the world outside. The first 'presbyteries' in
the Church have an undoubted connection with the corresponding
bodies in Judaism, as also the provision made for the poor and the
administration of cemeteries; while the treatment of women, certain
elements in the Christian calendar, fasting observances, and the like
are equally referable to the pagan hellenistic environment. On all
these questions a great deal of material, constantly increasing, is to be
found in the *Realwörterbuch für Antike und Christentum*, and much work
still remains for the researcher into the later history of Church law.
Yet we never come across the modern idea of a law valid *ab initio,* a
natural order which could be introduced as it is into the Church and
have force there. That would be contrary to the very nature of the
ecclesiastical order, which always originates and develops solely in
relation to the concrete facts of the Church's own spiritual life. This
position we find already adopted by Paul. On the one hand, he regards it as self-evident that the Church, in its moral and juridical
sentiments, cannot fall short of what illuminates 'even the heathens';
and, on the other hand, the Church is not to litigate in pagan courts—
it is capable itself of upholding order within its ranks, and, as the occasion requires, it finds the way of justice and right according to its own
premises.

The phrase 'as the occasion requires', brings me to a further characteristic of the quest for order in the ancient Church, one which, hardly

ever expressly formulated, is at once essential to the fundamental Christian attitude and indicative of it. It is the small number of express rules and prescriptions, and this corresponds to the little attention paid to the kind of questions about order on which we have embarked. The Church order was not always being added to and built up, but rather left, in a formal sense, unfinished. In this the ancient Church shows a marked difference from contemporary Judaism which, under the growing rabbinism, was never tired of propounding new questions of law, issuing firm decisions and answers, and so encompassing the freedom of life on all sides with a juridical structure. For in Judaism it was a question of fulfilling the law as such; this was what brought or ensured the promised salvation, which, in the Church, had long since, and without law, become a living reality. The Church, for this reason, kept largely to free exhortation and to the recalling of what had been done. How sparing, in the pastoral epistles or the Didache, for example, are the definite, concrete prescriptions on, say, the maintenance of the clergy or the admission of women to the service of the community. And even in the third and fourth centuries, the ecclesiastical legislation is surprisingly slight and therefore elastic, when we consider the rapid extension and development of the Church and, with it, of the ecclesiastical organization. The laws in question were, in fact, the outcome of the Church's life itself, rather than of the passion for theory of the canonist; and, precisely for this reason, they are a direct witness to the divine leading and guidance. The most famous example of a conscious restraint in the way of ordinances and enactments is the refusal to impose celibacy by law, as the Marcionites, for example, had done earlier, and as the anti-Marcionite Church must have been inclined to do as regards clerics, at least. We have seen how Paul himself had struggled with this question and only reluctantly allowed marriage. By the higher clergy at least celibacy was generally observed already in the third century, and had almost become the rule. Yet, even at the Nicene Council, Bishop Paphnutius, himself unmarried, protested successfully against the threat to prohibit the marriage of priests. Priests should not have any new, unbearable yoke laid upon them, and one should abide by ancient custom. The Church should not make enactments arbitrarily and as it pleases, but hold to what was given, to what is necessary and, in this sense, commanded.

This brings us to a final, highly significant element, closely related to the former: the basic conservatism of all the prescriptions of the ancient Church, and not only of the ancient. It is not absolute; we are always coming across change and reform, but they always remain within the tradition, that is, in the continuity of what was authentically established. The idea of solidarity works in conjunction with that of continuity. There is no separatist intention behind the new ordinances; the aim is always to hold fast to what was given originally and was common from the beginning. It is important to see how these ideas also, which even today play a significant role in the eastern Orthodox Church, originate, in fact, in the New Testament.

Paul himself puts forth explicitly the claim of ecumenical considerations in the sense of respect for general usage. Not only does he repeatedly emphasize—as in his judgement on slavery—that he gives the same directives to all the communities, but he adverts expressly to generally prevailing practice in the Church, for example, in the matter of women veiling their heads. To this practice one ought to hold and not lightly discard it without necessity. 'Did the word of God originate with you, or are you the only ones it has reached?' (1 Cor. 14.36). The idea of continuity with origins occurs in the New Testament not only in the pastoral epistles but also, where it is given special emphasis by Luke, in the Acts of the Apostles, which, while principally concerned with the doctrine of the apostles, also, and in connection with it, has the purpose of presenting their ethical pattern and preserving the wholesome ordinances they laid down. This by no means rules out changes consonant with the times, for example in missionary methods. A typical example of how the Church may be guided by the Holy Spirit in the formation of new institutions is provided in the account of the seven deacons. The first leaders of the Church, the twelve Apostles, in the changing conditions of a growing community, were no longer capable of satisfying all its demands. This led to a crisis and even to discord, till they themselves urged the creation of a new office with appropriate functions. The community then elected suitable persons, whom the Apostles accepted and blessed, and so peace and order were restored in the Church.

The primitive Church started, as we have seen, with, in almost every sphere of life, a multiplicity of forms and arrangements, to an extent embarrassing to Catholics and, indeed, astonishing even to us. Subsequently, it strove for unity with increasing insistence, and in a manner which makes it impossible to see this as no more than an imitation of the political unification of the Empire. Always, however, it permitted differences (as in the various forms of monasticism), and in the liturgical sphere there still existed, as we have seen, at the close of the first period, great differences between the larger interconnected Church groups. This was the time when considerable endeavours were initiated towards an adjustment, efforts of the kind that had been earlier prohibited. For the action of Victor, Bishop of Rome, in trying to compel, by breaking off communion, a uniform observance of Easter, met, at the close of the second century, with severe criticism and no success. It was only very much later, in the controversies between East and West, that such differences, and others far less important, sharpened as they were then by ecclesiastico-political rivalry, played a part both disgraceful in itself and fatal to the Church's unity.

No separation of law from faith, the safeguarding of the Church's independence in her decisions, the restraint of zeal for organization and rules, ecumenical cohesion and firm adherence to what was ancient and received—among all these characteristics of the development of order in the primitive Church none stands out more, and seems to us today more problematical, than the last, the constant insistence on what was from the beginning and on tradition. To us at least it becomes suspect when it oversteps the bounds of biblical teaching and tries to take in the whole field of ecclesiastical order, structure and morals. The tragedy of our Church is due entirely to the experience of the Reformation, which, in fact, not content with reforming the faith, went on largely to reject out of hand the received juridical order and morality of the Roman Church. We know that spiritual unity does not require uniformity in Church order and customs, and we like to insist that the Church must be flexible, not only in its preaching, but also in its juridical forms and the ordering of its life, if it is to fulfil its task in the present. The correctness of this is beyond dispute; it is a strong counterbalance to an over-rigid faith in the sanctity and sanity of order and tradition. But it may well be asked if this kind of corrective of the traditionalism of the old Church does really meet and rightly reject what the early centuries and what even, in part, early Christianity actually said and meant by its upholding of order, and therefore also of the old ordinances. Certainly, no Church lives by the continuity and ecumenical solidarity of its order, but neither, indeed, does it live by discontinuity and the capriciousness of perpetual change. It is of the essence of order—if desired at all—that it should be, as far as possible, uniform, coherent, and intended to last, that, though its form may change, it must be constantly borne with, upheld and preserved, provided that—and this is crucial—order does not become of greater moment than the spirit, that it can serve the uninhibited preaching of Christ and the bringing of his forgiveness, without impeding it in any way whatever. The question is: was the ancient Church already guilty of failure in this regard? or, more precisely, where, and to what extent, was this failure present in the ancient Church in defending its 'apostolic' order? When began the false apotheosis of order which raised it from an external means and instrument to an absolute value, and so to something contradicting or minimizing the 'one thing' that men should really be concerned with? This brings us to the final stage of these reflections.

III

The Reformation breached the established Catholic order of the Middle Ages mainly in two places. In the name of the Gospel it rejected the absolute authority of the Pope, who had elevated himself therewith, in the manner of 'antichrist', above the authority of scripture; it rejected the Catholic order of penance, which, in assigning a determinate value to man's deeds of expiation, rendered Christ's redemption meaningless. Without going into these two concrete points, it is, in my opinion, impossible to speak and judge of the meaning and nature of what happened at the Reformation, so certain is it that this and much else is conditioned and determined by a new understanding of the original Christian teaching. In the present connection, I must abstain from doctrinal questions, taking account now of only two points as regards the ancient Church. First, where did the acceptance of the ordained office limit the freedom of scripture, and second, to what extent did the order of penance impair the evangelical character of forgiveness? We have become today—in increasing reaction from the Middle Ages—far more suspicious in these matters than ever the Reformation epoch was against the ancient Church. How far, it may be asked, are we right? One thing, at all events, is certain, and, in a just, historical examination should never be ignored: it is not the same thing, whether errors, obscurities and malpractices are maintained and defended in the face of evangelical criticism, or whether they have crept in unobserved without being desired as such. The latter, indeed, is always the case, to some degree. As long, however, as error is not persisted in when confronted with truth, and the latter, once made clear, not condemned and rejected, one should beware of hastily judging past generations of Christianity.

On the first point—authority of Pope and of Scripture—I can be brief as regards the main issue, although in matters of detail much might be said and many questions asked. That holy scripture is the source and rule of the Church's profession of faith, that the original truth taught in the Church must agree with it and be, in content, identical with it, is, indeed, a fundamental principle of the ancient Church, acquired and confirmed in the hard struggle against gnosticism, and never revoked or forgotten. Certainly, we do not find in this principle—naturally enough—the polemical note of the reformers directed against false doctrines and misconceptions within the Church; but this does not alter the fact that there is nothing in the whole of antiquity that puts scripture in a subordinate place, nothing that restricts its importance in the Church. No doubt, if we put the question to any candidate at the present day, he will answer readily, following Harnack, that the ancient Catholic, anti-gnostic Church established three norms side by side and that they thereby became 'catholic' in the worst sense. These were the authority of the Canon, of the Confession of faith, and of the episcopal office in charge of tradition; and, as a result, the freedom of the original word was, from the outset, restricted and its meaning perverted in the interests of ecclesiastical order. This view, however, is false, or, at any rate, does not correspond at all points with the view of the ancient Church itself. It is based on the initial assumption of modern Protestantism that any definite assertion of Church order that is put forward without express reservations must be the work of the devil, and so directed against the freedom of God and of his sovereign word. (In reality, the sentence should, at most, be reversed, so as to mean that any order that is not expressly put before the truth of Christ and, in this sense, set up against it must be held theologically possible and permissible till the contrary be proved—otherwise, not even the New Testament and the Apostle

Paul himself would remain unaffected by the demands of our extreme Protestants.)

Let us, however, stick to the question. The sole, unrestricted and all-embracing authority that the ancient Church recognized *in concreto* was, as we have said, holy scripture. Admittedly, it agreed with the tradition that should be taught in the Church (and what evangelical Church would not assert the same for itself?); but the fatal attempt to derive this tradition from the Fathers, and then to set aside scripture as a true, formally binding canon, was not yet made. It was only in the controversies of the fifth century that something of the kind emerged to play its part. Till then there was certainly no talk about the infallibility of those who bore office. They, indeed, by their office were called and empowered to interpret scripture, and represented, in virtue of their commission, the original apostolic truth, as contained also in scripture, against all 'innovations' of heretics; but the bishops were not, on that account, made lords of scripture, and had no exclusive privilege of knowing and deciding what it really meant. Not only was the 'private use of scripture' taken for granted all through ecclesiastical antiquity; even the leading theologians were not always bishops, but laymen, and—notwithstanding the 'case of Origen'—this did not impair their reputation. One has only to think of Justin and Clement of Alexandria in the second century, Tertullian and Methodius in the third, Lactantius and Didymus in the fourth, and Maximus the Confessor in the seventh. Even in the ninth century, Scotus Eriugena was not, apparently, a cleric, nor even a monk, but a layman and a teacher of theology.

Throughout the early period of the Church there was only one authority which—beginning in the third century—raised the unheard-of claim, on the basis of a supposed scriptural and irrefragable right, to be able to ascertain the truth with certainty, to expound and establish it, over and above anyone else. This was the Roman Pontiff, in his papal authority as asserted and formulated by, for example, Leo the Great, about the middle of the fifth century. Then there was developed, in opposition to this, a correspondingly absolute and exclusive conciliar theory, which, owing to political complications, could not be made to prevail. The nature of these endeavours reveals their fatal intention of making the Church secure through a definite order of domination, though this became evident only in the High and Later

Middle Ages, when the authority of the Pope turned and established itself against the 'unauthorized' appeal to holy scripture. Thus the idea of a supposed God-given sacred order of the Church became, in fact, the mortal enemy of its true life, whose source was the word. It was only the Reformation that, 'by placing the Bible in the hands of every lay Christian, restored the confidence and simplicity of the ancient Church' (Harnack).

In addition, the Reformation won back spiritual freedom from the consecrated order of the sacerdotal office, by reverting to the conception of the *ministerium*, as viewed solely in relation to its evangelical task and to the order this entails. In this also it hardly differs from the ancient Church. The idea of a qualitative, sacramental distinction of the subject of the special priesthood, and so the doctrine of the sacerdotal character, gradually developed only from the end of the fourth century. It was prompted in the west and east respectively by very different motives; in the east, by concern for the purity of the cult, and in the west, by concern for the efficaciousness of the ecclesiastical means of grace, and its independence—against the Donatists—of the sanctity of the person administering; therefore, the 'efficacy' of the sacraments depends exclusively on the fact of ordination. This solution of the problem is certainly unscriptural and unacceptable; but neither in east nor west was it directly associated with any subjection of the laity or clerical desire to dominate.

We meet with much more difficulty in dealing with the second question; the menace to the duty and power of freely forgiving, and therefore to the true Christian approach in the administration of the office of the keys, owing to the emphasis placed on order as a mistaken conception of ecclesiastical discipline. The essence both of divine and human forgiveness, as taught in the Gospel, lies in its being unconditional and inexhaustible. The duty of indefinite forgiveness—'seventy times seven'—is, admittedly, not to be confused with overlooking or tolerating sin; indeed, it comprises a continuous struggle against it, the avowal, confession, and overcoming of sin. Nonetheless, there is absolutely no question, in this context, of any subsequent compensatory punishment or expiation, as can be seen from the Gospel of St. Matthew, chapter 18, and the whole teaching of the New Testament. Accordingly, the Church knew no such thing till well after the middle of the second century, though, admittedly, we find, in this early period hardly any trace of an evangelical exercise of the office of the keys. Then, however, in the second half of the century there arose the institution of penance with a pronounced and regularly administered Church discipline; that is to say, the principle was generally established—in spite of a large measure of freedom in detail—that a Christian who had lapsed from the faith or whose way of life was a violation of the basic Christian commandments, should not be received back then and there, but must first show in real earnest his sorrow and conversion, and prove them in act. Some time must elapse before he was admitted to the sacrament, to the exercise of his rights in the Church, and to complete 'peace' with God.

How should this procedure be judged in the light of the Gospel? The introduction of ecclesiastical discipline as such can hardly be held mistaken. It was not held so by the reformation Churches; in fact, they thought public discipline absolutely necessary, and, in spite of all the difficulties they encountered in its execution, they have never abandoned the claim to enforce it. No Church that takes God's commandments seriously can tolerate their being openly flouted by its members without doing anything about it; and, in the same way, no Church that has experienced persecution, apostasy, and betrayal can forego a certain testing and probation of those who return to her. It is somewhat incongruous if a sinner presumes on being received back as a matter of course and being fully reinstated unconditionally. One who is really penitent desires, rather, to evince his repentance in action, to do something and take on some burden, which, admittedly, should not be looked on as a punishment nor even as a condition of forgiveness. Accordingly, penitential practices were initially quite voluntary, and not in the nature of unpleasant impositions enjoined by the Church, as in the Middle Ages with their fixed tariffs. But public sins necessitated a public certification of repentance. Thus Ambrose, in dealing with no less a person than the emperor Theodosius the Great and the barbarous massacre enjoined by him in anger and revoked too late, refused to admit him to the sacrament till he had presented himself before the assembled community as a penitent and devoid of imperial pomp. There are other analogous examples which were not so spectacular.

Nevertheless, the ancient Church discipline of penance had begun to deteriorate on an essential point, and the longer it continued the more its true sense was imperilled. The fault lay not in the serious intention of the Church in the matter of public penance, though on this point also abuses crept in with time, nor in her judgement in insisting on the sinner giving real signs and proof of repentance. What the evangelical Christian really finds intolerable is that the Church, with her procedure of restoring to full ecclesiastical status, in principle supplanted divine forgiveness and the longed-for peace with God. The ancient Church —as opposed to primitive Christianity—recognized no absolution and, indeed, no pastoral exercise of the power of the keys that could, in principle, function apart from public discipline and penance. Consequently, it was inevitable that the sinner's prescribed penance and period of probation should come to be seen as the procedure which should make him, gradually, with the passage of time, worthy of divine grace, and that the bishop, as the authorized administrator of church discipline, should seem the lord of life and death, able to impart or withhold the forgiveness of God as he saw fit. It is true that these consequences were not at once drawn by the ancient Church. It had first to devote its whole energy to ensure the possibility of apostates and those fallen into grievous sin in the Church obtaining God's forgiveness; for the rigorist movements of the second, third, and fourth centuries all held the view, more or less, that this was quite out of the question, and so the protagonists of the penitential system rightly felt themselves to be performing an evangelical work.

But the exclusive attention paid to the struggle against gross sins by means of public ecclesiastical discipline involved a further danger. Hypocrisy and pharisaism, of a more or less blatant kind, could be avoided only if, at the same time, the struggle against the less obvious, but not less evil, private, daily sins of the apparently exemplary Christian were unremittingly pursued. Only thus could the awareness persist that all Christians are alike before God in that they live by forgiveness, and by that forgiveness alone which leads to full and generous forgiveness of one another. Here there was an obvious gap, not so much in the preaching, as in the pastoral practice of the ancient Church. For—apart from a few, barely established exceptions—it knew no private confession, no private acknowledgement of sins, and, in spite of the threefold imparting of authority in the Gospel, no personal pastoral functioning of the power of the keys. When something of the sort was introduced into monasticism in the fourth century, it was already too late for a thorough reform of the penitential process. In the Middle Ages progress was made in many ways, but, with the increasing dominance of ideas of good works and merit, there came about a fearful degeneration in the matter of penance, most obvious to us in the doctrine of indulgences. Only the Reformation changed the whole view of the matter. Taking its stand on the Gospel, it extricated and restored what had become confused and entangled in the Catholic practice of penance: the necessity, on the one hand, of an ecclesiastical order and discipline as regards obdurate and flagrant sinners, and the offer, on the other hand, to everyone of a free and unrestricted pardon, which, pronounced by the minister, brings to light the inmost sins of the heart and remits them.

I propose to stop here, as we have now come back to the starting-point of this essay. It now remains to indicate how the Reformation can be seen as a return to the beginning, not only in its teaching, but also in its new Church order. Whatever line of approach we care to choose— that of pastoral practice and Church discipline, the conception of authority or even the questions of public worship, administration of the sacraments, and the relationship to the State—the real 'renewal' of early Christianity does not consist in having restored to dignity and importance any of the ancient ways of ordering the matter. It is often questionable whether, when the reformers themselves thought they had done so, this was in reality the case. The crucial element in the Reformation, in fact, consists solely in that Christian teaching, our salvation, our justification, and our life were once more apprehended in the light of the Gospel and in their original sense, and that the Church, spiritually renewed in its faith, sought, in the light of this, to order afresh its functions and form. The Reformation revalidated the original relations of spirit and order, faith and works, doctrine and life, and, in asserting the fundamental character of the 'one thing', the first, regained for the second, third and fourth, freedom and the true orientation. This is what the Reformation meant.

In addition, Church history itself pre-eminently shows, with the utmost clarity, that the Church at all times can draw its life from one thing only, the original teaching of Christ, and faith in this word is and always remains its sole real function. Furthermore, the Church is truly alive, worthy of credence, and in order only when this teaching is something living and effectual. Yet this freedom in regard to any kind of superstition about order should make the Church freely disposed and inclined to order, an attitude which, taken for granted in the ancient Church, is not always favoured among us today. It may perhaps appear that I have judged rather too leniently the ancient Church's enthusiasm for order, and not brought out sharply enough the ever-present menace of perversion into the human, legalistic, and, as we like to say, 'catholic' spheres. But any order, taken by itself, is always open to objection, and at the very least, is conditioned by the period, is provisional, and is liable to abuse. In reality, therefore—as I have already said—the question of sin arises only when order comes to be an obstacle to the original truth and refuses to give it free course. The ancient Church did not prohibit any witness of the truth; it set up no absolute law contrary to what was originally given, and, even in its ordinances, aimed at protecting nothing other than the original life of the Church, its main responsibility. Today we see, indeed, how it went astray, and we refuse to forego the right to criticize freely. But we have, in my view, no right and, indeed, little cause, to adopt a lofty censorious attitude to the Church's desire for order and peace. The ancient Church, with its assertion of spiritual unity and spiritual governance, its maintenance of contact with and fidelity to the spirit, in its ordinances and life, always remained close to the New Testament. Even the order in the Church, the will to further 'whatsoever things are true, whatsoever modest, whatsoever just, whatsoever lovely, whatsoever of good fame' must be held a fruit of the Holy Spirit, and therefore, as says the Apostle Paul, the God of peace will also be with us (Phil. 4.8f.).

6

The Christian and Social Life
according to the New Testament

THE MODERN READER finds it strange that the New Testament in general has so little to say on all that has to do with public, political and social life. If we think exclusively of the State and political obligations in the strict sense, this may seem understandable. The state of affairs in Palestine and the situation of the early Christian communities in the Roman Empire were not such as to arouse and promote an active civic sense. This might incline us to explain the whole thing in a purely historical and sociological sense—the political problems, then, claimed such slight attention only because, in the existing environment and the situation of early Christianity, they could hardly play any part. But this explanation is inadequate. This becomes clear if, along with the political problems, we take into consideration those, in all their variety, of social life. These also were practically ignored; at most, they are discussed only when they arise within the Church and directly affect Christians. This can hardly be accidental. The crucial interests in the life of early Christianity were plainly of a fundamentally different kind, and not such as to further any participation in civil and political life.

This has often been remarked and stated, and cannot be disputed; but we cannot rest content with such a negative finding. Otherwise, Christianity might be taken to be a movement of flight from the world, 'gnostic' as it were, and, from the social standpoint, nihilistic, which, obviously, it is not. How, then, in fact, did early Christianity envisage the problems of civic life in the 'world'; and what role did they play, if, as such, they were neither emphasized nor ignored? The following historical survey is an attempt to answer this. It will deliberately eschew a detailed discussion of the evidence on the point, but use it solely to indicate the general tenor, the line followed by social and political developments, and, in the light of these, attempt to grasp the motives and basic approach of the early Christians, as expressed in the various texts and in such different ways. This is the approach of the historian rather than the philologist, however much he be, at every step, involved with and indebted to the latter's work. This is one way of getting to grips with the matter in hand; in fact, in picking out what is essential, one may be preserved from occasional misinterpretations and wrongly-placed emphases better than in an exegesis that keeps close to the individual texts.[1]

Primitive Christianity was pure religion, that is it directed man's gaze, in the first place, alone and exclusively to God. On God's action depended its whole destiny, its future and its salvation. But God is a reality and wills a reality, the bond with him is seen to have a determining influence on life, to be relevant to actual life, and to be, even in the social context, active and fraught with consequences. But the activity prompted by a faith is not the same as the faith itself, and where we are speaking of the thing, its effects can, for the moment, be ignored.

'Repent, for the kingdom of heaven is at hand' (Matt. 4.17 par.)— in these or similar words the first three evangelists comprise the whole teaching of Jesus. God's kingdom is at the door, God himself stands before each individual and, at this very moment, announces himself in Jesus as Word. Jesus addresses himself to each man be he even the most depraved of creatures, and encounters him directly, since he calls him, as a person, to penance, just as he does the most devout and exemplary. From this springs the decisive opposition in which Jesus became involved with the Pharisees. They did not inquire simply and directly after God, but, in the first place, after the right divine order, which thus interposed itself as a self-contained entity between God and man. Measured by its standard, men are of various kinds, and so can be divided into the just and the unjust. This indirect relation with God and this distinction between men is precisely what even the ordinary devout person seeks in every age. The

[1]To obtain an understanding of the whole question in the light of its history, one would, of course, not confine oneself to the canonical writings of the New Testament, but include the 'apocryphal' material, especially the so-called Apostolic Fathers. Here, however, we keep to these selected writings, since they alone were normative for the subsequent period, and, in fact, even from the historical standpoint, they are, to a great extent, representative.

struggle for the ideal, divinely appointed ends of order and sanctification in the world is what he can lose himself in as a person, and yet, in which, at the same time, gain an apparently heightened value. Jesus, however, did not allow the misconception of himself as a reformer or advocate of a programme, either in the ecclesiastical or political sphere. And since he was nothing of the sort, he did not by any means attack the Old Law as such, the Law guarded by the Pharisees, nor did he advocate any change in the political situation, as, for example, did the Zealots in his day. He confined himself to reminding men of the day when the world would be changed by God, before whom man would then have to answer for his whole life. Jesus kept man as a person, with his own will or 'heart', firmly in the presence of God. He called man to God, and wished to be understood as doing this; but in current affairs and ephemeral questions he declined to become involved.

'Man, who made me a judge or divider over you?'—with these words (Luke 12.14) Jesus dismissed someone who had come to him with the petition, not ill-intentioned, that he divide the inheritance between him and his brother. Still more significant is another incident, also reported by St. Luke. Pilate, who had no love for the Jews, and, in addition, lived in constant fear of an uprising, had, on a certain occasion when pilgrims from Galilee had gathered quite peacefully for a sacrifice, fearing a tumult, hurriedly given his soldiers the cruel order to hew them down, so that their blood was 'mingled with their sacrifice,' (Luke 13.1ff.). Jesus was 'told' of this, and his informants naturally expected an expression of indignation and a condemnation of the military power. Jesus, however, made no mention of the Romans. He addressed those standing by, devout persons, innocent and indignant, and answered quite a different question, one they had never asked: 'Do you think that these Galileans were worse sinners than all the other Galileans, because they suffered thus? I tell you, No; but unless you repent you will all likewise perish'.

There is, also, the well-known statement on the subject of the tribute-money, which is relevant in this connection. The way it is introduced brings out clearly that the intention of the questioners was to entrap Jesus (Mark 12.13 par.). Whatever answer he might give on this issue of politics, he would compromise himself: in the eyes of the Roman authorities, should he refuse the tax, or in the eyes of the disaffected people, should he approve it. Accordingly, the first point of the story, the most striking one, is how Jesus succeeded so adroitly in eluding the dilemma between loyalty and popularity, making his opponents themselves give, as it were, the answer on the basis of the image on the coin. Only then comes the real and essential answer, in the second part of his riposte: as the Imperial coin bears the image of the Emperor, so is man himself made according to the image of God and bears his stamp. You ask about the Emperor—as if God would keep back his property! 'Render unto Caesar the things that are Caesar's'—but, above all, give back now also to God what belongs to him, and what you have alienated from him, yourselves. Any further questions about the people of God, or the Imperial rights, or the extent to which honour may be given to the Emperor it is not necessary, in my judgement, to read into the episode.

This is the last of the passages in which Jesus takes up a position in regard to public or 'social' questions.[2] The images and comparisons occurring in his discourses and narratives are not significant for his attitude, and questions relating to marriage are hardly relevant here. His utterances on the point are all designed to ward off the subject, and so are wholly negative—this cannot be ignored. At the same time, it is equally clear that, however much Jesus—in contrast to John the Baptist—keeps away from all public questions, we never find a single word of his of express condemnation, no ascetic prohibition to take part in them, no general demand to withdraw from the world and secular affairs. The question with which we are concerned is left completely open.

A further stage of development is reflected in the epistles of St. Paul. He is not alone in presenting it, but here we may take him as representative. The Christian mission had cut loose from the familiar ground of Judaism and the accustomed relationships of his native land, and had pushed out into a new social world as alien, at least in part, to the Christians as they themselves seemed an alien body in its midst. The chasm was never bridged. Certainly, Christian preaching was directed, consciously and expressly, to 'all peoples' and to every man; but its whole endeavour was applied solely to win over to the

[2]The significance of what Christ said about care of the poor on the occasion of his anointing I will treat of in connection with St. John's Gospel, where it is more emphasized and not so isolated: see below p. 150.

Christian faith those whose eyes were opened, to incorporate them into the community as the mystical body of Christ, to save them from eternal perdition, and to bring them to blessedness. Apart from these concepts, it displayed no positive interest at all in the unconverted world, which drove forward—and how rightly so—to its inevitable catastrophe and the imminent judgement.

Yet, while attention was directed solely to the progress of the Gospel, inevitably the first relationships with the world claimed notice. For the mission to be able to go forward unhindered it was necessary that the young communities, in their manner of life, should put no difficulties in the way. In other words, they should not, as a new social structure within the existing society, make an unfavourable impression, particularly they should not act so as to disturb and unsettle it, or make themselves disliked in any way. Christians should, therefore, conduct themselves always with dignity and propriety, not over-reach anyone in business, and, as far as possible, preserve tranquillity and peace. Paul, of course, in urging all this, had not solely in view the effects on the environment; these demands were far from exhausting the obligations and potentialities of fraternal love within the community. Yet, as the first epistle to the Thessalonians shows in particular, they had to be made known and insisted upon to the new Christians. At least once these warnings were given explicitly as to be observed in view of 'those without'. Christians must not fall into evil repute, nor be idle, noisy enthusiasts, but 'use your endeavour to be quiet', to look after their own concerns, and work with their own hands, so that they may be judged an orderly people and 'want nothing of any man's' (1 Thess. 4.11). 'If any one will not work, let him not eat' (2 Thess. 3.10). Here we have, for the first time, the formulation of a universal principle of social ethics, valid not only for Christians but for all. Thus it was verbally adopted in the Soviet Constitution of 1936, as in the earlier one of 1918.

We see a similar approach to one of the basic institutions of the public life of the time, namely slavery, to which Paul has occasion to refer from time to time. Not Paul alone, but all in the ancient Church who speak of it, decline to support any aspirations of the slaves to liberty, whether by purchase or by any other means. 'In whatever state each was called, there let him remain with God' (1 Cor. 7.24). The order of slavery may be hard, but is not to be felt as unjust or criminal. It is enough for a Christian to be called henceforth a 'freed-man of the Lord', as, indeed, the free man is held a 'slave of Christ' (1 Cor. 7.22). 'You were bought with a price; do not become slaves of men' (1 Cor. 7.23; cf. Philem. 16). Paul would hold it derogatory to the divine redemption for anyone to try to use it to gain worldly, 'human' advantages; on this he is very emphatic. At the same time, it is true, he feels how perilous it would be to his whole mission for Christianity to appear in the hellenistic world as a movement for abolishing slavery or promoting any other kind of emancipation in the social order. To shift the primary concern of Christianity like this would not only endanger it, but be a betrayal of its true task.

In this connection may also be taken the celebrated section of the thirteenth chapter of Romans on subjection to the higher powers. It is, perhaps, no accident that Paul is led to speak on this precisely in a letter directed to Rome, where the problem was felt as especially pertinent, and was constantly present. We may observe that the passage does not answer the question which would be the first to be asked by a modern reader; for it speaks neither of the nature of the State, nor of the legitimacy or otherwise of a government, nor of the morality of revolution. The 'higher powers' he is thinking of have nothing particularly sacred about them, are not invested with that solemn character attributed to authority by the Church at a later date; his words refer directly to all the various police and fiscal officers with whom Christians then were most likely to come into contact. His point is that their concern is for justice, in that they punish the wicked and reward the good, and, in so doing, discharge a God-given task in the public sphere. And, because of this task of theirs even the Christian can and must show them honour and respect, and be obedient to them. This is thoroughly reasonable, since what the organs of public administration perform turns out to his interest, and is obnoxious only to the criminal. These statements cannot be watered down or otherwise explained away. And so once again we come up against the assertion that the public power—even in the form of the possessor of the *ius gladii*—is commissioned by God, indeed an absolutely universal principle, here applied not only to the social order but to politics, and, being universal, necessarily evident to the pagan, and certainly to every Jew. Thus, what Paul means is that to anyone, in virtue of his natural intelligence, it is evident that one is bound to accept the actual civil, police, and political authorities, since they are the guardians of justice, and God wills that justice should be preserved —from this duty even Christians are not exempt. But he does not go further than this. Over and above respect for authority Paul has nothing to say on any positive Christian duty in the general sphere of public life; he does not envisage any 'co-operation' or active participation. On the contrary, he is indignant if, for example, Christians make any approach to pagan tribunals, if they cannot settle their quarrels among themselves, and if they make pagans, so vastly inferior, judges over them (I Cor. 6.1ff.). Like every minority in an alien, more or less hostile environment, the Christian communities endeavour to solve their civil problems by themselves, by a kind of voluntary self-help. It was held beneath their spiritual dignity to expose themselves to the 'world', and, as it were, put themselves on the same footing.

Thus, by way of summary, we may say that Paul, as a missionary, was the first to consider certain questions relating to Christians and the social order, as affecting their vocation and existence and, therefore, of importance for the prosecution of their distinctive work. In so doing, he was led on to formulate general principles of social ethics, in which the justice of the pagan ordering of society was recognized. Christians should be seen, not only by other Christians, but by 'every man' to be people who desire and do what is good. 'If possible, so far as it depends upon you, live peaceably with all' (Rom. 12.18; cf. Gal. 6.10; I Thess. 3.12; 5.15; cf. 2.15). But, in such utterances, he was thinking more of what Christians were and ought always to be—not so much of what the world receives from them, at any rate in the temporal sphere. On this point, his ethical teaching is still wholly defensive in character, with its desire to avoid entanglement and friction with the world, and aiming at social autonomy rather than social integration with it.

The next generation goes somewhat further. Both works of Luke are explicitly addressed to an open-minded and interested pagan; his concern is to describe Christian doctrine and life in such terms as to commend them to a cultured upper class. For this it was necessary, above all, to refute the slanders of the Jews, who aimed at stirring up suspicion against the Christians as enemies of public order and the Roman Empire (as they had previously alleged of Christ himself). (Luke 23.24). In reality, they are, he says, an association of perfectly blameless, pious, and thoroughly reasonable and charitable persons, generous to the poor whom they receive among them, and 'take pains to have a clear conscience toward God and toward men' (Acts 24.16). It would seem as if Luke already had some idea of the excellent social effects Christianity was capable of producing. It is in Luke's Gospel that John the Baptist gives explicit directions on the conduct to be observed, in their respective callings, by those he stirred up to repentance. Furthermore, the story of Zachaeus the publican, the extortioner, which he alone relates, is the first and, for some time, the only instance where, not only is the conversion described, but also attention is drawn to the reparation made for former sins (here we may also recall Acts 19.18f.): 'Behold, Lord, the half of my goods I give to the poor; and if I have defrauded any one of anything, I restore it fourfold' (Luke 19.8).

Above all, the political innocuousness of Christianity is emphasized over and over again, both in the Gospel and, more particularly, in the Acts. Paul, who possessed Roman citizenship and its rights, was, more than once, judged completely innocent by the Roman authorities; he could have been set free, had he not himself appealed against the accusations of the Jews to Caesar's tribunal (Acts 26.32). It was the same with Jesus: Pilate formally declared that he found none of the accusations against him vindicated (Luke 23.14), and even the thief on the cross confessed that, though he and his companion were justly punished, Jesus had 'done nothing wrong' (Luke 23.41). In the same connection comes the remarkable section, already noticed, of John the Baptist's preaching. After the tax-collectors, there came also the soldiers, hardly just Jewish ones, but Gentile as well, to ask what they were to do in future, and he contented himself with the simple direction not to do violence to or calumniate any man, but to be content with their pay (Luke 3.14). Paul himself had previously spoken of the army as one of the normal elements, just like the judiciary and the financial machinery, of public life, and Christianity, far from disturbing these, only desired their representatives to proceed in a just and orderly fashion, as their service required. Must not, then, one is forced to ask, the Empire actually welcome such a movement? Surely it is no accident that Christ was born precisely at a time when the Empire, in drawing up a (supposedly) universal census, appeared for the first time as a self-contained unity (Luke 2.1f.)?

These are certainly questions which Luke wanted to provoke in the minds of his Gentile readers. Yet, although he, undoubtedly, was not describing Christianity otherwise than he himself understood it and wished it to be, he was very far from answering them, prematurely, in a positive and optimistic sense. He it is who records the sinister statement that all the kingdoms of the inhabited earth and their glory are given over to the devil, who can deliver them to whom he will (Luke 4.6). It is true that this is said by the devil; but it is not, for that reason, denied, as Irenaeus thought (*haer.* V, 22,2; 24,1), but is proved true. And what a melancholy, frightening certainty is expressed in his recording how Pilate and Herod Antipas, previously at enmity, became friends on the day when they found themselves sitting in judgement on Jesus! This event was symbolic: however great the discord and unrest in the world, the bitterest enemies join forces when it is a matter of rejecting the ultimate truth, incarnated in a person. Luke is not alone in this view of reality. He is only expressing the basic, unanimous conviction of primitive Christianity, of the entire New Testament, which seeks to arm Christians against persecution, to prepare them for suffering and martyrdom. Woe to the man of whom everyone speaks well, who enjoys universal public applause (Luke 6.26)! The advance, here indicated, beyond Paul is more an advance in the choice of standpoint than in the concrete judgement of the Christian's relation with the world. The demand that he should conduct himself without offence and commendably in the social and political spheres is now, as it were, seen from outside, and recognized to be just and reasonable. Christians ought to comply with it, since they are already obliged, by what they are, to follow such a way of life. Nonetheless, they are a specific community over against this world and their environment, and are always prepared, so precarious is their peace and the toleration they may enjoy, to be deemed enemies and treated accordingly.

No one expresses more incisively the ultimate incompatibility of the Christian faith with the aims of the world than the author of the fourth Gospel, perhaps a slightly younger contemporary of Luke. He wrote his Gospel with this relationship consciously and steadily in view, and it is therefore, I would say, of particular relevance today. Certainly, it presupposes and states that Jesus cannot be condemned on any just ground (John 7.43-52), that he was blameless even by the strictest standards of earthly justice and was hated 'without cause' (John 15.25).

Here also Jesus is not, on that account, against the world, but is rather its saviour, its Lord and salvation; he came unto his own, he is life and light to all men. But it goes on to reveal the strange fact that the world prefers its own darkness to the light of God. The world rejects Jesus precisely because he offers it a higher life than the one it possesses, and, in so doing, destroys the supposed security of its own special property. It even thinks that, in opposing him, it is doing what is right and 'a service to God' (John 16.2). Even when men accept Jesus and want to join with him, they understand him falsely, seeing in him a saviour and liberator from earthly needs and cares, with which alone they are concerned. This is precisely why they failed to understand him. The theme running through the whole Gospel is, as is well known, the constant misunderstandings that are the outcome. The earthly goods and necessities that usurp the foreground come now into a diabolical competition with the truth that Jesus brings. The elements of the world are seen as diabolic instruments, not excluding those of the social and political orders.

The five thousand in the desert were miraculously fed by Jesus, and the result was, apparently, a complete success; the crowd declared him forthwith the true 'prophet who is to come into the world', and tried to take him by force to make him king (John 6.14). But this only showed that they did not understand him, and he was obliged to make his escape. They followed him only because they had eaten their 'fill of the loaves', because they took him for a material benefactor. Jesus wished to be recognized for himself, so that they should 'labour for the food which endures' (John 6.27); they, however, took the 'sign' (John 6.26) for the reality, and so failed to recognize him. His own brethren now wanted him to come out into the open and gain adherents (7.3f.); in other words, his own apparent followers did not belong to him or 'believe' in him as he really was.

This fixation on the purely secular can even, in certain circumstances, assume the guise of concern for others. On the anointing of Jesus's feet with ointment of great value, Judas, who was a thief, became indignant at such a waste, considering it better to have sold it and given the money for the poor (John 12.3-6). The other disciples had a similar outlook, thinking that Jesus, at the last supper, was telling Judas to go and buy things for the poor, whereas he was speaking of the fulfilment of his passion and the salvation of the world (John 13.27-29).

Jesus defended Mary's action in anointing him. It had a more profound meaning: 'The poor you always have with you, but you do not always have me' to do something for (John 12.7f.).

This opposition between the two outlooks and aims takes its most sinister form in the strictly political sphere. Jesus had there no ambitions, no designs in any way dangerous; that is clear enough. His 'kingship is not of this world' (John 18.36), and Peter misunderstood the mind of his Lord when he drew the sword in his defence (John 18.10). Nevertheless, the rulers felt themselves threatened by his appearance on the scene; for it was the entrance of an ultimate authority and power, that of God, which was a menace to their own pretensions. The lords of the world wanted to rule exclusively, and without restrictions; they refused absolutely to admit the presence of an alien authority, one transcending the secular sphere. Anyone who joined Jesus was persecuted by the leaders of Judaism; those he healed, the witnesses of his glory and power, must be cast out or put to death (John 9.34; 12.10f.). Many, indeed, of the rulers believed secretly in Jesus; but they did not dare to come forward, through fear of being excommunicated and publicly outlawed, which would have been the consequence (John 12.42).

All these texts refer to the religious authorities of Judaism, who, notwithstanding, acted as secular potentates; but the clearest instance of the contrast between the spiritual and secular standpoints and aims is the celebrated encounter of Jesus and Pilate, the representative of the Roman Empire. Jesus, seemingly so helpless and abandoned, is, nevertheless, 'a king' (John 18.37), over whom Pilate would have no authority unless it were 'given from above', that is from God, so that he might fulfil his work (John 19.11). Pilate, on the other hand, who tried to impress him with his power of life and death (John 19.10), is shown more and more to be powerless and driven by circumstances, obliged for political reasons to do just what he would gladly have avoided and did not, in fact, desire at all. He felt certain that Jesus was innocent, and would have liked to set him free; but the Jews, who previously had opposed Jesus in case the Romans should invade and take over their country altogether (John 11.47-52), now, unscrupulously and recklessly, invoked the Emperor, intimating they could have Pilate dismissed, if he did not accede to their wishes. He sought for a compromise, which was impossible, and always is, where Jesus is concerned. And since, being the sort of man he was, he could not side with Jesus, and, since he could not break the bonds laid on him by his position in the world, he had to join with those who, in their injustice, condemned the king of truth. Pilate exemplifies the tragedy of the well-meaning official who, when it comes to the point, is unable to follow his kindly sentiments, but is obliged to obey the system of which he is a part.

What John intended to convey in all this is clear enough: 'no one can serve two masters' (Matt. 6.24 par.). Whoever says Jesus must not mean the world; whoever wishes to follow the world cannot remain with Jesus. But, over and above this, did John intend a judgement on secular power and authority as such, that is, did he wish to depict their possessors and concerns as essentially and always hostile to Jesus? This seems doubtful. At all events, he can hardly be held to have intended to discredit the whole field of public and social life, its concerns and tasks; they were simply not to be held as the end to which the message of Jesus was directed, and so stand in its way. It is obvious, for example, that John meant nothing against caring for the poor, in saying that Jesus meant something more than a summons to social feeling and active help. Of course, the poor must be cared for. And to Pilate, Jesus said that of course his adherents would be ready to fight for him, if his kingdom were an earthly one (John 18.36). Nor is it disputed that the political power represented by Pilate ought, in fact, to have decided otherwise and brought in a 'just judgement'; indeed, this is even taken for granted, in a sense. Yet all these questions, which occupy the modern reader who is interested in political, juridical, or social problems, are quite secondary; they are not of interest as such or in this connection. The peace which Jesus brings belongs to a completely different sphere (John 14.27; 16.33). One thing only is clear; that the world, which does not understand him, quite obviously retains, in all its dispositions and powers, the ineradicable tendency to deny to Jesus what he is in fact, and so to set itself above and against him.

This fact makes understandable why the Apocalypse of St. John (whose author was certainly not the evangelist) sees the kingdoms and powers of the world as simply demonic agents deployed against Christ and his Church, to which the faith has to oppose resistance and nothing more—and, in so doing, either suffer death or flee into the 'wilderness'. This is the ultimate decision required by the 'apocalyptic' situation; no other situations or decisions are even considered. For us, the important thing to see is that this exclusively negative attitude did not become, in fact, the determining factor in the further development of the Church and its relation to the world. Apart from the revivalist movement of Montanism in Asia Minor and its reactionary expectancy of the end, this 'apocalyptic' conception of the Christian's relation to the world never became established for long. In this regard, the Apocalypse is on the fringe of the New Testament, and the general development followed the lines laid down by Paul and Luke. We can see this already in the New Testament, if we consider the later epistles. They bring us to a final, fourth stage—after Jesus, Paul, Luke and John—in the development of the problem.

Here, at last, the general demands of social life emerge in such a way as to oblige Christians in particular to something positive. The factor prompting this new emphasis was, paradoxical though it sounds, the initiation of official oppression and persecution of the Christians. The persecutions and the slanders against the Church as an antisocial and criminal organization compelled it to set out clearly before the pagan environment, and for its own benefit, how far its adherence to Christianity and its inevitable resistance to the pagan cult-ordinances were other than the hostility to the State and public order with which they were reproached. It had to be shown convincingly that the Christians were, nonetheless, blameless citizens and obedient subjects, and that they acknowledged fully and sincerely the justice of the political order in general.

A significant document in this connection is the so-called first epistle of St. Peter, which follows, in part, the Pauline tradition. It was written by way of consolation and exhortation at a time when Christians were beginning to be oppressed and persecuted. They are, the writer points out, strangers and pilgrims in the world (1 Peter 2.11), and are not to wonder that they have to suffer like the Lord himself, whose followers they are. But the important thing is that it is as Christians, on account of their confession, that they are arraigned and punished: 'But let none of you suffer as a murderer, or a thief, or wrongdoer, or a mischief-maker' (1 Peter 4.15; cf. 2.16). Christians should, by their conduct, compel pagans to respect them and so 'glorify God on the day of visitation' (1 Peter 2.12), that is, when the time comes in their own lives for turning to God and to the good. The older theme of the mission which builds a bridge to the world is now amplified and made more general. Each individual Christian has his own part to play according to circumstances. He must be ready to do so before everyone 'with gentleness and reverence'—the sign of a good conscience (1 Peter 3.15)—and that can be done, at times, even 'without a word', solely through the goodness of his life (1 Peter 2.12; 3.1). The general principles of social behaviour are drawn from this and firmly underlined, as in the expanded form given to the old Pauline demand of obedience to public authority: 'Be subject for the Lord's sake to every human institution, whether it be to the emperor as supreme, or to governors as sent by him to punish those who do wrong and to praise those who do right. For it is God's will that by doing right you should put to silence the ignorance of foolish men. Live as free men, yet without using your freedom as a pretext for evil; but live as servants of God. Honour all men. Love the brotherhood. Fear God. Honour the emperor.' (1 Peter 2.13-17.) A special point is added for slaves, whose duty of obedience is not confined to good and gentle masters, but extends also to the 'overbearing' (1 Peter 2.18). But there is no corresponding injunction peculiar to those in authority; which means that, apart from oppression of religion, no injustice of theirs enters into consideration (1 Peter 3.13f.). As usual, no attention is paid to public institutions as such, but only to Christian conduct towards them.

The positive character of Christian loyalty is most strongly conveyed by the command to pray in general for all rulers and those in charge of public order, and to give God thanks on their account. This is a practice taken over from Judaism. In a Christian context it first appears in the extra-canonical first epistle of Clement, and afterwards in the first epistle to Timothy, which goes under the name of Paul, but is, in fact, later 'that we may lead a quiet and peaceable life, godly and respectful in every way' (1 Tim. 2.1f.; cf. Tit. 3.1). Paul's attitude of trust in those who govern and his confidence that they will uphold what is right is here adopted by the writer, and unreservedly placed in conjunction with the universal saving will of God: 'This is good, and it is acceptable in the sight of God our Saviour, who desires all men to be saved and to come to the knowledge of the truth' (1 Tim. 2.3f.). But even before this the first epistle of Clement had joined petition for the good estate of the rulers and for general peace with the wish that, for their part, they should not go against the will of God (1 Clem. 60.4*f.*), and, in the later epistle of Polycarp (Pol. 12.4), the emphatic inclusion of the persecutors in this petition indicates a further, explicitly Christian, application of the requirement. Very soon this prayer was expressly referred to in order to justify the Christian way of life in the eyes of pagans (Justin. *apol.* 1, 17.3), for great store was set on being held in good repute by 'outsiders' (1 Tim. 3.7). Christians must 'be ready to any honest work, to speak evil of no one, to avoid quarrelling, to be gentle, and show perfect courtesy toward all men' (Tit. 3.2). Those who are rich must 'do good, to be rich in good deeds, liberal and generous' (1 Tim. 6.18). 'And let our people learn to apply themselves to good deeds, so as to help cases of urgent need, and not to be unfruitful' (Tit. 3.14). They sincerely desire 'peace with all men' (Heb. 12.14).

We may sum it all up by saying that the social and political obligations incumbent on all must also be fulfilled by Christians, and as irreproachably as possible. Their obligations in this regard have now a positive character. In consequence, it is only natural, and by no means surprising, that the exhortations to this effect are formulated in traditional terms, and closely resemble the list of virtues enumerated by their Jewish and pagan contemporaries. The modest scope of civic requirements likewise reflects the conditions of the time and the position in which Christians found themselves. They, like most subjects of the Roman Empire, had no active political responsibility; for the time being, there was no question of their holding any political or communal office. Along with the obvious moral obligations, they only had to comply, as to public life, with the general requirements of peace and obedience—obligations of a typical subject-morality of a bourgeois or *petit-bourgeois* nature. Their own special character and task did not envisage social reforms or revolution, but, from the beginning, turned their activities and energies in a different direction. Nonetheless, they did not evade the question of public responsibility. They viewed it in the light of their own concerns, faced it positively, and answered it according as it presented itself at the time.

It is evident that all this was no solution to the actual problem of Christian resistance, which, in its exclusive confession of Christ, was to cause the breakdown of the old Roman Empire; but these matters could not come within the purview of anyone at that time. It is equally clear that the modest injunctions of a positive character relating to due subordination and decent behaviour, payment of taxes, respect for those in office, refraining from agitation, and regular intercession for rulers and governors could not, in the long run, meet all requirements. This became manifest even before Constantine, and, after his accession, a new ethical orientation was imperative. From the high Middle Ages onward, and at the time of the Reformation, the Church was faced with the new problem of the legitimacy and competency of rival political authorities. And the situation changed once again, and fundamentally, when public order and the ruling power were no longer held to be *ipso facto* authoritarian and static, but, in the widest sense, 'democratic', even though this conception was by no means universally realized. Today responsibility for the social structure has been transferred, to a certain extent, to each individual, and, therefore, also to the Christian members of the community. Fundamentally, there always exists the possibility of changing from below the existing structure, and of pressing for reforms, and the question even arises as to the conditions under which revolution would be permissible.

We are not going into all these matters here, since we are deliberately confining ourselves to the New Testament and, therefore, to the earliest stage. But these beginnings were not fortuitous, and what we conclude from them is far from being of secondary value for the understanding of the whole question; for their development was determined by the very nature of the Christian message, and so, rightly interpreted and applied, may serve as a permanent criterion. What, then, are the implications of the first decisions pronounced by the Church, and those it abstained from pronouncing, on political and social questions for its fundamental relation to public life outside the Church, and, within the limits stated, for the problem of the Church and the world? What follows is intended to be taken, not as a mere opinion of no binding force, but as a strictly logical conclusion.

1. The first thing that follows from the preceding survey of the New Testament evidence is almost self-evident, but must be explicitly stated: the original link joining Christianity to the world is the command and will to preach Christ. 'All nations' are to learn what God has done for the world, so that those who believe may be redeemed from the cramping godlessness of their previous existence and

begin a new life. The 'mission' in this sense is, in the first place, the only and, therefore, the real bridge joining the Church to the world. No one who is not primarily concerned about the peace which the world neither has nor can give, and about Christ and God, the Father of Christ and of all men, can be a real participant in the discussion on the Church and society; for these are what the discussion is about. This is what 'those outside' have to know when they turn their attention to the Church, so as to prevent any disappointment; this, more than anything else, Christians themselves need to know, and, most of all, those who have to proclaim Christ to the world. Anyone who holds that the Christian message and what it actually involves is not sufficient as the content of his preaching is not equal to his vocation as a spokesman for the Church, or, rather, has not yet found that vocation. On the other hand, should he hold the view that the Church has no longer anything to say to modern man, he is in error. If it were a fact that the world lacked nothing in this regard, there would not be all the attention paid to religious and pseudo-religious, psychological, social, and philosophical prescriptions and nostrums, nor would we have all this dissemination of political tenets as so many gospels offering salvation.

2. That Christians as such have no definite political or social order to proclaim does not, in the least, mean that they are basically indifferent to the life of society or that they must forgo, to the best of their ability, any expectations from that society. Christians are placed, along with the rest, in the world and in secular society, and, therefore, have to recognize and accept the duties and conditions it implies, with the very precise restriction that 'We must obey God rather than men' (Acts 5.29). Even if these duties were, at first, almost unnoticed, they were never simply rejected, and, as time went on, they became more and more clearly recognized and strongly emphasized. Thus we can see that Christians are not indifferent or neutral in the matter, but positively committed. For a community that derives from the Old Testament, this is self-evident in principle, and, therefore, it needed no new specifically Christian or christological foundation for its conduct in this respect. The fact that the degree of civic participation and responsibility was, at first, very slight is due, as we have said, to the situation at the time, and was to change along with the social and political circumstances. The New Testament presents no new pro-

gramme. It must, therefore, not be interpreted as prescribing a maximum or a minimum programme; it simply designates an orientation of the will and a state of preparedness that hold good in all circumstances.

3. Thus, the concrete and fundamental questions of social life and politics are neither settled nor anticipated. Christians cannot act as if their faith puts them into possession of a whole store of social and political knowledge, upon which they can draw and pass on to the world. Far from that, they have to learn, just like anyone else, their sociology, economics, psychology, jurisprudence, civics, and politics, if they desire to take part, by word and action, in public life, without making themselves ridiculous. What matters there is professional competence in the concrete situation. Certainly, the faith they possess should make them quick to detect when experts in a given field try to make their ideologies and subjective convictions pass for scientific findings and insist on both together. Above all, it should make them see through their fellow-Christians when they attempt to base political principles on alleged divine commands and directives from Christ, instead of producing relevant and convincing arguments. This is a procedure which not only prevents political discussion, but, far worse, obscures the very meaning of the Christian message.

Primitive Christianity turned its attention to the problems of social life in the interests of the Church's preaching. It did not go beyond this and consider them for their own sake, except when they seemed, from its own standpoint, to do with matters whose morality was self-evident, and about which there could be no rational doubt. Today, however—and not for the first time—it is not so easy to follow this line, since the nature of things hardly permits of a boundary marking off what is controvertible. Nonetheless, it seems to me that the same procedure is the basically correct one for all times. The Christian who pursues definite political and social aims has no need to be ashamed of the fact; but the Church is not the place for their advocacy. It can cause nothing but confusion if her representatives take sides in doubtful questions and deliver judgements, since these then become burdens laid, not merely on them, but on the Lord in whose name they should be speaking. It ought to be enough for the Church to speak only when there is no doubt of God's command to her, and when, in pursuance of her task, she proclaims the peace of Christ, which gives a new splendour and specific meaning to all earthly acts and intentions. The limits imposed in this way may seem, to political partisans and activists, to make her work fruitless, if not to destroy it altogether; but to those who see the matter from within the limitations serve essentially to recall them and to point them to life itself.

7

Christians and Military Service in the Early Church

THE QUESTION of the attitude towards military service adopted by early Christianity has been answered in an astonishing variety of ways. This is due not to the sources which have long since been collected and often discussed,[1] but to the modern approach, which states the question in such broad and undiscriminating terms, in a mode in which it never existed for the ancient Church, or for the Church in any age. The early Church had nothing whatever to say as to what non-Christians ought or ought not to do, nor had it any intention of changing the order of this passing world in a Christian sense. What it put forward in the way of concrete directions and demands was meant only for Christians. Certainly the truth can only be one at all times, and will, at some future date, alone prevail. But this world does not accept the truth to which Christians confess, even though, as the truth of the divine love, it is the salvation of every man. Christians are 'strangers' in the world; they do not wish to destroy it, but to heal it. They do, however, disturb it, since they do not let themselves be integrated into it and its chaotic laws, and so always remain an 'exception' in the world. Ethically, Christianity and paganism cannot be given a common denominator, as is evident from the way Christians explain themselves on matters of principle. If they comply with and accept

[1] Once and for all I would refer the reader to the well-known synthesis—still adequate on the main issue—in Harnack, *The Mission and Expansion of Christianity in the First Three Centuries* (1908). Among later contributions to the subject may be cited the article '*Militarisme*', in Cabrol–Leclercq, *Dict. d'archéol, chrét. et de liturgie* XI, 1 (1933). The fundamental problems have been discussed more especially by English writers, such as C. F. Cadoux, *The Early Christian Attitude to War* (1919) and R. H. Bainton, 'The Early Church and War', *HThR* 39 (1946) 189ff. Roman Catholic discussions in the manner of O. Schillings, *Naturrecht und Staat nach der Lehre der alten Kirche* (1914), nearly all have the drawback of confining the question within the framework of natural law and answering it from that standpoint.

some factor in the outside world, that does not mean that they approve it; it is simply that they cannot change the world and make it the Church. At the same time, if definite obligations are imposed on Christians by the Church and treated as self-evident, that does not mean that they are intended as principles to which all law must conform; it is simply that they cannot commit themselves wholly to the law of this world.

This explains the seemingly inconsistent ways in which the ancient Church judged war and military service. Not a single one of the Fathers doubted that, in the world as it is, war is inevitable, and, consequently, they saw no reason to condemn the military profession in particular. It is of the very essence of the world to be obliged to shed blood—whether in war, or by legal process (the two are nearly always taken together in this connection). It is only by force that external peace is preserved, for which Christians also are grateful. For this reason, they pray not only for rulers, but also for the army and its success in war.[2] They themselves, however, would not have anything to do with war service. The world may need its Caesars, but no emperor can be a Christian nor a Christian ever be an emperor.[3] The Church knows no war[4]; the military organizations in the world are not necessary on her account.[5] Christians are peacemakers and adhere to the commandments in the Sermon on the Mount. They are ready to suffer and die in testimony to their truth; but they do not kill.[6] The military requirements of bravery, moderation, and obedience they practise figuratively in a war wherein God himself has supreme command;[7] these are now 'spiritual' virtues.

How the early Church blandly assumed as self-evident the exceptional position of Christians, teaching and acting accordingly, is explicable only by the circumstances of the time. For little enclaves of a fairly humble status in the peaceful interior of a well-ordered empire, where there was practically no conscription, it was easy to avoid anything to do with the army; no difficulties were encountered from any source, external or internal. Christians were still outside the field

---

[2]Tert., *apol.* 30; Cypr., *ad Demetr.* 20; Arnob., *adv. nat.* IV, 36.
[3]Tert., *apol.* 21.   [4]Just., *dial.* 110.
[5]Clem. Al. *protr.*, 116; *paed.* I, 12.
[6]Just., *apol.* I, 39; *dial.* 110; Iren. *haer.* IV, 34; Tert., *adv. Jud.* 3; Minuc. Fel., *Oct.* 30.
[7]Thus, e.g., I Clem. 37.

of political responsibility, nor were they as yet much affected by the political philosophy of antiquity. But this state of affairs could not last. Development proceeded apace, and, with the growth of the Church, its responsibility for the inmost sphere of the spirit grew accordingly. A plain demarcation of the Church from the world on sociological lines proved impossible, both externally and internally. For a 'deliberate self-exclusion from the whole can only be maintained outwardly',[8] and the exceptional status of the Church was, fundamentally, considered not as external and sociological, but as spiritual. It was not possible to remain wholly negative as regards the 'world', industry, politics, or even the military organization; at the same time, these could not be unreservedly approved and accepted by the Church. The real, inner dialectic of Church and world began to unfold, and demanded definite attitudes according to historical conditions, attitudes which, however, could never be final, but must always remain flexible. The following outline is intended to bring to light only the initial stages of this development, the emergence of a dawning consciousness of the present problem, taking military service as an example. It does not propose to go into the question in all its historical and theological detail. We hope, however, that even so limited a study will be welcome to a philosopher,[9] whose essential concern has always been with the serious character of human decision, and who is never indifferent to the specific attitude of the Christian.

Till about A.D. 175 there were, as far as we can tell, no Christian soldiers, and, therefore, no actual question about military service arose. This was, at first, not a problem that called for the attention of Christians.[10] All attempts to adduce answers to it from early sources, especially the New Testament, are bound to be fruitless.[11] From the

---

[8]Karl Jaspers, *Von der Wahrheit* (1947), 749.

[9]Karl Jaspers; this paper is one of those in a *Festschrift* for him (*Translator*).

[10]It was touched upon once only, in the preaching of John the Baptist (Luke 3.14); here, in so far as the soldiers were admonished to a more controlled and ordered way of life, their profession, at any rate, was not condemned, but, under certain conditions, accepted. This argument was already used in Tertullian's time by the defenders of the military service of Christians, and rightly so. The only thing to notice is that the passage does not refer to Christian soldiers, and that Luke, the only one to report it, did so, probably, with a certain apologetic intention: to dissipate official misgivings about the new movement on this point.

[11]This is not quite the opinion of W. Bienert, who in *Krieg, Kriegsdienst und Kriegs-*

end of the second century, however, it became more and more frequent for soldiers to come in contact with the Christian mission and to be converted. Could they, then, as Christians, remain in their former calling? It is only in this form that the question arose; the possibility of born Christians enlisting voluntarily was not yet discussed.[12] Tertullian had already rejected it outright: 'The oath of allegiance to God and that to man, the standard of God and the standard of the devil, the camp of light and the camp of darkness are incompatible ... All uniforms are prohibited to us, since they are the signs of a forbidden calling.'[13] Here he is not thinking primarily of killing and bloodshed by soldiers.[14] What Tertullian feared was the denial of Christ and the taint of pagan worship, which seemed inevitable in view of the strictness of military discipline and the role played by pagan religion in the whole ceremonial and life of the army.

The views of others were less extreme. They held it far from desirable to put such great obstacles in the way of Christian propaganda in the army, and to stir up conflicts, by insisting that every soldier won over should leave the service at once. By way of justification, appeal was made to all the various examples in Scripture, from Moses and Joshua to the centurion of Capernaum.[15] Even Clement of Alexandria —in temperament far from being a 'militarist'—opposed an 'external' conception of the new Christian life. Not without reason had Paul commanded every Christian to remain in the state in which he was called; and that applied also to soldiers.[16] The only thing is that, henceforth, the soldier, as a Christian, must be ready to hear the voice of the one righteous commander, Christ, whose trumpet does not sound with wild martial music, and who has trained his followers for peace.[17] Altogether, theological opposition to the military service of

---

dienstverweigerung nach der Botschaft des Neuen Testaments (1952) adduces no fewer than twenty-eight theses he considers to bear on the subject; against this, see my review, Für Arbeit und Besinnung, appendix to Baden 6 (1952) 247.

[12]Cf. especially Can. Hipp. XIV, 74: christianus ne fiat propria voluntate miles.

[13]Tert., de cor. 11.

[14]Likewise, the arguments against taking official positions and becoming magistrates mention this only in passing and as purely secondary: de idol. 17f.; cf. de cor. 11.

[15]Tert. de idol. 19.

[16]Clem. Al. paed. I, 12; cf. protr. 116; Strom. IV, 61f.

[17]Euseb. hist. eccl. VII, 30, 8.

Christians was considerably reduced in the course of the third century. In the time of Diocletian, Christians formed a considerable proportion of the Roman army; obviously, they were not only converts, but, to a great extent, born Christians. Particularly in Rome, many Christians described themselves, not without pride, as 'soldiers'. At the same time, we must always remember that garrison-service was often of a quite pacific nature; also that the police and guards, postilions and firemen were held part of the 'militia' in a broad sense. Even a bishop, like Paul of Samosata, could maintain his own escort of δορυφορού-μενοι.

The discussion of the problem enters a new stage when the Christian attitude is no longer considered from a pastoral standpoint and in regard to the individual, but in the light of fundamental principles now beginning to emerge. These, understandably, form the starting-point of the pagan critique of Christian theology. This critique was what drew attention to the political problem which could arise from the Christian attitude on military service, and so prompted a different set of considerations and the adoption of new standpoints. The pagan philosopher, Celsus, is the first, to our knowledge, to express it openly. Christians, he says, are, politically speaking, parasites, since they refuse to give to the rulers, who maintain the Empire and peace, not only the honour due to them (that is, the cult), but also service, and, on the crucial matter, decline to take on the burdens which, in principle, every citizen ought to bear. It is 'unfair to take a share in the goods that the emperor possesses and not to contribute anything for them'.[18] 'If all behaved as you do', in the end no one could prevent 'the government of the earth falling into the hands of lawless and savage barbarians' and the extinction of culture and philosophy.[19] Or maybe Christians believe that 'God will come down from heaven and fight for them, so that they need no other help'.[20]

It was a long time before this attack was answered. No doubt, Christian apologists had always combated the idea that Christians were useless as citizens or desired so to be, and argued to this effect from their obedience, their law-abiding character, their payment of taxes and their regular public prayer for the Emperor. But the question had never yet been put to them in this pointed way. The reason for this

[18]Orig., *contra Cels.* VIII, 55.   [19]*Ibid.* VIII, 68.
[20]*Ibid.* VIII, 69.

incisive mode of presentation was that the apparently unshakable world-empire was beginning to be endangered and the Church itself was continually expanding. It was no accident that the man who finally took upon himself to answer the philosophical indictment was himself a philosopher, that is, a theologian thoroughly trained in the ancient philosophy and mode of thought, namely Origen. Accordingly, he had no hesitation in admitting outright the fundamental justification of the pagan demand. It goes without saying that all citizens are obliged to contribute to the common good of the State, and Christians also are perfectly ready to obey in bearing the burdens incumbent on them.[21] Nor had Origen any doubt that there must be wars, and that the Emperor had the right to defend the Empire. But, significantly enough, he prefaces his exposition of the Church's attitude to war and recognition of its lawfulness with the proviso that it be just and conducted with due order,[22] whereas habitually it is unleashed solely by hunger, greed and the lust for conquest.[23] All the same, soldiers who are Christians never actually enter the field of battle, even if the Emperor demands it.[24] In this respect, Origen is fully in accord with Tertullian. The vocation of Christians on earth is quite different from that of pagans: 'We are come in obedience to the exhortations of Jesus to break the swords wherewith we used to defend our opinions and assail our adversaries, and to change into ploughshares the lances which formerly we used in battle. No longer do we draw the sword against any nation whatever; we learn no more to fight, now that we are become children of peace.'[25] If Christians fight, it is only in a spiritual sense—they wash their hands and feet in the blood of sinners whom they convert; they slay whole battalions of devils, whose power over men is broken by their might.[26] This is the reason why it is not necessary that they should also take the field in an external sense. 'While others go out to war, we, as priests and servants of God, take part in the campaign in that we keep our hands clean and pray for the just cause, the lawful king and their victory . . . We form, through our prayers, a true army, an army of piety, which performs a better service to the emperor than all his visible soldiers'.[27]

---

[21]*Ibid.* IV, 81. [22]*Ibid.* IV, 82
[23]Orig., *Mt. comm. ser.* 36. [24]Orig., *contr. Cels.* VIII, 73.
[25]*Ibid.* V, 23. The allegorical development of the idea is significant.
[26]Orig., *Num. hom.* 26. [27]Orig., *contra. Cels.* VIII, 73.

Thus Origen sees the refusal of military service not as an avoidance by the Church of co-operation in the defence of the Empire. Just rulers and just wars are supported by Christians along with the rest, but in a different, directly spiritual fashion. In support of this, Origen expressly refers to the ancient idea of the special position of the priesthood in representing the people by their service, and thus the acknowledged privileges of the priestly caste are extended to the whole priestly people of the Christians. Evidently, for Origen, it is not merely the practice of idolatry and the danger of acting unjustly that keep Christians away from the army, but war itself, the bloody, earthly trade of the soldier, that is unbecoming to their vocation. A soft 'pacifist' undertone can be detected, which comes, not from the Bible, but from late neo-Platonic spirituality. This is also the source of the characteristic idea of gradation and representation, distinguishing the perfect spiritual men and ascetics—within and without the Church—from the mass, and raising them above the daily cares and concerns of life. It is precisely from this standpoint that, in the question of military service, the Christian attitude of withdrawal is not a disturbing element, but thoroughly 'reasonable'. It no longer means that they are wholly exceptional, but that they share the work in a perfectly real sense. We see philosophical reflection giving a new interpretation of Christian eschatology, when the providential co-ordination of the *pax romana* and the *pax christiana*, as seen perhaps already by Luke, and so frequently emphasized by the apologists later, is now seen no longer as a pure miracle wrought by God, but as, at the same time, the necessary outcome of an immanent process of development. World peace is seen as the result of Christian prayer, and the living Christian sentiment which brings it to pass by suppressing the '*operationes seminatrices bellorum*'. Conversely, the wars and confusion of the end of time are no longer held to be the 'cause',[28] but the effect of Christian love growing cold.[29] It is easy, on these lines, to harmonize and balance the demands of politics and the Christian attitude to life.

Already, however, it is clear where the proffered solution is bound to break down. The whole idea of Christians exercising a priesthood on behalf of the Empire presupposes that they will always be a distinct group in the world, that is to say a minority. What will happen,

[28]Matt. 24,12.　　　　　　　　　[29]Orig., *Mt. comm. ser.* 37.

Celsus asked, when the whole Empire becomes Christian? 'If all acted as you', where would the Emperor get his soldiers? The answer that then there would be peace throughout the Empire, and no need of police and army, is not applicable to the barbarians, who, by their nature, belong only to the fringe of the 'oecumene', and whose power could no longer be ignored in the third century. Even Origen could think of no better answer than that which Celsus justifiably rejects as inadequate: 'Were all the Romans to accept the faith, they would gain the victory over their enemies by prayer and supplication—or, rather, they would have no enemies at all to fight, since the divine power would preserve them'.[30] A Christian world-empire was always, for Origen, a quite Utopian idea; and therefore he makes bold to put forward a quite unreal, artificial possibility, which will free him from a Utopian kind of solution. Later Fathers availed themselves of their conviction that very soon the whole world would be Christian, and there would be no obstacle to the enjoyment of perpetual peace.[31]

The whole matter began to take a decisive turn with the reign of Constantine. When the supreme commander had himself become a Christian, the 'idealistic' approach was seen to be obviously untenable. It was no longer possible to shift the responsibility for wars to the heathen population exclusively. Christians had themselves to become members of the army—no longer just in isolated cases and by way of concession, but in general and on principle. The Church did not reach this decision easily.

Indeed, the atrocities committed in the preceding persecutions and civil wars powerfully reinforced the general horror of war on the part of civilians, as well as the Church's own impressions of the sordid character of the military profession. There had been Christians who, on being called up, chose rather to be martyrs, refusing even to attempt a Christian life in such a mob.[32] The just man could not be a soldier; for justice itself is his military status.[33] Consequently, even after the conquest of Paganism in the Empire and the army, there was enacted

---

[30]Orig., contr. Cels. VIII, 70.   [31]Thus Arnob., adv. nat. I,6.
[32]Cf. especially the martyrdom of Maximilian, who, in defiance of all persuasion, adhered to his 'non possum militare, non possum malefacere—Christianus sum'. In the later period, we find widespread instances of Christians in the army being involved in the question of participation in pagan religious rites.
[33]Lact., inst. VI, 20, 16.

a whole series of strange rules about desertion. It was not without cause that the Emperor Constantine hesitated so long to receive Christian baptism. It was often the practice to allow Christians to join the army, even to prescribe severe ecclesiastical penalties for desertion in time of peace,[34] yet to continue to forbid them to kill. 'Persons who possess authority to put to death' (that is to say, Christian judges) 'and soldiers, must, in no circumstances, kill, even when they are commanded to'.[35] Those who do so, even though hardly able to avoid it in an emergency, must be excluded from the sacraments, till they have done penance. A theologian, like Basil the Great, still held firm on this point towards the end of the century.[36] In the long run, of course, it was impossible to sustain. Already Athanasius declares on occasion that the killing of enemies, otherwise forbidden, is in war not only permitted, but even laudable,[37] and Ambrose has no hesitation in following Cicero in praising the bravery of soldiers in protecting the fatherland from the barbarians.[38] By an edict of Theodosius II of the year 416, only Christians were to be admitted into the army; and two centuries later, it was only with difficulty that the Emperor Phocas was dissuaded from his opinion that all his soldiers who met a heroic death in battle should be honoured as martyrs. From this it was but a step to the idea of the crusade, a holy war on behalf of the Christian Church.

Notwithstanding the development that took place, one cannot say that the Church, after its alleged 'decline' under Constantine, simply abandoned the original Christian idea of exemption from service in war. As we have seen, the Church had never insisted upon a dogmatic, absolute and anarchistic form of non-resistance. She could not then make it a law when Christians could no longer avoid taking on offices

---

[34]Thus must be understood, in particular, can. 3 of the Council of Arles in 314: *de his qui arma proiiciunt in pace placuit abstineri eos a communione.*

[35]Can. Hipp. 13*f.*

[36]Basil, *ep.* 188, 13. This, in spite of the fact that he expressly declares to be lawful the just war which is waged ὑπὲρ σωφροσύνης καὶ εὐσεβείας.

[37]Athan., *ep. ad Amunem*, where, it is true, the observation is made only by way of comparison, and has no special reference to Christians. But the change in view is at once evident, if we compare this with the related utterance of Cyprian, *ad Donat.,* where it appears utterly outrageous that the crime of murder '*virtus vocatur, cum publice geritur*'.

[38]Ambr., *de off.* I, 129.

in the State and political responsibility—unless the world had ceased to be what Scripture means by the term. But that does not mean that the Church simply capitulated to the world and its ideas about the rightness of war. We have seen how already Origen, with his insistence on justice, sought to preserve Christian liberty of decision, at least in principle, and this line of thought continued to be developed, and significantly, up to Augustine and beyond. The Church does not simply leave the world to judge for itself, but is bold enough to intervene actively within it on behalf of the right, and thus to bear witness to her own truth. Yet she herself would like always to remain a place where peace dwells undisturbed. The actual boundary is difficult to draw, and must, in fact, always be discovered anew. But there is a profound, and not only a symbolical meaning, in the accepted principle that, at the gates of the Church and the monastery, a halt is called to warfare and legal vengeance.

We can see, though not so clearly, similar considerations prevailing in the sphere of the individual, and governing the decision he must make. Notwithstanding the basic assertion that certain duties, political and military, are incumbent on all citizens, including Christians, war service is not held simply as an absolute law. There are possible exceptions, and, from the Christian standpoint, necessary ones. Monks, clerics, and 'spiritual persons' of all kinds are not obliged to fight, but may always restrict themselves to sacrifice and suffering. Perseverance and stability in these callings are a sign and a constant reminder of the possibility of exemption as a live issue.

For, in fact, the main thing is the freedom of such 'exceptions', which persist in full view of the world. The Christian readiness to share in all the burdens and responsibilities of civic life is not thereby revoked. It subsists unimpaired, and holds good even when—as in the case when war has become inevitable—it is clearly a matter of the *consequence* of human sin. At the same time, it is wholly indifferent whether, and to what extent, Christians share in the culpability or not. On the other hand, the impression should never be given that sin is itself a power to which Christians must submit, instead of fighting; and so their compliance with the political and military authorities never means that they take war to be an ultimate truth and a reality of life that suffers no impairment. The real and always valid truth is, rather, the truth of the peace given to the world, and this truth must

8

The Theological Problem of Images in the Early Church

I

IN ITS GENERAL rejection of images, especially of any image of God and any pictorial representation of saints, early Christianity was the heir of Judaism and, with it, of an age-old tradition, of which the extensive historical background has been described in detail by Hubert Schrade.[1] There is no doubt that the Judaism of the hellenistic Synagogue by no means adhered strictly to the Mosaic prohibition,[2] and even early Christianity occasionally transgressed it; this can be directly verified in the case of certain gnostic sects.[3] But these are exceptional cases. Fundamentally, the prohibition of divine images and of all 'Christian art' obtained throughout the pre-Constantinian age, just as the first commandment of the Old Covenant remained in force. And it received added emphasis in the missionary preaching to the pagan world. We can see[4] how the first article of the Creed was given, so to speak, priority over the second: the conversion to Christianity was, as it were, at the same time and primarily, also conversion to Judaism.

In reality, a problem is involved in these simultaneous conversions. The exact relation of the second to the first article is the crucial theological question at the basis of the subsequent disputes about images, and even the controversies of the Lutheran Church and the Reformed Church on their prohibition can be elucidated from this standpoint. The long time it took to discover the theological and christological

[1]Hubert Schrade, *Der verborgene Gott. Gottesbild und Gottesvorstellung in Israel und im alten Orient*, 1949. Also Gerhard v. Rad in *Verkündigung und Forschung*, 1952; for the Old Testament problems we now have also K. H. Bernhardt, *Gott und Bild. Ein Beitrag zum Bilderverbot*, 1956.
[2]*Cf.* Werner Georg Kümmel, 'Die älteste religiöse Kunst der Juden', *Judaica* 2 (1946) 1-56.
[3]Thus the Simonians. Eus. *hist. eccl.* VI, 1, 12.
[4]E.g., 1 Thess. 1.9*f*.

point of departure for the discussion, and the fact that its significance emerged only gradually do not tell in the least against its actual importance; in fact, that is absolutely typical. It is precisely when overwhelmed by new questions coming in from outside that the Church needs more and more time for an objective grasp of the matter, and for pervading it with her spirit.

What the discussion was about is already evident in the early Christian use of the image-concept.[5] The word 'eikon' (εἰκών), 'image' of God, is used in the New Testament not only for Christ, but for man, corresponding to the Old Testament tradition (Gen. 1.27). But primarily it is almost always used in early Christianity as a christological title, which—like the cognate concepts of splendour (ἀπαύγασμα) and others—is intended to stress not distance from God, but closeness to him, the essential divinity of its bearer and his belonging to God, a concept whose original meaning was only confused by being rationalized in the Aryan controversy. It was only through Christ's becoming man and revealing the divine glory as in a mirror that the concept becomes again applicable to men also. Through him they are drawn along into his divine image, and in their natural being 'transformed', in virtue of the marvellous revelation made a present reality by the Gospel, the testimony of God, the preaching of the word. The philosophical idea of the image and of man's original affinity to God was allowed a preponderant role only in Acts 17; in general, strikingly little attention was paid to it. In this, the character of early Christianity, with its tendency to gnosticism and to ignore creation and the natural order, and with its whole orientation to the marvellous redemption, comes out in clear contrast to the later 'catholic' theology. This tendency is so strong that the creation passage in Genesis, for example, is, in the epistle of Barnabas 5.5, held to refer primarily to Christ alone; also many Gnostics wanted to attribute the 'image' (as

[5] A collection of the principal texts is in Edmund Schlink, *Gottes Ebenbild als Gesetz und Evangelium. Ein Lehrstück der Dogmatik im Umriss in: Der alte und der neue Mensch, Aufsätze zur theol. Anthropologie—BEvTh.* 8 (1942) 86-87; further dogmatic discussions on the subject in the double volume 7/8 of the Evangel. Theol. 11 (1951-52); ecumenical conference of orthodox and evangelical theologians on problems of theological anthropology of June 1952. Jk. Jervell, *Imago Dei.* Gen. 1.26f. in late Judaism, Gnosticism and the Pauline epistles, 1960. The copious literature on the image-concept of the Fathers need not be cited in detail; *cf. ThR* 22 (1954) 335ff.; also H. Crouzel, *Théologie de l'image de Dieu chez Origène*, Paris 1956.

opposed to the 'likeness') of God only to the 'pneumatic', the perfect man, superior in his very nature, and to deny it expressly to the 'psychic' man (*Ecl. ex Theod.* 50, 54 *et al.*). Even Clement of Alexandria, despite his evident contact with the philosophical tradition, treats the divine image as an alien entity, merely dwelling in man, sharing his destiny, which originates only with Christ and remains identical with him (*protr.* 59, 2*f.*). Whenever, then, man is spoken of as being in the image of God, the reference is always, primarily, to the new and marvellous divine reality bestowed on the Christian, or, rather, on the community, something not pertaining to man as such, but which he has received in Christ or through the Spirit, and which dwells in him only as the divine Lord in an earthly temple.

The Church took over, as an inheritance from rational philosophy, the unremitting struggle against pagan anthropomorphism,[6] and this led her to insist more and more on the distance between man and the God-man. Aristides (7.1-3), for instance, is so decisive in rejecting any connection of man with the *divina natura* that he seems, from the standpoint of later theology, almost to overstep the limits of Christian tolerance. On the other hand, it was precisely this that made it possible to adduce against Judaism a scriptural proof of Christ from the Old Testament itself: the brazen serpent set up by Moses remained a flagrant contradiction of his own prohibition of images, so long as it was not recognized as a prototype of Christ crucified. It was only when seen as a symbol of Christ that what was apparently a divinization of the creature ceased to be such, since it was nothing else than a mysterious mode of worship paid to the incarnate Son of God (Justin, *dial.* 94; 112,1-3; *cf.* Tert., *idol.* 5). Thus, it was in the struggle on behalf of the divinity of Christ, the image of the Father, that the foundations were laid of the formulas and comparisons used later to justify corporeal images and their use by the Church.[7]

---

[6]Johannes Geffcken, '*Der Bilderstreit des heidnischen Altertums*', *ARW* 19 (1916/19) 286-315; also, on the philosophical justification of the use of images, N. H. Baynes, 'Idolatry and the early Church', pp. 128*ff.*, in *Byzantine Studies and other Essays*, Oxf. 1955, pp. 116*ff.*

[7]The image of the king, to which regard and honour were considered due, appears, though not fully developed in the later sense, in Iren. *haer.* I, 8, 1, and typically in Methodius, *resurrec.* II, 24. The frequently cited passage of Basil ἡ τῆς εἰκόνος τιμὴ εἰς τὸ πρωτότυπον διαβαίνει is part of his trinitarian speculation on the Holy Spirit 18, 45.

II

These conclusions would, of course, not be of any practical relevance so long as there was no such thing as Christian art, particularly no representative art appropriate to Christian worship. There was no question of this in the first three centuries of the Church. The proof furnished by Hugo Koch, and amplified by Walter Elliger, need not be adduced in this place.[8] The essentially decorative (if also symbolic) adornment of the Roman catacombs and of the early Christian sarcophagi, both of which date only from the third, or at any rate the end of the second, century, cannot seriously be taken as evidence to the contrary. Nor should we attribute much theological importance to the Simoniac cult-images of Simon Magus and Helena or to the 'authentic' images of Christ of the Carpocratians, spoken of by Irenaeus. There is no doubt that they were, in the first instance, what Irenaeus, Eusebius, and Epiphanios took them to be, namely a sign of gross paganization, of syncretism. They were the counterpart in Christianity of the same pagan phenomenon as that of the Lararium of the Emperor Alexander Severus, in which—according to the admittedly questionable account in the *Historia Augusta*—Christ and Abraham were placed alongside the images of the ancient gods and heroes. On this point, not only the diatribe of Tertullian, but also the later canonical ordinances, that put artists in the Church on a level with actors, brothel-keepers, and the like, speak with no uncertain voice.

The hostility of the early Church to images has nothing surprising about it, even if we disregard its origin in Judaism. One has only to realize how the Church of the first three centuries was in a state of uninterrupted conflict with the dominant paganism, its idols, its superstition, and its idolatrous abominations, and how the struggle was ever anew concentrated round the sacrifice for the 'images of idols', before which flowed the blood of the martyrs. In the Church's eyes, hostile

[8]Hugo Koch, *Die altchristliche Bilderfrage nach den literarischen Quellen*, 1917; Walter Elliger, *Die Stellung der alten Christen zu den Bildern in den ersten vier Jahrhunderten (nach den zeitgenössischen Schriftstellern)* 1930. For the texts used in what follows I content myself with a summary indication of these two studies; *cf.* also J. Kollwitz, *Zur Frühgeschichte der Bilderverehrung*, in *Das Gottesbild im Abendland* (1959) 57-76.

from the outset, this, more than anything else, showed the true nature of art. The whole art of antiquity was essentially orientated to religious practices, and as such—like the ecclesiastical art of the High Middle Ages—permeated the whole of life; and, although from the hellenistic age onwards there was growing a purely aesthetic conception and practice of art, it may well be asked whether it is possible to entertain the idea of a strictly speaking 'neutral', secular art before the time of Christ. The very themes of heroic mythology were bound to be felt by the Church as 'paganism', and seemed to demand that she take a firm line for or against. It is true that, in the legendary martyrdom of the Quattuor Coronati, these Christian artists did not hesitate to depict a Sol, and only became martyrs through refusing to make an image of Asclepius. Yet this differentiation between an idolatrous image and a nature-symbol is more the reflection of the feeling of a later age—or, at most, a practical rather than a theological attempt to find a middle way, and not an isolated instance either.

In addition, there was the general misgiving, moral and 'pietistic', about artists and art. The evil living of artists was notorious, and there was a sense of repulsion for the obscene subjects they preferred to treat. Also, at best, art remained a superfluous luxury, which withdrew support from the poor, an occasion of worldly vanity, which ought to have no place in the Church. These ideas have no direct connection with 'hostility to images', but were constantly coming to the fore and gaining influence until the reforming attempts of the monastic orders and the ravages of the iconoclasts. Altogether, the whole world-renouncing, ascetic and spiritualist tendency of ancient Christianity was anything but favourable to the development and acceptance of a Christian art. Of the pre-Nicene Fathers, Clement of Alexandria was the only one to have had any feeling at all for art and beauty;[9] but even he acknowledged no such thing as 'Christian' art,[10] and saw the true love of beauty as reaching out beyond the things of sense towards its end in God, the primal source of all spiritual beauty.

[9]It is even worse, though, when beauty is used for the service of false gods, which, without the splendour so imparted, would more quickly be seen in their nothingness: *protr.* 46.
[10]Harmless seal-images, alone permissible to Christians, must, according to *paed.* III, 59, 2-60, 2, be selected openly from pagan sellers. On the other hand, the chalices with representations of the good shepherd, of which Tertullian, *pud.* 7, 1; 10, 12 speaks, were perhaps already of Christian manufacture.

III

This is the general background against which we should view the special question as to whether images of Christ were to be allowed and tolerated. It emerges in acute form with Eusebius of Caesarea, who is, in any case, an opponent of images of Christian saints. There was a bronze image of Christ in Paneas, originally probably a statue of Asclepius, and then wrongly taken to be an image of Christ, which referred to the healing of the woman with a haemorrhage. Eusebius could explain it only on the ground that she, according to her pagan custom (ἐθνικῇ συνηθείᾳ), knew no better way of expressing her gratitude. And, on discovering that a certain woman had what were supposed to be images of Peter and Paul, but really, in his opinion, of two unnamed philosophers, he took them from her without more ado. But it was against an image of Christ that he expressed his views in most detail and as a matter of strict principle.

The occasion for this was provided by a desire on the part of no less a person than Constantia, the sister of the Emperor Constantine. She had requested the learned bishop to have a portrait of Christ made for her, and was obliged to receive, instead, a forthright instruction on the impropriety of such a wish. A portrait of Christ in his divine form is ruled out from the beginning, and would, in any case, contradict the express prohibition to portray God which applies throughout the Church. But also the image of his human appearance was, even in the lifetime of Jesus, so irradiated and permeated by the divine splendour that the disciples on the Mount of Transfiguration could not endure his countenance; and so it must be judged quite impossible to reproduce it 'with dead, lifeless colours'. And after the Ascension, which stripped off all the mortal part of his being and transformed the servile form into the splendour of God, it is wholly out of the question to paint a picture of his incomprehensible form—if, indeed, we can still call by the word 'form' (μορφή) a divine and spiritual essence! The only result would be what pagans experienced, who, in attempting to represent God, did not, in fact, achieve the slightest resemblance, but could succeed only in producing human forms.

This early fourth century explanation of the matter is particularly instructive and interesting, since it is quite unaffected by the later controversies about the two natures in Christ. It is a naïve and frank avowal of the same inclination to minimize the human in the person of Jesus, as was evident earlier and more bluntly in the docetism of the gnosis, and appeared later more subtly in the monophysite christology. What was mortal is held to be outshone, transformed, and absorbed by the overpowering force of the heavenly glory. This was the basic tendency of the entire christology of the ancient Church, or, rather, a basic danger with which it had always to fight, and later, in fact, did so in full consciousness. It is the opposite danger to that of the modern conception of Christ; for today it is the humanity of Christ that appears unassailable and self-evident, and only its relation to the divinity difficult to grasp and problematical. Christ was, according to Eusebius (*demonstr. evan.* IV, 10,20), 'born like us, and clothed himself with a mortal man, yet no longer as man, but as God' (τικτόμενος μὲν ἡμῖν ὁμοίως και θνητοῦ δίκην ἀνθρώπου ἀμφιεννύομενος, ὡς δ'οὐκέτι ἄνθρωπος, ἀλλὰ θεός). From this point of view, it is especially his marvellous virgin birth that is significant, and the Resurrection set the seal on the whole preceding course of his deification: 'The man was wholly "absorbed" by the godhead, and God the Word was again God in the way he was before becoming man, and he made the man co-divine with himself' (ὁ πᾶς ἄνθρωπος ὑπὸ τῆς θεότητος "κατεπίνετο", καὶ πάλιν θεὸς ἦν ὁ θεὸς λόγος, οἷος καὶ πρὶν γενέσθαι ἄνθρωπος, καὶ συναπεθέον γε τὸν ἄνθρωπον).

This has absolutely nothing to do with the 'Arianism' of Eusebius. It is simply the application of the line of thought generally prevalent, and attributed even to the strictly Nicene thinker Apollinaris, at the end of the same century. For he could only conceive and make theologically acceptable the union of the divine and human natures in the God-man by admitting a certain truncation of the human nature. This christology, with its affinity to docetism, was conditioned by a strictly spiritualized and transcendental understanding of God and holiness in general, which rejected totally, not only any image of Christ, but all 'material' and sensible intermediaries, and, with them, all sacred images. In this, Eusebius had directly in view the terribly seductive power of pagan idolatry.

IV

It was only after Constantine that ideas developed rapidly. He himself, to all appearances, never went beyond the Old Testament prohibition of depicting God, nor did he allow any other kinds of sacred image or their public veneration. But in raising the Labarum to the status of a Christian symbol, which, as a battle-standard, was honoured even by pagan forms of sacred worship, he, for the first time, opened a breach in the Church's closely-guarded theological defences. This was not without far-reaching consequences.[11]

In addition, there arose the necessity for the official State Church to represent itself in outward form, and its magnificent buildings and their furnishings enlisted the services of art and sumptuous adornment. The old pietistic aversion to pomp and display did not disappear entirely; in fact, it even gained, to some extent, a heightened emphasis from monastic asceticism; but, generally speaking, it could not be maintained unalloyed. Alongside the representation of the cross and other more decorative and genre motives, there soon appeared in the churches pictures of events in the Bible and particularly of the deaths of martyrs; these, far from causing offence, were even welcomed by theologians for the most part.[12] Images also of saints, even living ones (Paulinus along with Martin of Tours), of Christ himself, and the Apostles were not wanting. Only, as before, there was absolutely no question of allowing any representation of God the Father, any more than in ancient times.[13]

[11]On the other hand, Minucius Felix, Oct. 28, 6 declared: *cruces nec colimus nec optamus*, and none of the Fathers before Constantine approved or even mentioned representations of the cross. In spite of the extended, and in part revised, knowledge gained from archaeology, I still think that what Hugo Koch, pp. 45 ff., says on the historical importance of the Constantinian cult of the Labarum is essentially correct.

[12]The first allusions to ecclesiastical images in Basil, Gregory of Nyssa, Asterios, Prudentius, etc. are almost always connected with representations of martyrdom, which, for the most part, may correspond to the special purpose of the buildings. I purposely refrain here from adding to the literary evidence that of archaeology as supplementary or corroborative (Dura, S. Constanza? San Pietro?).

[13]The only possible exception may be certain popular representations, such as the celebrated sarcophagus reliefs of subjects from early history, which perhaps Augustine had in mind in *fid. et symb.* 7. I am not so sure as Adolf Krücke that there was here no

Yet this development was far from proceeding unopposed.[14] The researches of Holl[15] make it quite clear that, at all events, Bishop Epiphanios of Salamis inaugurated a fierce struggle against Christian images, and this was still before the end of the fourth century. Nor till the day of his death did he cease from stirring up the conscience of his colleagues, of the Emperor and—in view of the failure of his efforts— at least of his own community, to make them abide by the strict rule of former times. Neither in the churches nor in Christian cemeteries do images serve any purpose. And Epiphanios, on discovering in a country church of Palestine a curtain on which figures of saints were woven, tore it down with his own hands, and had the material made into burial-cloths for the poor. Anyone who undertakes to depict saints or incorporeal angels, 'to honour their memory', as it is said (εἰς μνημόσυνον καὶ τιμήν), does, in fact, commit an outrage against them. It is absurd and smacks of paganism to try to confine the super-natural life to dead matter, instead of worshipping God in spirit and truth. Epiphanios goes on to appeal with particular emphasis to ecclesiastical tradition, the 'traditions you have received' (παραδόσεις, ἃς παρελάβετε), and not to be abandoned: 'Which of the ancient Fathers would have painted a picture of Christ and put it in the Church or his own house or on the door-curtains? Which of the ancient bishops would have dishonoured Christ by having him painted?'

Once again, particular significance attaches to the christological turn given by Epiphanios. His opponents, indeed, assert 'that Christ was born of the virgin Mary as a perfect man,' and that they 'therefore may represent him as man'. But the incomprehensible divine Logos of God has not become man that we should daub him with

---

question of representing God the Father, though, in general, I find him thoroughly convincing in his essay 'Über einige angebliche Darstellungen Gott-Vaters im frühen Mittelalter', Marburg, Jahrb. f. Kunstwiss. 10 (1937) 5-36.

[14]Cf. for example, Jerome; see Rud. Eiswirth, Hieronymus' Stellung zur Literatur und Kunst (1955) 53 ff.

[15]Karl Holl, 'Die Schriften des Epiphanios gegen die Bilderverehrung', Sitzungsber. d. preuss. Akad. 1916 XXXV=Gesammelte Aufsätze z. Kirchengeschichte 2 (1928) 351-387 (containing the complete text of the fragments cited in the following). The objections adduced by Georg Ostrogorsky, Studien (cf. p. 191 below, n. 48) pp. 61ff., are rightly held unconvincing.

colours on walls. For, according to Epiphanios, he is 'described as man, but not as mere man'. He is 'a mediator between God and man, in that he has become God and man without changing his nature, but rather mediating on each side in relation to both' (*anc.* 44,5*f.*). Divinity and humanity are so closely conjoined, the humanity is so profoundly elevated and immersed in the divine essence that it is impossible now still to apprehend it as simple humanity. 'How will one describe in painting the incomprehensible, inexpressible, unthinkable and un-describable, whom not even Moses could look upon?' There are, therefore, absolutely no real images, but only 'falsely styled images' of Christ (ψευδώνυμοι εἰκόνες).

We can see from this that, in his rejection of images of Christ, Epiphanios no longer argues from Christ's human nature being swallowed up and transformed—which he himself would not now consider orthodox—but solely from the indissoluble unity of the natures in the one person of the mediator; in this way, he achieves the same result in regard to the possibility of an image. Thus his line of thought is the same as that of the later 'Alexandrian' speculation about Christ. And perhaps it is no accident that even Gregory of Nazianzus, who developed, more excellently and forcefully than any theologian of this time, the idea of the unity of the divine-human person of Christ as so wonderfully significant for the redemption, is silent about images of Christ and images in general, although he refers quite un-concernedly to the great painters of classical antiquity.

On the other hand, Basil was already becoming enthusiastic about the paintings of martyrdoms, in which Christ also appeared in semi-symbolic form as presiding over the conflict. 'For what the words of the historical account bring to the hearing is presented by painting and brought silently before the eye'.[16] And with Gregory of Nyssa it becomes quite clear that images of Christ are most readily justifiable by the adoption of a more 'antiochene' dyophysite christology. His theology stresses that the humanity of Christ is by no means fused with the divinity. It is simply God's dwelling (θεοῦ δοχεῖον); the man Jesus is a God-receiving man (θεοδόχος ἄνθρωπος), and possesses the God-receiving flesh, but remains unmixed. It is allowable to con-

---

[16]Eusebius, on the contrary (at the end of the fragment of his letter to Constantia), concludes from the pictorial force of the word of God that any actual painting of Christ is unnecessary and prohibited.

template the physical and the divine attributes, so long as they are always regarded as such. In the light of this we can understand his observation that a representation of Christ presiding over the conflict which he approves, depicts Christ only in his human aspect—the divine remains unattainable by art, and fails to emerge, and absorbs the humanity wholly into itself only after the Ascension.

v

Karl Holl has, on more than one occasion, drawn attention to a fact that is, at first sight, surprising. In the development of image-worship, it was 'only the first, innocuous step', admitting in the Church images of religious subjects, that roused opposition, whereas 'the second, and worse, step, the adoption of the pagan conception and worship of images' was taken unopposed, so that the reaction, resulting in the image controversy centuries later, came too late.[17] However strange this may seem, it is partly explained by the fact that, to men in ancient times and in the south, and to simple men generally, images and their worship, broadly speaking a 'cult' attitude to the image itself, were interconnected far more closely than they are to modern man with his detached, purely aesthetic approach. The first attitude is instinctive and primordial, and prior to any theological standpoint; it is taken as a matter of course in the political and purely human sphere, just as much as in the strictly religious. The image is, quite simply, loved, saluted, adorned, and honoured; one who looks upon the image of someone held in honour thereby 'venerates' it.[18] An instructive example of this in Christianity can be found in the gnostically-inclined 'Acts of John', from the latter part of the second century. A recent convert, Lycomedes, had persuaded a skilful painter to do a portrait of the Apostle, which he hung in his bedroom, crowned, with a miniature altar in front, and lamps upon it. John spoke to him about it, viewing it as a case of worshipping a pagan idol. When, however, the matter was explained to him, he confined himself to pointing out the futility

[17]Karl Holl, 'Der Anteil der Styliten am Aufkommen der Bilderverehrung', Ges. Aufs. 2 (1928) 388. The conclusion, however, needs to be narrowed down; cf. pp. 187-8 below.
[18]Epiphanios attacks, at one and the same time, images and their veneration in the Church.

of the art of portraiture in general, restricted, as it is, to what is external. One's concern should be, rather, to paint the invisible image of the soul with the colours of spiritual virtues. The question of idolatry and worship of the image is thereby solved, and no further attention is paid to it.[19] It seems, therefore, more or less natural that anyone who possesses a picture of a distinguished man pays him respect and worship by the very fact of possession.

A result of the first stage in the Church's adoption and approval of images, on grounds furnished by theologians of the end of the fourth century, was the sharp distinction between the instructive and commemorative qualities of 'mere' images on the one hand and, on the other, of the person therewith depicted.[20] The use of images was justified mainly on the ground of their subject-matter, by which they served as what was called a *Biblia Pauperum*. They were valuable for what they showed and called to mind, and for everyone, especially simple, illiterate people, the 'poor in spirit', they were a useful, almost indispensable means of instruction. This was the standpoint already adopted by Basil and Gregory of Nyssa, and, in the west also, was implied by the action of Paulinus of Nola, who, in the churches he built, made extensive use of representative art, and thereby emphasized its value for the *rusticitas non lassa fide neque docta legendi*. The same idea was first explicitly developed by St. Nilus, a pupil of Chrysostom, who recommended, for church interiors, scenes from the Old and New Testaments as a substitute for the suggested secular subjects, 'so that those unversed in writing, who could not even read the holy scriptures, might, through the contemplation of the picture, recall the excellence of the genuine servant of the true God, and be stimulated to imitate noble and glorious works of virtue'. To Theodoret, this educational function of the image was so obvious that he considered the pagan Cyrus must himself have had it in mind when—prompted, of course, by the devil—he set up pagan idols for people who were unable to read and were strangers to philosophy.

[19]The striking, almost jesting form in which the question of idolatry is treated may be connected with the gnostic character of the work. I cannot agree with Holl, *op. cit.*, p. 392, n. 1, that the point of the story is that what was condemned was depicting an *Apostle*. It concerned, rather, the quite general, gnostic and spiritual idea of the superior and unique value of the soul and the spiritual (similarly Origen, *Cels*. VIII, 18).

[20]The first example is Methodius himself, *autex*. XV, 6.

This idea is familiar to us, above all, in its classical formulation by Gregory the Great. In expressly condemning image-worship, as well as the iconoclasm set in motion by Bishop Serenus of Marseilles, he instructs on the right use of Christian images: *aliud est enim picturam adorare, aliud picturae historia, quid sit adorandum, addiscere.* At the same time, what occasioned the letter shows that resistance to religious images was still not completely broken down at the close of the sixth century. In fact, it later arose repeatedly from the time of Claudius of Turin right up to the Reformation iconoclasts. But in general the west was satisfied with this didactic and pedagogic conception of the Christian image and its function of giving an easy acquaintance with history; and this idea was steadily maintained.[21] According to Thomas Aquinas, images in the Church had the threefold purpose, *ad instructionem rudium*, strengthening the *memoria*, and *ad excitandum devotionis affectum*. The counter-Reformation theologians, in view of Protestant criticism, expressed themselves perhaps with yet greater caution,[22] and even Martin Luther, in his defence against iconoclastic and reformist extremists, endorsed essentially the old idea of the *Biblia Pauperum*.[23] However gross the practice of the cult of relics and of the Sacrament had become in the west,[24] it was only in the ecclesiastical underworld that veneration of images played a clearly defined, 'superstitious' role.[25]

We may well ask to what this general attitude was due. It is not enough to point to the greater 'sobriety' of northern and western man, a quality which we may consider doubtful in view of the conduct of many monks and nuns. A more likely cause might be the ever-increasing importance of the missionary task, with its strong opposition to idolatry and the explanatory method of teaching which it favoured.

[21]G. Ladner, '*Der Bilderstreit und die Kunstlehren der byzantinischen und abendländischen Theologie*', *Zeitschr. f. Kirchengesch.* 50 (1931) 1ff., and 12ff.

[22]They gave up the defence of image-worship based on the connection between prototype and eikon, which Thomas, as a southern Italian, used and approved: Lukas Koch, '*Zur Theologie der Christusikone*', *Bened. Monatschr.* 20 (1938) 172.

[23]H. v. Campenhausen, *Die Bilderfrage in der Reformation* in *Tradition und Leben* (1960) 392f.

[24]The cults of relics and of the Sacrament are interconnected, and easily lead to pictorial representations.

[25]In the east, on the contrary, the relic goes behind the picture, which derives its holiness only from the former: A. Grabar, *Martyrium. Recherches sur le culte des reliques et l'art chrétien antique* II: *Iconographie* (1946) 343ff. ('*Des reliques aux icones*').

But the chief cause was the greater depth characteristic of western devotional life and theology as a whole, with its attachment to the *deus crucifixus*, rather than to the *deus incarnatus*. This is shown in the particular moralistic, juristic, and political conception of the Christian scheme of redemption and, correspondingly, of how salvation is appropriated. Western man seeks salvation from the salvific act— whether of God, or of man encountering God, or acting for him. In the Church too he holds fast to the word of God—either active itself or interpreted—which of its nature cannot be understood as an 'image' nor can be replaced by one. In this way an essential quality of the early Christian, historical conception of salvation remained actually in full vigour throughout all modifications and distortions.

VI

On the other hand, the theology of the Greek upholders of images showed, from the outset, a characteristic preference for visual and aesthetic ideas and concepts, as opposed to aural and historical ones. Here we see the working out of a genuine Greek heritage, transmitted by Plato and the neo-Platonists and determining the thought of all the Greek Fathers. Already it coloured the earlier utterances on the lines of the *Biblia Pauperum*, and was fully established by the defenders of images in the eighth and ninth centuries.[26] According to them, the artists who paint 'from the life' and 'with words' (ζωγράφος and λογογράφος) belong together in the Church; they were complementary, just as in certain codices the text and illustrations are placed opposite each other. They both have the same significance, 'to announce one and the same good tidings' (ὅτι ἀμφότεροι μίαν ἐξήγησιν εὐαγγελίζονται) (Ps. John Damascene). Accordingly, early Christian narrators, such as Luke, Nicodemus, and others, were willingly accepted as being also painters of pictures or originators of them;[27] and, conversely, one who was no longer allowed to preach

---

[26]For what follows the evidence is to be found in Lukas Koch, *op. cit.*, especially *Bened. Monatschrift* 19 (1937) 381ff.

[27]Ernst von Dobschütz, *Christusbilder. Untersuchungen zur christlichen Legende* (1899) 28. I am indebted to Fredirich Matz for the suggestion that the story of Socrates being a sculptor might be a parallel from antiquity.

and teach might not paint either: the Council of Constantinople of 869 forbade excommunicated persons to paint ikons, as well as forbidding them to teach.

In reality, word and picture did not merely stand on the same footing; the picture was given clear preference over the word. It strikes more deeply and has a stronger hold, it comprises everything in a far briefer time and excludes all misunderstanding; it means precisely 'autopsy', in which there is no question of deception. Images in the Church are quite indispensable. The sense of history is the first human sense and so must, before all the others, be sanctified by looking on the image of Christ. On this account, the word already has no pre-eminence over the image, since words themselves are but images, abstractions from things seen. Consequently, Holy Scripture can also be designated an image.[28] 'All is an image, and the image is all.'[29] The image also corresponds in a special way to our whole earthly nature: 'For since we consist of flesh and blood, we are impelled to confirm by sight what we are wholly convinced of in the soul' (Germanus of Constantinople).

Nor is Greek theology confined to these general considerations. It enters also on a particular justification of the sacred image from the ancient tradition of Greek philosophy, and in this way becomes the inheritor of the pro-image outcome of an older philosophical 'image-controversy'. This had passed through many stages since the rational criticism of Xenophanes, and ended finally with the complete vindication, at the hands of Iamblichos and Julian, of the sacred images of the gods.[30] Thus it was that the growing dominance of barbarian and oriental trends from the third century, the mounting hostility to the Christians, the need of political reserve on the part of philosophers, and the strengthening of its 'world-view' on the part of the Empire, all

---

[28] A typical example often cited is the liturgical veneration of the book of the Gospels. Even merely looking on the sacred books, αὐτὴ καθ' ἑαυτὴν τῶν βιβλίων ἡ ὄψις, makes one, according to a statement attributed to Epiphanios (*apopht.* 8), slower to sin, and is an incentive to righteousness.

[29] Harnack, *Lehrbuch der Dogmengeschichte* 2 (1914) 484.

[30] On this, see Johannes Geffcken, *Der Bilderstreit des heidnischen Altertums* ARW 19 (1916-19) p. 35, n. 1; also *Der Ausgang des griechisch-römischen Heidentums*, 1920; Charly Clerc, *Les théories relatives au culte des images chez les auteurs grecs du 2ème siècle après J-C.*, 1915; Pierre de Labriolle, *La réaction païenne. Étude sur la polémique antichrétienne du 1er au 6e siècle*, 1934. Mainly philological is P. Aubin, 'L'image dans l'oeuvre de Plotin', *Rech. sc. rel.* 41 (1953) 348ff.

united, strangely enough, in fostering the inner development of late Platonic philosophy. And now the theory also met the theological tendencies and practical needs of the victorious Church.

It was a question of applying the allegorical principle of interpretation to the world as a whole. It is a mysterious world, a reflection down below of what is above, and then returning upwards from below. The God beyond the world is encompassed by spiritual archetypes which bring forth sensible images, and these in turn witness, for the receptive sense, to the beauty of the spiritual archetype, and so point out the way to those able to see aright. According to this general pattern, it was possible to assess the sensible images by the archetype of spiritual truth and beauty, and so to judge them deficient or wholly to reject them, as, for example, Clement and Origen did within the Church. At the same time, however, or soon afterwards, the late pagan philosophy decided in favour of images and their more or less extensive cult, mixing together symbolic and aesthetic interpretations with arguments referring to popular instruction and others of a historical romanticizing and magico-fantastical flavour. Already Celsus, on these lines, rebutted the Christian objections in a tone of lofty condescension. And, according to Porphyry, those who tax the pagans with religious materialism and idolatry have failed to grasp the profound, spiritual meaning of their religion. But, while the earlier Fathers like Origen, Lactantius, and others, rejected such explanations with disdain, a fundamental change was in preparation from about the turn of the fifth century. The Church adopted the line of thought previously opposed in regard to 'images', just as she had already previously adopted it in justification of her cult and sacraments.[31] And now she proceeded to honour the transcendental (as symbolized) in the material, even if, of course, only by way of analogy ($\sigma\chi\eta\mu\acute{a}\tau\omega\nu$ $\mathring{a}\nu\alpha\lambda o\gamma o\acute{v}\nu\tau\omega\nu$), as stated by John Damascene.

In precisely the same way as in paganism, for example in Porphyry, there arose a conflict between the more psychological and artistic theory of the image and a materialistic and magical conception. The former prevailed in the highly developed theology, which held fast to the Greek traditions. It looked for the connection with the archetype in emphasizing the meaning of the representation and of the form made present, which the image brings home to the consciousness of

[31]The Pseudo-Areopagite did not yet envisage the question of image-worship.

the beholder. Here, to use the words of Thomas Aquinas, the image is honoured not *in quantum est res quaedam*, but only *in quantum est imago*. But the more faith deteriorated spiritually and morally, the more primitive, magical, and material became the understanding of the sacred image presented to the eye of man.

We will not rehearse here the historical development of image-worship. It went on unceasingly, and, clearly enough, it cannot be really opposed on the basis of the line of thought stemming from the neo-Platonic tradition. The Stylites and the monks generally were the most zealous protagonists of the cult of images, sometimes in the crudest forms.[32] In the time of Justinian, an important role began to be attached to images coming down from heaven, or originating in some other miraculous way; they were the so-called 'not made with hands' (ἀχειροποίητοι), the successors of the ancient pagan images 'fallen from heaven' (διπετῆ). It seemed that the grossest materialism was to predominate in the matter of images. What is interesting however, is to see how the idea of authenticity, in the sense of the historical genuineness of the image form, and of the fidelity of the representation, came, with time, to supplant belief in the holiness of the individual miraculous object, and finally remained the sole essential factor. In the iconoclastic controversy, images of miraculous origin played no particular part. There grew up, however, a strict tradition, to which each particular type of image had to conform—a 'succession', in fact, of images and their copies, just like the succession of bishops.[33]

Popular devotion to images admitted all kinds of superstition. It was said that they irradiated a supernatural splendour, that oil poured out from painted jars, that they bled if anyone disfigured them, that they gave credit, or at least, guarantees to impecunious Christians[34] —they were even petitioned to be sponsors[35]—and more after the

---

[32]*Cf.* Holl (p. 181 above, n. 17) pp. 388-398.

[33]Dobschütz, *op. cit.* pp. 268*ff.*

[34]There are some charming stories in Erich Caspar, '*Papst Gregor II und der Bilderstreit*', ZKG 52 (1933) 51*f.*

[35]Theodorus Studita, *ep.* I, 17, who relates an instance of this, admittedly goes on to say that it was really the saint represented 'who *by means of* his ikon lifted the child from the baptismal font', and Lukas Koch, *Ben. Monatschr.* 20 (1938) 174, considers it necessary to adduce this explanation 'against the scepticism and criticism of our day', as in Schwarzlose (*cf.* n. 38 below). He would, however, have made little impression on Lactantius, as we can see from *div. inst.* II, 2, 1*ff.*

same fashion.[36] Superstition even went to the length of scraping the paint of ikons into the Communion wine, or, alternatively, mixing pulverized relics with the colours used for painting so as to enhance the material holiness of the image itself.[37] All these abuses were bound to lead to a reaction; but, even so, that is not sufficient to account for the whole problem of iconoclasm.

VII

The great dispute over images,[38] which raged for a century and a half, did not break out suddenly. It was long fomenting in the east. Image-worship was not uniformly widespread in the different provinces and classes, which was why the question of images was never completely at rest, even in the preceding centuries.[39] Nor was it an isolated question, but formed part of the great east-west conflict. We should not, therefore, in approaching the problem, think first of Islam, whose hostility to images might, in fact, have been due to the theology of the iconoclasts.[40] More important was the influence of the Jews, who were particularly widespread in the Asiatic provinces, and whom the inaugurator of the image-controversy, Leo III, offended with compulsory baptism. Equally important was the regard paid to various

[36]Further evidence in Kollwitz, *op. cit.* pp. 9*ff.*, 16*f.*

[37]This last information, referring to a later period, I owe to a letter written me by Georg Ostrogorsky, who refers also to the Moscow review *Voprosy Restavracii* (1926); *cf.* also R. v. Walter in '*Der christlichen Osten*', *Geist und Gestalt* (1939) 114.

[38]For what follows, see especially Georg Ostrogorsky, *Geschichte des byzantinischen Staates*, 1940. There is also much material in the old, in many ways superseded, account of Karl Schwarzlose, *Der Bilderstreit—der Kampf der griechischen Kirche um ihre Eigenart und Freiheit*, 1890, and in Leclercq, art. '*Images (culte et querelle des)*', *Dict. d'archéol., chrét. et de liturgie* VII, 1 (1926) 180*ff.* I was unable to obtain E. J. Martin, *A History of Iconoclastic Controversy*, London 1930, or G. B. Ladner, 'Origin and significance of the Byzantine iconoclastic controversy', *Medieval Studies* 2 (1940) 127-149.

[39]On this, see Sirarpie the Nersessian, '*Une apologie des images du septième siècle*', *Byzantion* 17 (1944-45) 58-87, and especially N. H. Baynes, *The Icons before Iconoclasm*, *loc. cit.*, pp. 226-239.

[40]C. H. Becker, '*Christliche Polemik und islamische Dogmenbildung* in: *Islamstudien* 1 (1924) 432-449. It is true that the first edict against Christian images was issued by the Egyptian caliph Jazid II in 723; but even John Damascene directed his polemic only against iconoclasts and Jews, not against Mohammedans.

eastern sects, such as the Marcionites and Paulicians;[41] the Nestorian and Monophysite secondary Churches also rejected sacred images.

Furthermore, the image-controversy was only one factor in a comprehensive *kulturkampf*; the *iconomachia* was, from the beginning, part of a political *monomachia*,[42] or, at least, it very quickly became such. The excessive influence of the monks, the power exercised by monastic feudalism and the Church generally in public life, had to be broken in the interests of the government of the State. The struggle allied itself with the hostile instincts of a primitive, military 'enlightenment' —the army was, to the very end, the strongest support of the iconoclastic movement. Even the rulers were, for the most part, filled with purely religious zeal, not only against the use of images, but also against the exaggerated worship of Mary, prayer to the saints, and the 'civil' piety of the monks and ecclesiastics generally. Constantine V, 'Copronymus', must, like Justinian, have composed no fewer than thirteen works of theological controversy, of which a few fragments are extant.

Nonetheless, it would be perverse to attribute this convinced hostility to images to a higher degree of spirituality and culture. The opposite was the case. The classical Greek tradition was everywhere opposed to the iconoclasts. One of the first results of the anti-image edict of 730 was the closing of the School of Constantinople (οἰκουμενικὸν διδασκαλεῖον) by Leo III. The enemies of images were held by their opponents to be not only satanical heretics, but also cultural barbarians. Even a Westerner like Pope Gregory II[43] wrote to that effect to the Emperor, in a letter, which is now generally again held to be authentic: 'Go anywhere where a school is held, and say: I am the destroyer and persecutor of images. They will at once beat you over the head with their slates, and what you have not learned from the wise, little children, unable yet to reason, will teach you'. This was the epoch when the political leaders of the Byzantine Empire became rigidly fixed mainly in the east, and the greater part of Italy

[41]The Paulicians, in their rejection of images, may have been influenced by the Marcionites: F. Scheidweiker, *'Paulikianerprobleme'*, *Byz. Zeitschr.* 44 (1951) 371.
[42]A. A. Vasiliev, *History of the Byzantine Empire*, 1928, p. 317.
[43]Who, however, had particular reliance on Byzantine ideas in general: Georg Ostrogorsky, *'Rom und Byzanz im Kampf um die Bilderverehrung'*, *Semin. Kondakov.* 6 (1933) 83f.

was lost to them. The European, highly refined provinces, especially those of the Balkans, resisted their cultural policies strongly to the end.[44]

It was, however, precisely as a dispute over images that the great struggle of the time directly revealed its political significance and character.[45] The ancient religious worship of the imperial image had become, especially since the Diocletian reform, a fixed element of the political ceremonial, and had been taken over—with occasional theological reinterpretations—in this meaning even, without opposition, by the Christian Church. It was most firmly established in the religious practices of the military camps with their banners, but in civil life also, in the law courts, the theatre, etc., the imperial image appeared in accordance with the official rules, and received all the honours due to the Emperor in person. 'The image *is* the emperor'; the two things were, according to Athanasius even, 'one and the same,' (ἔντι). Every revolt immediately manifested itself in the treatment meted out to the public images, which were torn from the standards and thrown down from their pedestals. One of the regular official acts of a new ruler was the sending out of his image to all provinces and cities, where it was solemnly received in a great procession with candles, incense, etc., and then set up (sometimes even in churches). Accordingly, the comparison of the image of Christ with that of the Emperor was one of the most convincing and frequent arguments in favour of images, when it was a matter of reinforcing the idea that the honour paid to the image directly flowed to, and was attributed to, the prototype, otherwise invisible, namely the person himself.[46]

Thus the war of the iconoclastic emperors against the sacred images

[44]An Armenian monk of the early seventh century, Vrt'ames K'ert'ogh, himself a defender of images, saw in ecclesiastical images a Grecian import: '*Car jusqu'à présent personne chez les Arméniens ne savait faire des images, mais on les apportait de chez les Grecs, et notre culture venait aussi de chez eux, et ils n'étaient pas perdus*'; thus the translation by von der Nersessian, *loc. cit.* 67; also p. 75.

[45]For what follows see Helmut Kruse, *Studien zur offiziellen Geltung des Kaiserbildes im römischen Reiche*, 1934; André Grabar. 'L'empereur dans l'art byzantin'. *Recherches sur l'art officiel de l'empire d'orient*, 1936; Lukas Koch, '*Christusbild-Kaiserbild. Zugleich ein Beitrag zur Lösung der Frage nach dem Anteil der byzantinischen Kaiser am griechischen Bilderstreit*', *Bened. Monatschr.* 21 (1939) 85-105; Kenneth M. Setton, *Christian Attitude towards the Emperor in the Fourth Century* (New York 1941) 196-211 ('Imperial images').

[46]*Cf.* p. 173 above, n. 7.

of the Church was particularly embittered by the fact that, far from giving up the veneration of their own public images, they insisted on it more than ever; and, furthermore, they tried to revive the old, largely obsolete, iconography of a politically representative character. And its sacred, quasi-religious significance was brought out all the more clearly in that the emperors did not confine their authority to the 'secular', political sphere, but brazenly flaunted the old 'Byzantine' pretension to be both 'emperor and priest'. Thus, the removal of the images of Christ was a twofold challenge, appearing, as it did, to the convinced image-worshippers as a deliberate, demonic substitution of godless princes of this world for Christ the king. Under Justinian II, there had been minted coins showing, on one side Christ enthroned, and on the other the Emperor standing; but now there appeared coins on which the Emperor was enthroned and from which Christ had disappeared completely. It was quite understandable that Stephen, martyred in the cause of images, threw the coin on the ground and stamped on the Emperor's image, in order to demonstrate in the most dramatic way *per analogiam* the connection between Christ's image and person which was denied by his adversaries. It was, therefore, a question of a 'Church struggle' in the fullest sense. Not only the spiritual, but also the intellectual superiority lay with the opposition to the Emperor, and this was not the least of the reasons why the policy of the government against images was bound, in the end, to collapse.[47]

Nonetheless, the theological position of the iconoclasts is not without interest.[48] The attack was conducted on a broad front, and the old appeal to the Mosaic command, charges of idolatry and superstition were, naturally, not neglected. What was new was the prominence given to the christological aspect of the problem. After three and a half centuries of theological dispute over this question, it became almost self-evident that every 'false doctrine' must be judged primarily from this standpoint, and the central importance of christological consequences and presuppositions was clearly evident to all. Now the iconoclastic polemic against images of Christ followed the line already taken

[47]*Cf.* on the later effects of the image-disputes from 843 onward Dvornik, *Le schisme de Photius* (1948), and F. X. Seppelt, '*Das Schisma des Photius in neuer Sicht*', *Theol. Rev.* 48 (1952) 82f.
[48]For what follows, see Georg Ostrogorsky, *Studien zur Geschichte des byzantinischen Bilderstreites*, 1929.

by Epiphanios; that is to say, the idea of unity, 'the profundity of the dogma of the union of the two natures of Christ' (τὸ βάθος τοῦ δόγματος τῆς ἐνώσεως τῶν δύο φύσεων τοῦ Χριστοῦ) is so strongly emphasized as to seem to prohibit any representation of the man Jesus. Consequently, the anti-image theology had a certain 'monophysite' tendency, a suspicion reinforced by the fact that Constantine V, in his contribution to the dispute, repeated the Chalcedonian formula in a not quite correct, 'monophysiting' fashion; for him the unity of the person of the God-man was not a unity 'in two natures', but 'out of two natures'. Thereby the human nature seemed not to continue essentially in being, but to be merged in a higher unity and so to cease.[49] Yet I do not believe it permissible to lay such stress on this and similar slips as to impute to Constantine, and those who thought like him, a clear awareness of their doctrinal deviations. At all events, the great iconoclastic Council of 754 was absolutely correct in its formulations, and showed itself concerned rather, by somewhat subtle means, to impute to the pro-image party an infringement of christological orthodoxy. The two natures, it said, are neither to be separated in Christ nor commingled. Whoever aims at completely describing in an image the God-man becomes thereby a Monophysite and, in addition, offends against the Mosaic prohibition of images. Whosoever takes the human person by itself and paints only the humanity is a Nestorian, and, in addition, enlarges the Trinity through the monstrosity of a fourth hypostasis. Of interest also is the thesis that the Last Supper is the sole permissible 'image' of Christ; for this alone is 'identical in essence' (ὁμοούσιος) to its prototype, which the actual images can never be. If the theory here does not originate solely from the one-sided demands of controversy, we have in it an example of a thoroughly unclassical, magico-physical conception of the sacred image, such as would well accord with the place of iconoclasm in the general history of ideas. This kind of oriental 'enlightenment' is closely akin to spiritualism and magic.

---

[49]How uncertain is this conclusion is clear from the account of Jos. Lebons, *La christologie du monophysitisme Syrien*, pp. 510ff., in A. Grillmeier–H. Bacht, *Das Konzil von Chalkedon* I (1951) 425ff.

VIII

On the pro-image theology which proved victorious we are much better informed.[50] Apart from the acts of the Nicaean Council of 787, our main source for it is John Damascene and Theodore of Studios who go into it thoroughly; their material and reasonings were worked on further by lesser theologians, such as the patriarch Nicephorus. All of these upheld the validity of the use and veneration of images as corresponding to an age-old norm of the Church, a part of the 'unwritten tradition' of the Apostles. The proof of this, laborious enough, was conducted with an astonishing expenditure of industry and ingenuity, the references to the Fathers being no less copious than those of the opponents. In John Damascene alone are to be found one hundred and nineteen citations, many of them, however, unauthentic.

The Christian faith and faith in Christ in the strict sense make images, especially images of Christ, imperative, an unavoidable necessity from the standpoint of dogma and for whole-hearted belief in the incarnate Lord. 'I saw the human form of God', said John Damascene, 'and my soul was saved'. 'Those who say he may not be "described", that is, not acknowledged as Christ, thereby take him as without the flesh', in other words, are Docetists and Monophysites in disguise. Their assertion that it were sin, 'for us to long to see his countenance', denies the mystery of the incarnation, the fleshly dispensation (ἔνσαρκος οἰκονομία) of our redemption. It is on these ideas that now is concentrated the whole energy of the dogmatic proofs; nor can one say, in view of the above exposition, that it was only a matter of theological subtlety for the purpose of justifying their own standpoint at all costs. The fact is that the latter seemed to the Greek theologians absolutely essential, so that they had no compunction about adding an interpolation in its support to the letter of the pro-image Pope Adrian

[50]For what follows, see Ostrogorsky, *Studien* (p. 191 above, n. 48); Lukas Koch, 'Zur Theologie der Christus-Ikone', *Bened. Monatschr.* 19 (1937) 375-387; 20 (1938) 32-47; 168-175; 281-288; 437-452; Hieronymus Menges, *Die Bilderlehre des hl. Johannes von Damaskus* (1938), only available to me in the form of the (somewhat altered) *Münster theol. diss. of* 1937; A. J. Visser, *Nikaphoros und der Bilderstreit* (Hague 1952).

I, sent to be read at the Ecumenical Council of 787. They were not content with his merely agreeing to the use of images, as Gregory the Great had done before him. Certainly, the idea of a connection of the problem of images with christological doctrine had never established itself in the west, where it always seemed strange and unaccountable; in the east, on the contrary, it was held to be the central point of the whole discussion. Here the preoccupation was to establish images as the indispensable means by which we are 'borne aloft to faith and remembrance of the salvific work in the flesh of our Lord Jesus Christ'.[51]

This idea, then, rests on a broad theological and philosophical foundation. The principal characteristic ($\pi\rho\hat{\omega}\tau o\nu$ $\dot{\iota}\delta\dot{\iota}\omega\mu\alpha$) of man is that he can be represented by an image. In every pattern, the 'prototype', the copy is contained virtually ($\delta\upsilon\nu\dot{\alpha}\mu\epsilon\iota$); it lies hid there, just as the body always has its shadow with it, even when there is no light for it to be actually thrown. It thus pertains to the value of the prototype that this happens, that it gives rise to images *in concreto*, just as the seal becomes wholly such only when something is sealed with it. What this means as regards the humanity of Christ is that only by its appearance in the image is its full truth brought out. 'What is wholly real must become an image; only by becoming an image does it bear testimony to its reality'.[52] God was himself the first image-maker by generating Christ as his image and then creating men after this, his true image. For us, however, it is indispensable to have images of Christ, and it is not enough to represent him merely intellectually, as the enemies of images would have us do. Of our very nature, in fact, we can never dissociate ourselves from the earthly element, nor can we ascend to spiritual things independently of those of the body. One day we will be able to contemplate our Lord with our own eyes ($\alpha\dot{\upsilon}\tau o\pi\tau\iota\kappa\hat{\omega}s$), freed from all material attributes; but so long as we live, we pray to him not only in the spirit ($\nu o\epsilon\rho\hat{\omega}s$), but also in figure and 'in the image' ($\dot{o}\mu o\iota\omega\mu\alpha\tau\iota\kappa\hat{\omega}s$). Hatred of images, therefore, is, as the second Nicene Council declares, the worst of all heresies, since, whatever is said to the contrary, it denies our redemption.

These explanations were completed by a corresponding theory,

[51]This is the Byzantine insertion in the epistle of St. John; cf. Ostrogorsky, *Rom und Byzanz im Kampf um die Bilderverehrung*, pp. 73-87.
[52]Thus, in a different context, Hubert Schrade, *op. cit.* p. 23.

carefully elaborated, elucidating the nature of an image. The assertion that image and prototype must of their nature be equal is false. It is valid, certainly, of the 'natural image', the εἰκὼν φυσική, which a living man and above all the God-man are in themselves and embody: Christ was, in fact, of one nature with the Father in his divinity and with his mother in his humanity, and only distinct in the hypostasis. But the reverse is the case with the 'art-image' (εἰκὼν τεχνητή), the image in the narrower sense. An image is, in its substance, different from the one it represents, and only in the person, that is, in its meaning and content, is it hypostatically equal. The image is, as compared with the prototype, something other, but not another. Between the two there is a 'homonymy'. The Emperor's image can be directly designated as 'the Emperor', and thus the image of Christ, in that which as image it represents, is Christ himself. Therefore the death suffered in defence of Christ's image is also a martyrdom, a true martyrdom for Christ.

This means that Christ is made present through the ikon, not merely in his humanity, but wholly in his divine and human power. The cautious limitation prescribed on this point by Gregory of Nyssa is now observed only in a formal, logical sense; the religious significance of the image is concerned with the whole Christ. The basis of this conception is provided now by the principle of the enhypostasis, and the *communicatio idiomatum* that follows from it—and therefore the idea itself of unity which the iconoclasts had adduced *against* the possibility of a representation of Christ, on the ground that the divinity is 'indescribable'. Certainly, said Theodore of Studios, it is so; but yet the Logos himself appeared in human form, 'although he is not in that described nor represented as in an image, since in his nature he is invisible and wholly incomprehensible. But since in his person he is one and indivisible, he is therefore at the same time (with his human nature) brought to our consciousness'. If we observe the artistic form of the Byzantine ikons of Christ, we can see how serious was this conviction.[53] They convey the 'struggle for the vision of the unseeable, without betraying its transcendence of the visible'.[54]

[53]The details furnished by A. Grillmeier, *Der Logos am Kreuz* (1956), are certainly instructive, however doubtful be his special interpretation of the 'christological symbolism of the ancient representation of the crucifixion'.
[54]Thus Hans v. Soden, '*Vom Wesen christlicher Kunst*' in: '*Urchristentum und Geschichte*',

It is now absolutely understandable and justifiable that the image should, according to the belief of the theologians, not only be accorded the same honour as befits the 'prototype', but also work the same effects as the latter produced. In the presence of the sacred images devils departed; light shone round about them, they healed the sick, and worked other miracles; people prayed before the image and to him whom it represented and made present, not indeed in his essence (κατ' οὐσίαν), but with his divine grace and power (χάριτι καὶ ἐνεργείᾳ). The city of Camulia, where a miraculous image of Christ made its appearance, was called 'Bethlehem'. John Damascene entirely accepts the edifying fable he relates, that the wax image of an escaped slave, on being placed before the image of a saint compelled the slave to return to his master, and to give back the stolen money. All this is not to be considered magic or superstition, but follows from the nature of images and their religious meaning. If anyone still doubted their power, he would be reminded of the long-established cult of relics and the similar effects attributed to them. The new custom under attack was fortified by the older, no longer dubious one.

It is well known that the Greek Church, as a defence against the allegation of idolatry in regard to images, introduced a distinction in the idea of worship. Worship in the full sense (προσκύνησις λατρευτική) is, as always, reserved to God alone, while the worship performed to images is 'relative', and only in view of the prototype; furthermore, it is attenuated, mere 'honour', rather than worship (προσκύνησις σχετική or τιμητική). One may well doubt whether, according to the whole tenor of the theology of images, this second limitation has any real application to Christ and images of him, and even in John Damascene it is far from being clearly formulated.[55] In view of the accepted 'hypostatic' homonymy between prototype and image, it is hard to see why a relative worship, one directed to the prototype, should not also be accorded, without restriction, to the image. Admittedly, this would imply complete agreement with the corresponding pagan theories in Porphyry and others, and that had to

---

Ges. Aufs. u. Vorträge I (1951) 105 on the 'symbolic ideality' of Christian art in general.

[55]P. Matzerath in discussing the book of Menges (p. 193 above, n. 50), ThRv. 38 1939) 22.

be avoided. In addition, in framing the theory, it was necessary to bear in mind its application to other sacred images: it had to establish a contrast not only between the image and the prototype, but also between the saints in general and the divine person of Jesus Christ. On the whole, therefore, this theory is to be deemed a compromise of a sort, framed to meet not only the actual objections of the iconoclasts, but also the misgivings and 'misconceptions' of the west.

A further concession was the definite renunciation of the use of the plastic arts for images in liturgical use. This had been long preparing,[56] and was in agreement with the general trend of the time towards painting. Any confusion of image and reality, into which men had been misled by the statues of pagan idolatry, seemed to be ruled out from the beginning by the two-dimensional nature of the painted image (and totally so, in the case of mosaic, with its mysterious effect of a lighted painting detaching itself from the wall behind). No longer had the image any substantial reality, being, as the theory required, only a 'symbol', pointing back to the prototype. In addition, the fidelity with which the types of Christ and the saints, as stamped once and for all and believed to be historical, were steadily adhered to was reinforced by the dogmatic controversy, and finally erected into a principle. Nor was any attempt ever made in the Greek Orthodox Church to represent God the Father. The west, on the other hand, very soon ignored the prohibition of the use of statues in public worship, and, from the late Middle Ages, did not hesitate to depict the Father himself. But, as we have seen, here there was never any real iconoclastic crisis. The full development and prosecution of the theology of images, in countering objections on the score of doctrine, was confined to the Greek Church. It was there, consequently, that the results of the developments in the ancient Church and the early Byzantine period were permanently established.

---

[56]Epiphanios, *ancor.* 107, 2; *haer.* 3, 4*f.*, had already declared the veneration of icons to be the more innocuous form of idolatry, preceding the veneration of statues, which was worse. A more just conception of the course of historical development is that of Clement of Alexandria, *protr.* 46. Even the polemic of Eusebius seems primarily directed against pictures (and mosaics): Hugo Koch, *op. cit.*, p. 64, n. 1. The first express prohibition of plastic representations is found in a fragment of Julian of Atramution (6th cent.), contained in Frz. Diekamp, *Analecta patristica* (Rome 1938) 127*ff.*

IX

In the history of ideas, the victory of those who defended images may be considered a victory of Greek thought over the amorphous quality of Eastern thought. With this resolution of the iconoclastic crisis, Byzantium squarely placed itself once and for all on the side of Europe. It is more difficult to pass a theological judgement on the decision reached. The friends of images hailed it as the triumph of Christianity over Judaism. Through Christ and the miracle of the Incarnation, human nature has been transformed. The union of the divine and human nature is not to be confined to his person, but extends to the whole of mankind redeemed by him.[57] Even corporeal matter, the ὕλη itself, has since then changed, and, 'by the analogy of faith ' (κατ' ἀναλογίαν τῆς πίστεως), as John Damascene says, is to be honoured by us. In Judaism, no man's memory could be celebrated, and the dead were held unclean. 'Now however that the Godhead has united itself with our nature (συνανεκράθη), this nature of ours is glorified (ἐδοξάσθη) and changed so as to be incorruptible (πρὸς ἀφθαρσίαν μετεστοιχειώθη) through this channel of life and salvation'. This idea also, as every reader of The Brothers Karamazov knows, did not remain in the confines of 'theology'; for Christians of genuine holiness it was a reality of experience and belief accepted in full.

If we consider the actual development of devotion to images, and its 'decadence' in popular piety, we are bound to ask whether the victory of the Church over 'Judaism' was not bought, to a great extent, at the price of a victory of paganism over the genuine Christian heritage. It was not only that Greek theology actually took over completely the pagan philosophical justification of images and their worship; it also remained, to an astonishing degree, heedless and unguarded in respect of the temptations to paganism that were bound to arise. What was the reason for this? The orthodox theology of glorification cannot be

---

[57]This is the principle on which rests the christological justification of the cult of saints and their images; for the former, cf. Origen, Cels. VII, 65f., and for the latter (in a contrary sense) Epiphanios, frag. 6. In Epiphanios we can see how, along with the worship of saints, the old problem of the cult of the angels still played a part. Frag. 4, 7, 9, 11.

reproached as neglecting Christ in its preoccupation with the numerous saints—the doctrine of the Incarnation was firmly held as the central point of faith. It is equally clear that this theology did not become, in its way of thinking, simply 'secularized' and mundane: the expectation of the final, 'eschatological' transformation and vision remained the soul of all eastern theology, and—except in the west—a theological virtue, hope, which was never underrated. The weakness, however, of the Greeks—a theological weakness with well-nigh fatal repercussions in the question of images—was their defective knowledge of what was meant by 'word' in early Christianity and biblical thought in general. They put both the word and the Bible on the same footing with the 'image', and understood them after the manner of an image. This prevented them from grasping the special character of the early Christian message of salvation, and of the obedience in faith which was spoken of in the Gospel. Faith itself, along with the word, lost its pre-eminence; hearing became a sublime form of vision, and encounter with the word of God became encounter with the divine image. And then, as we have seen, this divine image was not taken merely as representational; it became itself a real 'manifestation' of the prototype, and was publicly venerated as such. Furthermore, even the greatest, the sacramental, mystery of divine worship was indicated by concealing and obscuring the altar with curtain and iconostasis, and was thereby conveyed optically, whereas the west, with the solemn 'elevation', visible to all, expressed the mystery 'acoustically' through the strange language and silent prayer.[58]

But, whatever opinion we may have about these differences, there is no doubt that on one point the image-theology of the ancient Church saw correctly, and brought the development of so many centuries to a lasting conclusion. For it showed that the question of the divine image and of images generally in the Christian Church must be answered in terms of christology, for in no other way can a real answer be found. If, indeed, it is true that God became man in order to be 'humanly' near to us, then it is obviously no longer blasphemous to contemplate him in the image of this one man, to know him, in fact, familiarly in a new way in his humanity. Christianity, seen in this light, is the only religion that need not concern itself about its anthropomorphism, and

[58]Gerhard Kunze, Lehre—Gottesdienst—Kirchenbau in ihren gegenseitigen Beziehungen ᵀ (1949) 97.

which, 'in giving to God a human countenance, lays the foundation for an anthropology which, in the figure of Christ, provides for man a true way of access to God himself.'[59] But the religious freedom thus imparted is not restricted to the sphere of art and painting. These are but the outstanding examples of what we are here concerned with generally. It is always the case that any approach to the reality of God must be by way of the imagination,[60] and in all theological thought and speech there is, therefore, present an anthropomorphic, and to that extent a blasphemous, element that no injunction about images or command to keep silent can eliminate. Only the Christian idea of revelation can take us beyond this, further, in fact, than Judaism. It is, therefore, to be deemed wholly reasonable that Christianity should have cancelled the Jewish prohibition of images, although it maintained uncompromisingly the Old Testament idea of God as above the world, 'transcendent'. However, the consequences which could result from this new approach to the things of God as regards not only the divine and other sacred images, but also the problems of knowledge, art, and beauty in general, were hardly perceived by the ancient Church, nor need we enter upon them further in the present survey.

[59]Gerardus van der Leeuw, *Der Anthropomorphismus als Problem der Anthropologie in: Gottesbild und Menschenbild* (1948) 18; *cf.* the same author's *Der Mensch und der Religion. Ein anthropologischer Versuch* (1941) 119*ff.*, and the Dutch collection of essays I was unable to see, *Wegen en Grenzen*. For a critical view, H. van Oyen, 'Zur Frage der christlichen Kunst,' *ThZ*7 (1951) 423-445.

[60]Erich Frank, *Philosophical Understanding and Religious Truth* (1945), ch. 4.

9
Augustine and the Fall of Rome

(An inaugural lecture)

IN ACCORDANCE with an old academic custom, I propose today to speak on a special subject in my field of study, and, like all engaged in research who are not content with being merely specialists, the Church historian welcomes such an opportunity. In fact, Church history itself is not a specialist science; for its object, the Church, by reason of what it has to say to the world, is intimately bound up with world history of all epochs, being related to all that takes place on the human and spiritual levels, and, of its very nature, affected and swayed by the questions arising. Church history is not about a corner of human life; it is the history of all mankind in its encounter and confrontation with God's word. At the same time, in this continuous reference to its original, distinct, ever freshly apprehended task lies its special character; this holds it together as a living whole in all the diversity of its periods and phenomena. If, in Ranke's celebrated words, every epoch of world history stands in a direct relation to God, Church history, in a still more decided and comprehensible sense, is, in all its epochs, directly related to Christ, since all Churches see their sole legitimate meaning and purpose to be that of witnessing to him and making him present. For this reason, and because this is the origin and centre of its existence, even the most remote epochs of Church history again and again suddenly converge and enter on a dialogue with our own present time; and what long seemed buried in the past, presents itself to us afresh, as if it had happened only yesterday. It is true that history never repeats itself, and our task lies exclusively in the present. Yet, in what we have to endure today, we are not left solitary before God and history. In turning to Christ, we find, both in near and distant times, companions and helpers in our destiny and sufferings, who interpret to us our own reality, in the common hearing of the unique Word, become in time all flesh and all reality, and, therefore, intended for all times.

With this in mind, I should like to speak to you of the answer given to his time by one who, a millennium and a half ago, was the leading spokesman of the Church, in a period which, like our own, had experienced the collapse of an empire with all its success and pride, and seen its people abandoned without resource. I refer to Augustine and the fall of Rome.

On the 28th of August in the year 410, Alaric penetrated into the age-old capital of the Roman Empire,[1] at the head of his army of Goths, followed by other barbarian tribes, Huns, and escaped slaves from Rome itself. It was night, the city was burning in a number of places, further resistance was out of the question. Soon the streets were full of dead bodies, although the king had forbidden any needless killing. For three days the population was abandoned to every sort of ill-treatment, the women violated, houses and palaces indiscriminately plundered. A great number of the inhabitants were dragged off as slaves, a still greater number took to flight, and were soon scattered over all the Mediterranean countries. Other parts of the Empire were also devastated, and, in the eastern parts which were spared, complaints arose of congestion and excessive infiltration. Thus, Jerome wrote from Palestine that he was compelled either to keep the door of his house shut or to abandon his studies, so unceasing was the stream of arrivals, to whom he could only give sympathy but not help, beggars who had lately wallowed in riches, maimed persons destitute of food and clothing—even the scanty baggage they had with them had been opened and searched for valuables by their hard-hearted fellow-creatures.[2]

Wretchedness was everywhere, but, worse than all the outward misery, was the terrible knowledge that the venerable, supposedly eternal, city was itself polluted and fallen, that the whole order of things was shaken to its foundation.[3] 'The world has lost its Rome'.[4] It was a current saying that no one knew 'his own word any longer',[5]

---

[1]For a description of what happened in Rome, see Gibbon, *Decline and Fall of the Roman Empire*, vol. V, chap. 31; Gregorovius, *Geschichte der Stadt Rom im Mittelalter*, I, 4; the sources in Otto Seeck, *Geschichte des Untergangs der antiken Welt*, V, 6.
[2]Jerome, *comm. in Ezech. III praef.*; *comm. in Ezech. VII praef.*
[3]Aug. *sermo* 296, 6 (Morin p. 404): *mundus concutitur*; *cf. sermo* 81, 7*f.*; 105, 11.
[4]Arsen. *apophthegm*, 21.   [5]Jerome, *in Aug. ep.* 165, 2 . . .

that is, understanding had ceased and could not grasp what had happened.

We know now that this was not yet the absolute end of the Empire. It was still to drag on for a few more decades, before its total collapse in the West. At the time, then, people soon plucked up a little courage and denied the seriousness of what had happened in Rome as a symbolical foretaste of the fate of the whole ancient culture, although the charred ruins of the city continued to stand up, as the years passed, conspicuously against the sky.[6] The refugees even—'a later generation will hardly credit it'—soon crowded once more the circuses and theatres in the cities to which they had fled,[7] and if, for a short time, the chill of fear had reduced men to silence, disputes very soon arose, as malicious as they were heated, about the disaster and those responsible for it.

As usual, the political catastrophe brought in its wake a change, not without bloodshed, in the principal personages in the Court. But, apart from this, no change in the forms of government was admissible in the late Roman absolute monarchy; there was no political 'system' that could be attacked and condemned in itself. The only change admittedly accomplished by the government in the past century was in its religious policy, and, shortly before the fall of Rome, its insistence on the exclusive validity of Christianity had been intensified by repeated measures.[8] Naturally, then, criticism was directed to this point, and, such was the strength of superstitious feeling at the time, it was powerfully re-echoed in the pagan camp, and also found Christians in a state of doubt and perplexity.[9] Was not, perhaps, the fall of Rome the result of traducing and dethroning the ancient tutelary deities of the city? Why could not Christ have protected the Empire and his followers, as had indeed been promised in his name and generally believed? The Church was challenged to answer, and Augustine, though only bishop of a secondary city of North Africa, was, as the recognized theologian of the West, compelled by the anxiety of his friends to undertake the task. This was the origin of his most important work, the twenty-two books of *The City of God, De Civitate Dei*.[10]

---

[6]Oros. *hist.* VII, 40, 1. [7]Aug. *De civ. Dei.* I, 32.
[8]*Cod. Theod.* XVI, 5, 42 of the 14. 11. 408.
[9]*Cf.* besides the details in the *Retractationes* (n. 10) and in *Civ. Dei, Aug. serm.* 81, 7*ff.*; 105, 8. 11*ff.*; 296, 9-11 (Morin, pp. 406-409).
[10]Aug. *retr.* II, 69; *cf. ep.* 136.

It is not my intention to expound systematically the entire content of what Augustine himself called the *'opus ingens.'*[11] As the last and greatest apologia of Christian antiquity, it displays a vast wealth of material assembled over the centuries, and combines a refutation of pagan religion and philosophy with a positive exposition of the whole of Christian theology and ethics. Yet, in two respects, the book, on which Augustine worked, with intervals, for half a lifetime, remains always close to the particular circumstances of its origin, as the answer to a question posed in this form by the fall of Rome and now become imperative. His aim was to vindicate the Christian faith in God, precisely at the point where its emptiness was apparently unmasked by the catastrophes that had occurred; and further to conduct the defence against the pagan attacks on this front, not only on 'purely religious' grounds—the usual, but misleading, form of approach—but also on political ones, going thoroughly and critically into the real status and value of political life in general, and, first of all, in the Roman state now so severely shaken. Only two aspects of the book, which made it a direct answer to its own time, will be considered in what follows.

The first question that Augustine had to put to himself was whether the fall of Rome had shown the absurdity of the Christian faith and vindicated the pagan gods that had been rejected. The answer to the second part about the pagan gods was comparatively simple, for the literary tradition had already provided the material from which to prove the futility and vanity of idolatry. It was only a question of bringing definite historical considerations to bear on the point. The numerous reversals recorded in ancient Roman history were to corroborate his judgement that the pagan gods were powerless or, in any event, did not protect the State in earlier times any more than did Christ, with whom they were being contrasted, in the present crisis.[12] By way of direct rejoinder on this point, Augustine did not disdain to use more weighty arguments insisting especially on the fact that it was precisely the Christian sanctuaries, and they alone, which, while the city was being sacked, afforded a refuge equally to pagans and Christians

[11]*De civ.* XXII, 30; *cf.* I *praef.*; *retr.* II, 69.
[12]*De civ. Dei*, II, 3; IV, 2; VI, *praef.*; *cf. serm.* 81, 9.

alike.[13] Basically, however, Augustine had no need to fear any longer a serious revival of paganism,[14] and what was new and significant in his achievement was not the range and learning of the argument in which he prosecuted the ancient controversy between the religions, but rather the manner in which he grappled with the first question, that of the meaning of the Christian faith. He had a clear awareness that the shock of the catastrophe struck not merely at this or that form of belief, but at all belief in God and the meaning of life, and that it weakened man's feeling for life at its root, whatever camp he belonged to. As regards popular paganism this was evident at first sight: if, indeed, the overthrow of the gods of the Capitol was deplored— for no one really believed in their power—it was simply that men brooded in resigned scepticism over the meaningless dispositions of a Fate dominating all things.[15] But the Christians also had lost the assurance of their faith, when, under the impact of the catastrophe, they faced, bewildered and vacillating, the question how God could have permitted it all and why Christ did not protect at least those who confessed his name. This also had to be answered and supported against attack both from without and within.[16] Thus *De Civitate Dei* was written both for Christians and for pagans. In the context of an apologia it undertook to lay anew the foundations of Christian belief itself, in the course of developing a definite theodicy relating to the cares and hardships of the time.

Why are Christians put to death in such numbers, even tortured to death,[17] tortured too on account of alleged treasure which they never in fact possessed?[18] Why do they go starving,[19] why are they torn from their land,[20] allowed to die, and often deprived of proper burial?[21] What can one say to women and girls who have been violated,[22] and what account can be given of all those who destroyed themselves to avoid falling alive into the hands of the enemy and being

---

[13]*De civ.* I, 1, 7ff. 34; II, 2; IV, 2; but against an illicit use of the argument see, in particular, *serm.* 296, 6f. (Morin pp. 404f.)   [14]*Cf. De civ.* V, 26.

[15]*De civ.* VIII, 23f.; mention of Fate already in *De civ.* I, 1; *cf.* also V, 8ff. (refutation of astrology V, 1ff.); the unbelief of the 'augurs' IV, 30; VI, 2.

[16]Augustine himself stresses his intention to afford consolation to Christians: *De civ.* I, 16; II, 2.

[17]*De civ.* I, 11.   [18]*De civ.* I, 10.   [19]*De civ.* I, 10.

[20]*De civ.* I, 14.   [21]*De civ.* I, 12.   [22]*De civ.* I, 16.

made the victims of his depravity?[23] It is obviously quite meaningless to speak of God's justice or mercy in view of individual cases of preservation, when these are often the least deserving.[24] Constantly, in all possible forms, the question arises where in the present day are we to find God's purpose, his power, and reality—'where is God?'[25]

Such a question, Augustine feels, is highly revealing. Anyone who asks it shows that he does not yet possess God or know him, or else knows him only as the pagans claim to do, and so must remain silent before their objections. No one truly believes in God if he seeks him only as the means to ensure the good things of this life and its happiness, and despairs of him as soon as disaster overtakes him. Further, it shows a complete misunderstanding of life to expect its fulfilment in time, and to dare to claim it as one's due from God's governance. The meaning of life is attained only by those men who always remain humble before God, accept in the world of time what God disposes, and abide in his pilgrimage with their hearts attuned to God's will and desire, believing in an eternity where all is fulfilled, and which will be just as much God's as are all the sufferings of the present time.

Statements such as these do but re-echo the fundamental ideas of Augustinian theology; but they are not developed primarily for themselves alone. Augustine is fully aware that this is not the time to speak as a systematic theologian, and that his answers would sound in the void unless, by his words, he enters deeply into the torment and dereliction that was the fate of his fellow-citizens, and can manage to kindle anew, in a direct confrontation with reality, their hope and faith. And so he applies his whole art of dialectic and rhetoric, so that no possible question or objection may be left unanswered. He has to show that suffering is not simply that and nothing else, but, according to how it is borne it is, already in this life, either a curse or a blessing, since it hardens and degrades the godless, but purifies the devout and frees them from the inner burden they still carry.[26] Furthermore, independently of this, the apparent meaninglessness of God's judgement, which strikes equally the good and the bad, is in fact a religious necessity, making man seek God, not in the hope of earthly well-

[23] *De civ.* I, 17, 22, 27.　　　　[24] *De civ.* I, 8; II, 2.

[25] *De civ.* I, 29: '*Ubi est Deus tuus?*' (Ps. 41.4).

[26] *De civ.* I, 8. On this the young Luther wrote in 1509 the enthusiastic annotation: *Hoc capitulum super aurum et topasion et solo Augustino dignum auctre, signa memoriam tuam hac illustrissima nota (WA IX, 24).*

being, but for himself. This statement in turn is dissected into rules and exceptions, and the latter explained and assigned their seemingly necessary place.[27]

All this, admittedly, is not fundamentally a matter of actual proof. In reality, however, Augustine wants to reach the hearts and consciences of Christians at a deeper level than logic can go, so as to persuade them to abandon the teachings of the sceptics, the disbelief that offers no security or salvation and makes for contention with God. Instead, they must take the decision in faith to recognize and assent to his will, and so find their way back to reality, truth, and life. Where there is faith in God, making him present once again and a living reality, nothing is without meaning and nothing wholly in vain. Perhaps this basic idea does not come out at first in full clarity on account of the exigencies of pastoral and controversial argumentation, and in view of the wealth of possible interpretations and standpoints so subtly interconnected, complementary, and overlapping. At the end of his work, years after the publication of this first provisional answer as a pamphlet for the time, he returns to the whole question of evil in the world, and issues something like a deliberate corrective, excluding all misunderstanding. He now presents, in clear-cut and unambiguous language, the Christian faith, and that alone, as the force that can withstand the enigma of life. We must accept God's discipline as what is best, even though its purpose is not yet evident to us. We do not know at present why God does not prosper the devout, why he spares the sinner; nor do we know why even this statement has its exceptions, and why, at times, the reverse is the rule. All we may know is that, fundamentally, what matters is, not the distribution of so-called fortune and misfortune in this world, but our future division, one from the other, at the last day before the judgement-seat of God. Then, at the last day, all riddles will be solved, even the last one of all, why it was necessary that God's justice should so often, in fact always, have remained hidden. But that it persists and determines all that happens—so much is already certain to those with faith in Christ, and that is enough.[28]

But is it really enough? Is this directive to naked faith sufficient in the presence of the catastrophe of Rome and the approaching end of

[27]*De civ.* I, 8-29.   [28]*De civ.* XX, 2 . . .

an epoch of national history? Augustine's answer could be seen as a total and despairing withdrawal from the world of reality and its political issues, as finally establishing a purely individualistic, ascetic attitude to life, one which foregoes all concern with the process of world history, and abandons it, without a struggle, to earthly forces and to those of the devil. Then, indeed, his work would be the historical document of an inner collapse, paralleled by the outer collapse of the Empire, the end of active political force and responsibility in the Roman Church as in the whole Roman Empire. But the matter is not to be explained so simply. Augustine was not writing '*de vanitate mundi*', but '*de civitate Dei*'. Certainly, the community it refers to is not of this world, its end and aspiration reach beyond. Nonetheless, it is a real community, '*civitas*',[29] one that 'is more enduringly founded and works more profoundly than all the merely political, ever-changing, and vanishing entities of this world'.[30] The contrast between the *civitas Dei* and the *civitas terrena* is what determines the further structure of his massive work, and gives it, against the background of the disasters of the time, its political significance and historical importance.

We have already drawn attention to the fact that, from the beginning, the religious objections urged by the pagans included a certain political grievance. Now, once again, in the attack on Christ and Christianity, the ancient gods stood for the age-old kingdom taken from them, for Rome once great and now humbled, for its traditions, seemingly betrayed and abandoned by the Christians, and for its political greatness. Augustine is wise enough not simply to turn the tables on them and to turn back on to the pagans their own accusation that the Christians were to blame for the city's fall. Certainly, the pagans must convert themselves, and we must all become new men, different from what we have been up to now.[31] But Augustine does not, in so saying, speak in the tone of those preachers of penitence who see in political misfortune simply a payment for definite sins, and flourish the receipt triumphantly before those who alone were supposedly guilty.[32] He has nothing in common with those interpreters of history, whether pagan or Christian, who check up, as it were, the

[29]*De civ.* XIX, 5. *Cf.* XIX, 17; II, 24.
[30]*De civ.* I. *praef.* (n. 63 below).
[31]*Serm.* 296, 6 (*excutitur vetus homo*). 12 (Morin, pp. 404, 409).
[32]*Cf. serm.* 105, 12.

divine interventions in world history, and supply each instance with theological and moral explanations.[33] But Augustine feels that, with the exercising of the national greatness and the past, there has been summoned up a moral strength and an emotion, which the Church cannot ignore, which she cannot simply leave to her pagan adversaries and condemn untested. The matter requires to be discussed, and the outcome is that the religious apologia becomes a critical revision of the prevailing conception of history, a struggle for a right understanding of the Church's own past, and of political history in general.

Obviously, this does not mean that the religious standpoint is eliminated. Augustine agrees with his pagan adversaries that the political and religious elements in the life of a people cannot, in fact, be separated. But now this idea is raised by him to a fundamental principle, and turned against the prevalent national ideology of the pagan historians and philosophers. As he is constantly insisting, religion and politics are always concerned with one and the same life of man. Consequently, there is, for states and individuals, only one ultimate source of all salvation,[34] which Christians recognize as the one God, ruler of all peoples in all times. The fundamental error of all pagan—or, as we should say, all political—religion is that it fails to accord such recognition. It does not seek the One, the determining factor 'for its own sake', but contents itself with a multiplicity of gods, who are not really gods, but merely instruments and an expression of one's own greatness and dominance, and accepted as such. Or, more exactly, the real tragedy of Rome was that it was unable to find the one true God, and so necessarily lapsed, irredeemably, into the worship of devils and of its own greatness.[35] Thus the real basis of life, justice, which upholds men and kingdoms, was absent,[36] and in its place came impious pride, the *superbia* of man. The same misconception of religion, this-worldly and egocentric, that Augustine indicated and condemned in the life of the individual as the distortion, so decisive in its effects, of his relation with God, is thus seen also as the inner driving force of the life of the State. It is precisely here, mag-

---

[33]Augustine, therefore, decisively rejects any kind of preview of history, unlike the apocalyptic writers of the Middle Ages: *cf. De civ.* XVIII, 53; XX, 30.
[34]*Ep.* 155, 7: *non aliunde esse beatum hominem, aliunde civitatem*; 137, 17; 138, 10; *cf. De civ.* IV, 3.
[35]*De civ.* II, 3*ff.*; XIX, 21.   [36]*De civ.* IV, 3; XIX, 21.

nified enormously, that its presence is most clearly to be seen. And Roman history has become, as it were, the prototype of this demonic character of the political will, and presents Augustine with its most perfect model.[37]

Augustine is not wholly insensible to the magnitude of the Roman achievement. He acknowledges that the Romans attained political results without parallel in history because they possessed political virtues, which will always be worthy of admiration.[38] But, if these achievements are virtues and to be rightly assessed, they must not be taken in isolation. They grew, in fact, from the soil of man's original sin, from *superbia*; and what Virgil wrote about his people's vocation to rule, '*parcere subjectis et debellare superbos*', was to appropriate the honour due to God, who alone accords mercy to the humble and has the right to punish.[39] The deliberate and conscious cultivation of ambition for glory on the part of the Romans could, indeed, inhibit avarice, as well as countless other vices, and impel them to fantastic achievements;[40] but still it was radically an evil force, making for disorder at a profounder level and ever new forms of corruption.[41] Always human pride can exalt itself only by humiliating and crushing others. This attitude of theirs was the real reason why there was never peace in the world. It was the source of all the bloody wars and conquests which made her for centuries the terror of her neighbours, and, finally, the all-devouring Empire. Rome herself, indeed, extolled her justice as the quality which laid the world at her feet; but history, as it really is, knows otherwise.[42] How can there be justice in the true sense when the first and most sacred order of all right has been abandoned: the law of humility obliging man to honour, not himself, but God alone, and him alone to serve.[43]

---

[37]*De civ.* 30; V, 17; XVIII, 2, 22.

[38]*De civ.* I, 24 on Regulus: *inter omnes suos laudabiles et virtutibus insignibus inlustres viros non proferunt Romani meliorem . . .* II, 2, 13; V, 15.

[39]*De civ.* I *praef.*; V, 12.

[40]*De civ.* V, 13: *pro isto uno vitio, id est amore laudis, pecuniae cupiditatem et multa alia vitia comprimentes*; likewise V, 12.

[41]In this connection occurs the celebrated passage on the so-called '*splendida vitia*', *De civ.* XIX, 25.

[42]*De civ.* I, 6; II, 17, 21; XIX, 19, 24.

[43]*De civ.* XIX, 21*ff.*

With this in mind, Augustine, using Sallust and other classical writers, embarks on a long and terrible summary of the whole of Roman history, from the fratricide of Romulus to the last horrors of the republic. It is an assault, such as had never been previously attempted, on the ancient tradition, carried out in order to tear from Roman cant its sanctimonious mask, in the name of God.[44] Certainly, the strict religious sense of reverence, the steadfast ordered respect for law and the common good, which were characteristic of the true historic Rome, is here too often presented in the distorting mirror of a completely altered world. But Augustine is not now concerned with historical justice, but with bringing out what is fundamental to the whole, and the opponents, with whom he is brought into direct contact thereby, are not, by any means, the Romans of old, but, as he emphasizes, the successors, a very different type, of the superb race;[45] these invoke those glorious exemplars only in order to close their minds to the truth now proclaimed, so as not to be obliged to acknowledge Christ. The true race of the ancient Scipios and Fabricii ought no longer to stay aloof, but to follow Christ and recognize in Christianity the nobler commonwealth, in the Church their true home.[46] Then would their political virtues also rise again in a new spirit.[47]

Civitas terrena—civitas Dei! Augustine, in summoning the old nobility and ruling class to a new standard and a new vocation, comes now to the crucial opposition which is his basic concern. There are, in general, two fundamental attitudes which determine the world and its history. They are called pride and humility, *superbia* and *humilitas,* the tyrannical power of the proud and the God-directed humility of the believers. Their most perfect characterization is found in the Roman state, on the one hand, and in the kingdom of the Church, on the other; but their contrast is not simply on a par with that between Church and State as definite organizations within this world—precisely because it is a question of attitudes and basic decisions in regard to God and life. The humility and sobriety of faith has to be maintained everywhere, even in the environment of political and social life. There is no happier state than that in which these alone bear rule,[48]

[44]*De civ.* II-V.
[46]*De civ.* II, 29.
[48]*De. civ.* II, 19.

[45]*De civ.* II, 2; I, 30, 33; II, 20, 23.
[47]*De civ.* V, 16, 18.

just as it is great good fortune for the world when a Christian, who understands something of how to govern, comes, by the mercy of God, to actual government,[49] and then assumes the burden of ruling, not for his own sake, but for that of others.[50] For then the thought of God, who alone has power and imparts it, will preserve him from the intoxication of power;[51] his interior attitude will always be one of service, even when he has to command and, at the worst, to employ force.[52] And in thus restoring to power its proper bounds and true significance, he refutes in action the opinion that Christ's doctrine necessarily runs counter to the conditions governing the life of the State.[53]

Admittedly, such a case will always be exceptional. Augustine has no illusions about a steady Christianization of the world. He accepts the crude early Christian verdict on the world and the persistent power of evil within it; he knows too that only God himself, at the end of time, will bring about that eternal peace for which everyone fundamentally longs.[54] The citizens of the city of God remain strangers and pilgrims on the earth. They are always the few and persecuted, and for that very reason are ready to co-operate with anyone for the practical ends of this life, as they must always be prepared, when occasion demands, to endure patiently any government, even the worst and most hostile.[55] Not without reason do they discard, in salutary disenchantment, all pretentious speech about glory and victory, conquest and empire,[56] proclaiming rather the 'mild law' of their kingdom as more conducive to human welfare than pride, with all its strivings, to which the world is so prone.

What characterizes Augustine's criticism is not the absence of political responsibility, but his positive refusal to take the political situation as tragic, his utter freedom from all illusion and his clear insight into the inviolable limits set to the political life of his time, indeed, of all times. He holds as spurious the romantic nationalism of Roman paganism, always delighting in the ultimately futile role of a city state dominating the world. Yet he dissociates himself no less sharply from the apologetic of the court pamphleteers and their idea

[49]*De civ.* V, 19.
[50]*De civ.* IV, 3; XIX, 19.
[51]*De civ.* V, 19.
[52]*De civ.* V, 24; XIX, 14.
[53]*Ep.* 138, 9; *De civ.* V, 25.
[54]*De civ.* XIX, 10ff.
[55]*De civ.* II, 19.
[56]*De civ.* IV, 3.

of a Christian society, their expectation of a world empire become Christian, and enduring for ever. Whether Rome will ever recover is a question Augustine leaves aside.[57] In any case, the *imperium sine fine*, the eternal empire of the pagan poets, was, as history has shown, a lie.[58] But, not even Constantinople will last for ever, simply because it is a Christian foundation and capital city.[59] No city, no kingdom, not even the world, is eternal.[60] God alone and his kingdom are eternal, and it is the knowledge of this that should make us willing, in the light of God's future, to do and accept in time what God lays upon us. Thus the outcome of Augustine's criticism of the State is the same practical decision as he had already enjoined on each single person: 'Love the law given by God, instead of rebelling against it. I beseech, I adjure, I exhort you: be generous, have pity on those who suffer, receive the sick! Now that there is such a multitude of refugees, of the necessitous and helpless, your readiness to receive them, the good you do them, must be superabundant. What Christ commands, that must Christians do; only pagans complain against their fate and blaspheme'.[61]

That is the historical answer that Augustine made to his time and his world, in the name of Christ and the Church, in the lucid, sober, and resolute frame of mind in which the Christian Church surmounted the collapse of the ancient world and began a new period. His intention was no other than to expound what Jesus and early Christianity had proclaimed about the nature of this world and the vocation of Christians. The manner, however, in which he apprehended their message certainly reveals the special character and the limitations of his century and of his nature. In contrast to Jesus, Augustine was an ascetic and a spiritualist, and his mistrust of material goods on account of their physical nature and, in the social sphere, his view of political activity as tending pre-eminently to evil, were, in that form, not shared by early Christianity. The pure New Testament demand that all should be prompted by faith and the obedience of faith alone was, in his case, combined with a pronounced depreciation, a deliberate indifference as regards all earthly things; and, in his longing for the

[57]*Serm.* 105, 11.

[59]*Serm.* 105, 12.

[61]*Serm.* 81, 9.

[58]*Serm.* 105, 10; *De civ.* II, 29.

[60]*Serm.* 105, 11; 81, 9.

heavenly fatherland, to make good the deficiences of the earthly one, there is admixed at times an alien, almost a 'narcotic' element.[62] But this does not really affect the basic presuppositions of his work and the demands it makes. The hope, assurance, and confidence in the future kingdom of God, the serious character of the great decision set before us by Christ, by which he calls us to conversion and frees us from the doomed forces of this world—this, in fact, is what constitutes, from earliest times, the starting-point of all Christian teaching, the source of the new life, and the new form of service in the community of the Church. In the breakdown of the political ideals and institutions of his time, Augustine seeks to affirm and establish anew the truth of Christ, the reality of the Church, and its mission of help. His aim, as he says at the outset, is to use all the force at his command to bring home to the proud that the power of humility is a real power, which, through the grace of God, reaches greater heights than all the peaks of this world now tottering to their fall.[63]

Starting with this conception, Augustine becomes, as his work proceeds, the historian of the Church—or, more exactly, the first universal historian and theologian of history of the west. Under the old idea of divine salvation-history comprising 'all peoples' he subsumes the historical tradition of the Bible and antiquity in a 'world history', and gives it a uniform interpretation as an incessant struggle between the two primordial mentalities of *humilitas* and *superbia*, between the two communities of a people of God journeying in obedience, and a kingdom of this world stubbornly setting itself up in opposition to it. This world history includes the story of Cain and Abel, equally with that of Babylon and Rome; it recounts the triumphs and disasters of the powers of the world equally with the hidden sufferings and hopes of the saints and lowly in the land. All the lines of history, from the beginning, run towards a point in time and converge on Jesus Christ, in whom the meaning and purpose of the entire movement mysteriously manifest themselves. With him begins the history of our present time, which again flows on ceaselessly towards the same Christ, to his return at the end of time for its fulfilment and for judgement. He alone, the incarnate God, and no man setting himself up as God, such as

[62]Harnack, *Lehrbuch der Dogmengeschichte* III, (1890), 66.
[63]*De civ.* I, *praef.*

Romulus, has built us in the heavens, and not here, an eternal city for our home, 'where victory consists in truth and rank in holiness, where peace is in blessedness and life in eternity'.[64] But, he goes on to say, 'the salvation of this city of God is of such a kind that he alone can retain it, can attain to it at all, who is empowered in faith and through faith; while one who abandons faith will never be able to reach it'.[65]

Our idea of world history has, in fact, its root in this theological conception of a salvation-history orientated to Christ, its end point being the fulfilment of all things in the kingdom of God. Augustine was the first to allow himself to be guided by this postulate, a sort of general prospectus, in accordance with which to outline, with the means afforded by his historical knowledge, a survey of world history. It is clear that we cannot today force world history into the Procrustes bed of the biblical theological framework which for him was authoritative.[66] On the other hand, whether and how it is possible to see and treat world history as a unity without the Christian standpoint as the dominating factor is a different question, which we here leave open. At all events, the Church historian has no occasion to leave aside the task bequeathed to him by Augustine; but he has to grapple with it anew with fresh means. Admittedly, we have a long way to go before we can attain a comprehensive history of the Church that meets the demands of modern historical science and, as its purpose requires, puts each epoch in direct relation to Christ, and judges it by the original teaching of Jesus. And it must, in addition, to form a real whole, comprise a corresponding theological grasp of the history of Israel and the Near East as a movement towards Christ, with, naturally as its central point, an account of early Christianity and of Jesus himself that looks both backwards and forwards. Only then will specialists in the theology of history be able to achieve a unified and comprehensive work such as Augustine, on his own initiative, intended and accomplished. The magnitude of the task ought not to deter us, for it is simply the consequence of the magnitude, the range, the importance of the problem facing us. And perhaps the example of Augustine's

[64]*De civ.* II, 29.
[65]*De civ.* XXII, 6. Here also we find the contrast between Romulus and Christ brought out; *cf.* III, 15.
[66]*De civ.* XVIII, 40.

10
The Origins of the Idea of
the Priesthood in the Early Church

I

THE WORD 'PRIEST' is one that is in constant use, the meaning of which everyone thinks he knows. But it is not infrequently the fate of such words and concepts that, when used in a scientific context, they are the cause of confusion, since they are in reality not so unequivocal, and mean very different things for different writers. We can observe this over and over again in the controversy about the origins of the Christian priesthood. It will, therefore, be useful to agree at the outset on what the words 'priest' and 'priesthood' were intended to convey at any given time. In my view, the facts of the case require that certain distinctions be drawn and adhered to, and that we have to admit a twofold idea of the priesthood, a wider and a narrower, and, accordingly, the question of its origins in the Christian Church must have different answers.

The basic prerequisite for the priesthood in the wider sense is that there be a fixed *cultus*, a definite, consecrated form of divine worship, and especially of sacrifice, by which a human society seeks to draw near to the divinity. The priest is the one who presides over this act of worship, who offers this sacrifice as representative of all. The idea of the priest so understood lacks any sharp differentiation from that of the 'layman'. In this sense of the word, the father acts as priest for his family, the leader for the army. This priesthood means primarily a function to be rightly understood, an activity incumbent on an individual to which he must be duly called, and even a permanent, vocational priesthood can come into being on this basis. It will then involve certain rights, will have a certain holiness of its own; but the rights inhere fundamentally in the position accorded to it, the holiness springs from the service the priest performs, and, in the case of his exclusion from the priestly calling, he personally no longer possesses them.

A second stage is reached, the priesthood in the narrower sense, when to the priest as such, independently of his position in the community, a definite religious capacity and quality is attributed, distinguishing him, once and for all, from the laity, and making him privileged to perform his special, in fact his 'priestly', service. A priest in this sense resembles, in his extraordinary, 'magical' nature, the miracle-men and the prophets with their special gifts, only that, as van der Leeuw expresses it, the divine gift is, in his case, 'as it were, frozen, crystallized', and, as such, has always to do with a definite service 'bound to definite times, places, actions, words', the priestly service of the cult, sacrifice, and the magico-sacramental actions—but independently of all questions of right and authorization, independently, too, of any charge by the community, as it were, behind and above him.

Certainly the boundary between right and magic, between a priesthood bound up with an order and a community, and a priesthood existing in itself and as an individual thing, cannot, as a rule, be so sharply drawn. Magic and right, personal endowment and the power derived from office, overlap one another and become more and more intertwined. Yet, in the case of the Christian priesthood, and in the history of the idea of the priest from its roots in the ancient Church, such a distinction is both possible and imperative. At first there was no fixed human priesthood at all, just as there was no fixed cult to which it would be related. But even after cult and priesthood in the wider sense were both established, it was long before the special priesthood, understood as something individual and magical, was formed. The main reason for this delay was the significance of its support, the sacred community, the Church, then so strongly insisted upon in all its range and depth as never since. There was no holiness and no divine worship outside the one Catholic Church; none was conceivable otherwise than in and through the Church, which was filled by the Spirit of God. And so neither was there any priestly 'character' that might mean anything independently of the priest's position in the Church, however firmly established might be the rights and duties of the priestly state.

Thus, the acceptance of the idea of the priesthood in the ancient

Church involved, as we have said, two different processes, which must be clearly separated both as to their content and their time. First came the conception of a special Christian service of worship and sacrifice, which at once brought about the corresponding conception of a special priestly calling and status. From the cult there came into being a sacred right of the priestly order. But this right always remained primarily the right and order of the Christian Church, in which the priest of God had to perform his functions. The Church is holy, the Church possesses the Spirit on whom depends the holiness of the cult and the sacrifice, and, therefore, the priest is neither holy nor competent to act independently of his actual union with the true Church, which he has to serve. His ordination, his priesthood, taken in itself, means nothing at all; a deposed priest, a priest outside the Catholic community, is no more than a layman.

Over against this concept we have that, however it may be understood, of a *character indelebilis*, that is to say permanently inherent in the person of the priest and therefore of a sacerdotal power independent of the idea of the Church. This is something quite new, and contrary to the old Catholic idea of the Church, which at first held the field alone. Its adoption needs explaining. To do so it is not sufficient simply to start from the completed medieval doctrine and to work backwards from it, using it to interpret the earlier development. Nor may we present the idea of the character simply as the outcome of a clearer insight into, or a culmination of the idea of, the priesthood in general, which, once this was accepted, was bound to follow sooner or later. The only man to have at least perceived the problem that here emerges, even though his solution is far too dependent on assumptions, is, to my knowledge, Rudolf Sohm. Not only did he see, what is now admitted, a sharp cleavage between primitive Christianity and ancient Catholicism, which is indicated by the adoption of a 'divine law' as the basis for ecclesiastical authority; he finds a cleavage also between 'ancient Catholicism' and the 'neo-Catholicism' of the Middle Ages. The boundary line between these two epochs, first apparent in the sphere of ecclesiastical law and dogma, is seen also, according to Sohm, in the conception of the spiritual office. This, in antiquity, depended solely on 'institution' by the Church; only in the high Middle Ages was it made to depend instead on ordination and the priestly quality of the ordained person.

Undoubtedly, Sohm's explanation is, in many respects, over-subtle, and, in any case, it implies a serious misapprehension in drawing the boundary between the two epochs only at the twelfth century. This may be one of the reasons why his assertions on this point have generally received, especially from evangelical theologians, far less notice than his statements on Catholicism and primitive Christianity, which, in my view, are far more dubious. I should like to think that Sohm, with his second distinction, has, in fact, seen something of essential importance and seen it rightly; and, though we cannot here unfold the problem in its full range, a close examination of one individual point—the admission of the priesthood—may be welcome as a contribution to its solution.

II

The admission of the 'general' concept of the priesthood came about in the second century. It has been frequently studied, and we are concerned, in what follows, solely to bring out, somewhat more sharply and decisively, its distinction from the neo-Catholic concept.

The idea of the priesthood follows, as we have said, the conception of the liturgical sacrifice. The word 'sacrifice' (θυσία) first occurs in this connection in the Didache. But something similar is meant when the first epistle of Clement (44.4)—in the last decade of the first century—speaks of an 'offering of the gifts', which the bishops perform for the communities during the service. With this in view it is perfectly understandable that these Christian bishops should very soon be seen as closely parallel with the priests of the Old Covenant, and this, in the opinion of the writer of the epistle, should firmly secure their permanent rights in the execution of the cult. The word 'sacerdos', priest, first appears as applied to the Christian bishops and presbyters in Tertullian. Evidently, he alludes, not so much to the idea of a special priestly dignity accruing to the clergy, as to the distinct function the priest has to exercise in virtue of his office. The order, which distinguishes the office from the community, is still based exclusively on a regulation issued by 'the Church': *differentiam inter ordinem et plebem constituit ecclesiae auctoritas (exh. cast. 7)*. Tertullian is fully aware of the fundamental implications of this. He concludes from it that the authority which the bishop can exert for his part is not by any means his own authority, but simply *auctoritas ecclesiae*, and the service he performs is not, strictly speaking, the service and privilege of his order, but the service and rule of the Church. Consequently, in case of necessity, any layman who belongs to the Church can become a priest. Even a layman can, if no priest in the official sense is at hand, offer sacrifice, baptize, and, in the authority of the universal priesthood, 'be his own priest'. For where two or three are gathered together, there is the Church, and God is no respecter of persons. It is clear here that the idea of the Church rules out completely any idea of a sacerdotal character, and any kind of fundamental, religiously decisive distinction between priest and layman, although the idea of sacrifice and the normal fixed rule of the office are stated unequivocally, and, indeed, taught.

It may, indeed, be said that Tertullian was the last representative of a passing epoch, and that the succeeding one did not endorse his ideas. Nonetheless, it did not affirm anything contrary to them, and, on two points at least, it is perfectly clear that the ecclesiastical concept of the priesthood was upheld as essential rather than the idea of special rights of the priestly order. For the bishop—which means the actual, 'supreme' priest of the community, from whom the other priests derive all their rights—became such at this time only by unanimous election on the part of his community; and, further, an episcopal or priestly office outside the true Catholic Church was held impossible and never admitted. And so it disappeared, if the bishop personally, by his conduct or false belief, cut himself off from the Church—which means, from the Holy Spirit.

There is no need to embark here on a long study of the history of episcopal elections and their forms. The crucial question is not the form in which the community as a whole actually took part in the election, and how far it was able in practice to enforce its will, even against that of the clergy. What is crucial is solely the principle, reiterated up to the fourth and fifth centuries, a modest remnant of which survived even into the high Middle Ages, that a bishop must be chosen *ab omni populo* and ordained *consentientibus omnibus*. It would be a complete misconception of this principle to take it only as a provision, albeit a secular provision, of Church law, a rational rule prompted by tact and human considerations of the needs and desires of the community, while the really decisive spiritual procedure of the consecration was reserved to the priests. Such a juridical splitting up of the unitary ecclesiastical event into choice and ordination is the outcome of the modern Catholic mentality; it is completely absent from the ancient Catholic sources. Even the choice by the community, which at first was the principal factor, had a spiritual character, and was, in conjunction with the consecration, indispensable to and inherent in the right and authority of bishops—and indeed for their sacerdotal authority. The fact that, already in the time of Hippolytus, this consecration was performed only by clerics may be connected with the idea of the apostolic succession, apart from which such a rule would be inexplicable. Nevertheless, the emphasis was not on this as a 'succession in consecration'; the decisive factor was the succession in office. Choice, ordination, and succession, not consecration and character, made the bishop a bishop, and the priest a priest.

The essential dependence of the priest on the Church and the community as a whole is further shown—this is our second point—in the ever-present possibility of his forfeiting his sacerdotal office and power, if he should leave the community of the true Church. In such a case, he could no longer ordain, even if he was a consecrated bishop, nor even, according to Cyprian, baptize; and the Council of Nicaea expressly laid down that any schismatical priest entering the ranks of the Catholic clergy was to be ordained anew. In fact, the Council of Chalcedon (sixth century), declared null ($\check{a}\kappa\nu\rho\sigma\varsigma$ $\chi\epsilon\iota\rho\sigma\tau\sigma\nu\acute{\iota}a$) even a Catholic ordination as a priest of someone perfectly orthodox if performed without reference to a definite community, null, therefore, as an 'absolute ordination'. In other words, it is not merely, as most Catholic scholars make out, illegal, but absolutely ineffective and meaningless, and the person receiving such ordination remains a layman. Behind the priest must stand the Church, the community of God, which sustains him and his service in the same Holy Spirit as that with which he, in his priestly capacity, represents it before God. Apart from this community, any supposed priesthood, any consecration and ordination, mean in fact nothing.

This is, in a way, proved by the fact that in all the first three centuries of the Church not a single bishop appealed to his consecration to claim for the clergy a privileged position as priests over against the laity. The distinction came more to the fore only in the middle of the fourth century, and even then it was not so much a matter of developing a distinctively priestly ideology as of protecting the bishop, by marking the boundary against the interference in the Church of the political power, which was in the hands of laymen. This began with Athanasius, and, significantly enough, only very quietly and indirectly, and then found expression in, for example, Lucifer of Cagliari and definitively in Ambrose of Milan. On a certain definite occasion (*gesta conc. Aquil.* 52), the latter declared a bishop deserving of censure for daring to appeal against a conciliar judgement to the imperial tribunal; for it would be an outrage for a priest, however unworthy, to be condemned by laymen. It is perfectly clear what was the intention behind this and similar statements; they can hardly be adduced to explain the acceptance of an idea of the priesthood as separate from the concept of Church and community. The basic idea, in fact, is that of a comprehensive Church order and constitution, which assign to the 'office'—in much the same way as later in orthodox Lutheranism—a definite, inalienable place in the Church and community. The roots of the individual and 'special' concept of the priesthood are not to be found in the sphere of ecclesiastical politics.

III

The decisive transition to a new, absolute concept of the priesthood occurred at the turn of the fourth to the fifth centuries. It is, nevertheless, well established that in none of the older Fathers is there any demonstrable trace of a '*character indelebilis*', or of a 'sacrament' of priestly ordination, and if anything of the kind is thought to be present, this is due to a misconception. This is roundly admitted even by a Catholic scholar like Cardinal van Rossum in his study of the fourth-century Fathers, published in 1932, though he chooses to explain the fact as pure 'chance'. If we now turn to the new epoch, we must take separately the development in the west and the east, the Latin and the Greek worlds. Though the time at which the change occurred was roughly the same in both parts, the motives were different. Once again we must start with the history of the cult and of the priest's place within it.

In the west, to inquire into the significance of the priestly ministry is tantamount to inquiring into the relationship of the priest to the sacraments. It was the development of sacramental doctrine that determined the development of the idea of the priesthood. It first proceeded on its own lines, with hardly any direct effect on the priesthood, and here, in the doctrine of baptism, there first began to appear a special, sacred entity within the community over against the idea of the Church and community. Originally, even baptism was considered holy only when administered in the Holy Spirit, that is within the true, holy Church. Baptism conferred by heretics was invalid and had to be 'repeated'. But already, in the course of the third century, we see men beginning to vacillate on the point. The holiness of the sacramental rite and the revulsion in practice against insisting on a new baptism for those returning combined to establish more and more firmly the principle that baptism as such, independently of the place where it was conferred, imparted the specific quality of a Christian, even though not of a true Christian, deserving of blessedness. From then on, this idea gained wider currency, so that, at a later date, a corresponding line was taken by Augustine as regards the ordination of priests, agreeing in this with Tyconius, and always appealing to the analogy of baptism. In his view, ordination, as such, and independent of the ordaining priest's relation to the Church, confers a definite, irremovable imprint, in fact the '*character*' which empowers its recipient to perform valid priestly functions, even though not efficacious for salvation; consequently, schismatic priests, on their return, could be recognized as priests. And, in addition, the ordinations they had performed could be held valid, instead of having to be repeated. Again, therefore, we see the rite made into something absolute as before. The only thing we have to do now is to look more closely at the practical presuppositions of this line of thought so as to bring out its significance. It was all part of the struggle of the African Catholic Church against the Donatists; its effects on the idea of the sacraments and of the priesthood were already perceptible before Augustine, as we see in Optatus of Milevis.

The long-drawn-out struggle between the Catholics and the Donatists started, as is well known, with the purely factual question whether a certain bishop, from whom the ordinations of the Catholic clergy more or less directly derived, was cut off from the Church, that is, had fallen away in the pagan persecution, or not. The Donatists, who held that he had, concluded therefrom—fully in accord with the older Church and especially the great African teacher Cyprian—what seemed quite evident, that the priesthood of the priest in question had ceased, so that all the ordinations he had performed, all the sacraments he had administered, and also all the sacraments and ordinations of the clerics ordained by him, were absolutely invalid. Consequently, the communities joined with him were no longer Christian communities —observe, not because the priesthood, but because the Christianity of the bishop in question had been defective. No one can give what he does not possess. A bishop, who has lapsed from the true Church, no longer has the Spirit, and cannot, therefore, have, dispense, and administer the sacraments of the Church, filled as they are with the Spirit. Indirectly, then, through the sacraments, we recognize once again the primacy of the idea of the Church over that of the priesthood.

The Catholics at first contested only the fact alleged by the Donatists. The bishop in question, now long dead, was no apostate, they asserted; his ordinations and the sacraments he conferred were, therefore, to be considered valid. But the more the impossibility came to be realized of elucidating the matter finally and in a way convincing to all, doubts of a fundamental nature were bound, with time, to be felt and voiced. Surely it might often happen that a bishop, exercising his priestly office within a community, was in reality an apostate, secretly in a state of sin, and so no longer in possession of the Spirit and not in the community of the Church. Must, then, the faithful, who unsuspectingly received the sacraments from his hands, be defrauded of salvation? To evade this consequence, which would exclude any assurance of salvation, the line of thinking had to be reversed: the sacrament imparted by the priest must remain a sacrament even if he himself no longer has the Spirit. It is enough that he should have once received ecclesiastical ordination, that, as Optatus so well says, 'God's name was spoken over him', for him, once and for all, to be empowered for the priestly service that the community requires of him. Precisely, then, for the sake of the laity is it necessary to hold as valid, in such cases, as Augustine says, the *dominicus character indelebilis*, of priests, once and for all, independently of their personal state and disposition. *Neque enim episcopi propter nos sumus, sed propter eos, quibus verbum et sacramentum dominicum ministravimus (c. Cresc. II, 13).*

Thus, the establishment of the Roman Catholic concept of the priest had nothing whatever to do with hierarchical pretension and the subjugation of the laity. The priestly character was introduced not with a view to making the priest independent of the community, but independent, as it were, of his own person, whose human weaknesses were not to be allowed to impair the service he had to render. What was significant, therefore, about the idea of the character, when it originated, was not only the total abstraction from the personal qualities of the priest, but also that the whole question was approached not so much from the side of the priest as from that of the Church and the community; and that, finally, the question of the certainty of salvation —or at any rate the certainty of the sacraments—came to be preponderant. The interpretation of the character as a privilege and a personal distinction, making the priest indispensable to the laity and unimpeachable was, on the other hand, a later line of thought, attaining its full significance only in the Middle Ages.

IV

The eastern Church also recognized the doctrine of the sacrament of orders and of a *character indelebilis*; in fact, it took it over, in its essentials, from the west. Occasionally, as in John Chrysostom and John Damascene, we find also the characteristic motive of the certainty of the sacramental graces imparted by the ordained priest, independently of his personal qualities. But, in reality, these ideas were borrowed ones, and the definite formation of the absolute idea of the priesthood took a different course in the east. This is evident in that the idea, crucial for the west, of the inamissibility of the priestly character, never wholly prevailed without question in the east; in fact even in the last century it could still be formally condemned in the Russian Orthodox Church. We must, however, start, not from here, but, as before, from the liturgical functions of the priest.

If in the west, as we have seen, the idea of the priesthood was mainly determined in reference to the sacrament the priest had to consecrate, in the east this was much less the case. There, the liturgy, in which the celebration of the eucharist was enshrined, preserved much more the full range of its meaning. The regular divine service of the Church is the sacred event, which, in a marvellous way, joins heaven and earth, in which God stoops down to the community, and Christians ascend to the choirs of angels. It is, at one and the same time, the holy service that is offered to God, a sacrifice that possesses, as such, an objective value, as it were. But the holiness of this event cannot be simply encapsulated in the sacrament and given an independent standing. As is well known, even today, in the Greek Church, the validity of heretical baptism is disputed, and it would perhaps have never been admitted were it not for the influence of western theology. For the priesthood is not held to be something absolute in its validity; it always remains related to the true cult, and so to the true Catholic Church. But here the whole man must be holy and pure, and worthy of God, if he is to perform the service of God, if he is to represent the Christian Church before God, and to lead up the community in the way to God. It is not enough to ascribe to him some kind of formal capacity, enabling him to administer validly a sacrament and exercise priestly 'functions'. Thus, the question of the priesthood in its right sense comes back to the idea of true 'perfection', of *teleiotes* (τελειότης), and so to a fundamental problem of Greek theology.

The priest, who performs the divine service by and in which the Church lives, should be the most perfect and holy of Christians. But can he be simply assumed to be such? The disparity between what ought to be and what is, so evident in this matter, had already occupied Origen. But with him its full importance is not yet apparent, since he treated the question only, as it were, from outside, from the standpoint of the Gnostic, who sought and acknowledged a perfection and an ascent to God independent of the priesthood. Origen's religious practice did not really draw its life from the liturgy. The same may be said of the first monks, who often judged the priesthood of the Church very unfavourably, and had no need of it themselves. The question is really urgent for the priest himself, who believes in the greatness of his task as mediating salvation, but equally knows what tremendous demands it makes on him, both religiously and morally.

This comes out again and again in works of pastoral theology, those, for instance, of Gregory of Nazianzus, Chrysostom, and Cyril. They all extol the glory of the liturgical service, in which the priest—a constantly recurring image—enters, as it were, the choir of angels; their language is so profuse as to give the simple expositions of Ambrose or Augustine of the duties of the clergy—*de officiis ministrorum*—a jejune air. But they all emphasize the danger lying in wait for the priest, should he fail to live up to the holiness of his service, for, by reason of the gift of this service, which elevates him above the rest, God will demand more of the priest. This enables us to understand the avoidance, the flight from the assumption of the priestly office, which is so often witnessed to from the fourth century on. It must not be taken simply as an expression of 'monastic' humility, but must be seen precisely in the 'sacerdotal' aspect also. Men did not dare to undertake so holy an office, and the refusal was, in many cases, obviously meant seriously; it was not always just convention or affectation, as was then the mode in the west, and of course occurred in the east also.

How does man, in fact, become holy enough to be able to serve in the choir of angels? This gave rise to a problem which, towards the end of the fourth century, brought Greek theology itself to outline something like a doctrine of the sacerdotal character, independently of the west and its anti-Donatist preoccupations. The attempt was made in the east also to maintain a uniqueness of the person of the priest, grounded, not in his natural capabilities, but in the charismatic powers of ordination. The stream of divine graces, which flowed in the services and sacramental rites of the Church, makes his person also into a server with the requisite qualities, makes him, in fact, a new and fit instrument for God. But now the significance of priestly ordination does not consist in a mere impregnation of a spiritual colouring, which makes no further change in the man himself. It establishes no character in the western sense, but its effect is a real, if invisible, inward transforming of the 'old man', which makes him mature and competent for the whole range of his priestly tasks.

I have not found these ideas generally held by the fourth century Fathers. Especially in Basil, whose correspondence on these questions provides abundant material, there is no trace of any sacerdotal endowment imparted sacramentally; such an idea, in fact, would hardly accord with his general personality, clarity of thought, and strictly ethical approach. But, on the other hand, it does appear—as far as I know, for the first time—quite clearly in Gregory of Nyssa. The passage in question (Migne, PG 46, 581) has not been considered up to now, and I will, therefore, reproduce it in translation. 'The same power of the word that hallows the simple water of baptism,' says Gregory—

he is reflecting on baptism—'also makes the priest holy (σεμνός) and worthy of honour, when he is set apart by the new blessing from the multitude. Just now he was but one of many, one of the people; suddenly he appears as leader, as Superior, as teacher of piety, and as director (μυσταγωγός) of the hidden mysteries. And this happens without his being changed in body or appearance; but, externally and apparently the same as he was, he is, by an invisible power and gift changed in his invisible soul to something better'. Ordination, then, has made the priest, invisibly but actually, a different, a better man, and so has raised him up above the laity.

The ideas here so graphically expressed were, a century later, inserted by the pseudo-Dionysius into a vast system of theology of the Church, a system which, henceforth, finds support in them, just as they find support in it. There the eastern idea of the priest appears fully complete in its independence and in its specific nature. Now the power of the Greek priest also rests entirely on ordination, which signifies a divine bestowal of grace, and so the ideas of the community and calling by it are totally set aside. By this divine transformation the priest is marvellously incorporated into the great hierarchy of spirits which leads up from the earth to the throne of God. Each new Order he receives signifies a corresponding ascent of his moral personality, by which he is sanctified and sanctifies others, in virtue of his special priestly power (κατὰ οἰκείαν δύναμιν). This power not only permits him to perform the holy, divine functions of his service, it makes him alone capable of performing them. The image-concept, the conviction that the ecclesiastical ordinations must always somehow transmit the power they show forth, these are what make possible the underlying fiction that the degrees of the priestly state always signify degrees of actual perfection. It is precisely this that makes the eastern idea of the priest essentially different from the western idea, with its formalism.

For this reason, it is fundamentally impossible to see the sacerdotal character as a *character indelebilis*. Such a fiction would have been in blatant contradiction with reality. Those guilty of apostasy, sinners excommunicated and degraded, of course, completely lose their priestly power. The question how the community, if their priest is secretly a sinner, can be certain of salvation is, significantly enough, not even put by the Areopagite. All he gives on the point is a warning not to ordain any unworthy person. In fact, the whole theory of the priesthood is not worked out, as in the west, from the standpoint of the community; it is the priest himself who occupies the foreground, together with his objective service of public worship, by which the Church lives. Even where the ideas seem to bear the same meaning as those of the west, their inner tendency is quite different.

At first sight, the eastern idea of the priest may seem the more pagan, and so in fact it is, having a purely sacred foundation in public worship. On the other hand, in regard to the person of the priest, it is also more consonant with primitive Christianity, in that it holds that the essence of priestly perfection is that the whole man becomes new and holy. At the opposite extreme, the purely formal, detached concept of the character in the west is strongly suggestive of magic; as far as I know, the doctrine, in this respect, is cruder than that of any non-Christian priesthood. Yet the motive behind is, once again, a Christian one. In the question of the imparting and the assurance of salvation, the approach is almost that of primitive Christianity, the person of the priest being left out of account.

In any case—and I should like to conclude by insisting on this— the acceptance of the absolute idea of the priesthood cannot really be understood so long as its explanation is confined to the usual, general, and timeless categories of the history of religion, without taking into account the unique characteristics of Church history. Certainly, universal and primitive instincts of religious awe, ideas of cultic purity, of the magic power of blessings and rites, and such like things have played their part also in the history of the Christian priesthood, probably much earlier, and perhaps at a far deeper level than the theological sources tell us today. Yet they became clearly potent, their force assured and definite, only in the context of belief in the Church and in the special, salvific functions of her servants. And, therefore, the persistent strength they ever anew display lies not only in the darkness of an instinctive religious sensibility on the human level, whether genuine or superstitious, but also, and mainly, in their close connection, contestable but seriously held and asserted, with the saving faith of the Christian.

11

The Ascetic Idea of Exile
in Ancient and Early
Medieval Monasticism

'By faith Abraham obeyed when he was called to go out to a place
which he was to receive as an inheritance; and he went out, not knowing where he was to go. By faith he sojourned in the land of promise
as in a foreign land . . . For he looked forward to the city which has
foundations, whose builder and maker is God'.[1] The Old Testament
has nothing to say about the actual state of mind of Abraham, expressed
in this passage of the epistle to the Hebrews; but already in pre-
Christian times it is found in the hellenistic Jewish philosopher, Philo
of Alexandria, and from the time of the epistle onwards it finds
frequent expression in the Christian Church in similar words. 'Go
from your country and your kindred and your father's house to the
land that I will show you'.[2] This divine command seems to go beyond
its literal meaning to the more profound one of indicating the duty of
every devout soul to be detached from the transitory world and to
look to the eternal, heavenly Jerusalem promised by God. Or else,
as the philosophers taught, the soul should now already, by a spiritual
ascent, leave this physical world as far as possible, and find its true
homeland in the realm of transcendental truth, from which the soul of
man himself originates. With the appeal to Abraham is readily conjoined the words of Paul understood in a similar sense, 'while we are at
home in the body we are away from the Lord'.[3] The Christian is a
pilgrim on earth, where he has no abiding city. Whether he moves
from place to place or remains at home, his life, properly understood,
is always but 'a crusade towards the promised land'.

In the pages that follow, we do not propose to speak of this figurative

[1]Heb. 11.8-10.   [2]Gen. 12.1.
[3]2 Cor. 5.6.

231

state of exile and pilgrimage, but of a religious migration of a wholly concrete kind into strange lands, whose history, little known and more than a little ambiguous, runs into centuries. Appeal was also readily made to the model of Abraham in urging a literal abandonment of country for the sake of the 'faith', and at times use was made of the more elevated standpoint of allegorical interpretation. But basically, this requirement was more in the nature of a contrast to the pattern of Abraham. Its root was neither the primitive Christian longing for the start of the kingdom of God, nor the spiritualism of a world-renouncing, idealist philosophy. The decisive factor was, rather, the ascetic striving after detachment from the senses and for divinization, and so the monks have become the classical representatives of this ideal. As the ascetic seeks to free himself from all earthly ties, so finally he cuts himself loose also from the exterior life-sphere of his native land, in order to go into a strange land as a completely solitary stranger.

Homelessness as an ascetic ideal was considered exemplified by Christ, 'who became a stranger for our sakes', and, next to him, by the Apostles in particular. This attribution may seem strange to us today, but perhaps it is not really so unfounded as it appears at first sight. After all, Paul himself, who wished to traverse all the provinces of the Empire to preach the Gospel, and to sustain the young communities who needed his support, had been a wanderer on earth without rest or home. Nor was he alone in this mode of life. In primitive Christianity there was a whole class of lesser 'apostles', 'prophets' and 'teachers', who needed not to belong to any fixed community, and often, like him, were unmarried and without possessions, and went from place to place as 'travelling preachers'.[4] Admittedly, they took on this life of movement not in regard to themselves, as ascetics, but 'for the growth and building up of the divine word', to look after the communities, and to preach to the pagans. It was for them a reasonable Christian service, and this, to our way of thinking, sharply differentiates them from their ascetic successors. Yet, at the same time, a certain historical connection between the two seems possible and even probable, though it is more a matter of presumption than of strict proof.

[4]*Cf.* on this Harnack, *Die Mission und Ausbreitung des Christentums in den ersten drei Jahrhunderten* I, pp. 357ff.

It was a necessary consequence of the establishment of local hierarchies that the old unsettled teachers, actuated by the Spirit, should lose their original importance; but they did not, for all that, disappear. The ascetic tendency, so prominent in the beginning in the leaders of the Church and rapidly growing in the succeeding epoch, assured their continuance as ascetics by vocation, as it were. As such they were soon to be found in every community, and were held in the highest regard as heroes of Christian morality. 'Out of free evangelists and teachers who were also continent arose practitioners of continence who were also teachers';[5] and under the influence of the dualistic environment and of the idea of merit now once more coming to the fore, asceticism came to be looked on as the characteristic quality of the 'apostolic way of life'.[6] This view of the matter is supported by the fact that the wandering life did not cease altogether in the changed circumstances, but simply received a new meaning under the influence of the new ideal, being held a mark of the 'spiritual', that is, ascetic, life. According to a brilliant hypothesis of Reitzenstein, we may recognize as heirs of the old apostolic way of life the 'Circumcellions' in Africa in the fourth century, adherents of the Donatist schism. With them Catholic monasticism, newly brought in from the east, engaged in sharp competition and conflict. Possibly certain wandering kinds of monks, censured by ecclesiastical writers of the west as 'circuitae' and 'monachi gyrovagi', roaming monks, belong also to this connection.[7] In the east, particularly in Syria, they seem to have held out longer still, and to have continued in a special branch of monasticism as 'wandering monks'.[8] From a Syrian writing of the sixth century, we can gain a clear idea of its peculiar features. These ascetics, who did not count themselves as actual monks, lived by begging and in privation, wandering about quite uncontrolled, either

---

[5]Harnack, 'Die pseudoklementinischen Briefe de virginitate und die Entstehung des Mönchtums', Sitzungsber. d. preuss. Ak. XXI (1891), p. 381.
[6]See R. Reitzenstein, 'Des Athanasius Werk über das Leben des Antonius', Sitzungsber. d. Heidelb. Ak., Phil-hist. Kl. V (1914), Nr. 8, pp. 54ff.
[7]R. Reitzenstein, Historia monachorum und Historia Lausiaca (1916), pp. 50ff.; 'Ein donatistisches Corpus cyprianischer Schriften', Nachr. d. Göttinger Ak. 1914, Phil-hist. Klasse, p. 90, n. 1.
[8]Harnack, Sitzungsber. d. preuss. Ak. XXI (1891), p. 382, and W. Bousset, 'Das Mönchtum der sketischen Wüste, ZKG42 (1923), pp. 40f.

singly or in groups. In winter they spent the night in some hut or other, in summer, out in the open. It was their highest glory to be taken, from time to time, as idiots or outcasts, this being the severest test of their humility. Other accounts bring out as specially striking the practice of these homeless enthusiasts of eating nothing but grass, which led their opponents to make them into a special sect of Grass-eaters (Βόσκοι). In addition, we hear frequently of homeless ascetics going stark naked (in reality, this was seldom practised). In both these cases, it was, of course, not a question of a romantic 'return to nature', but the condition, or else the sign, of their spiritual mode of being, and their angelic superiority to all human needs and natural sexuality and shame. The non-Christian influences affecting the formation of this ideal and suggestive of the east need not be considered in this place.[9]

Now and then, the ideal of ceaseless wandering through the deserts, homelessness in its most extreme form, seems to have found adherents even outside Syria. Anthony himself, according to an interesting conjecture of Bousset, may have been one of these.[10] In addition, traces of this form of life are to be found in the stories of the Egyptian monks.[11] As a general rule, however, this ideal contradicted the spirit of the classical *Egyptian anachoretism*, with its habitual aversion to the fantastic and superhuman, and, in particular, it came up against decided opposition in the desert of Scete. There, it was not to perpetual wandering and travelling that importance was attached; nor to instability of life, with its sufferings and uncertainties. 'Wandering through the desert', as practised by the 'travelling monk', was rejected,[12] and the naked saint, subsisting on vegetables, was here merely

---

[9]See R. Reitzenstein, *Hist. Mon.*, pp. 52ff., 256, and W. Bousset, '*Der verborgene Heilige*', *Arch f. Religionswissensch.* XXI (1922), pp. 1-17.

[10]W. Bousset, *ZKG* 42 (1923), pp. 27ff.

[11]*Cf.* for example Bessarion's *Apophthegma* 12 (PG LXV 142f), kindly pointed out to me by Dörries: Δεῖ γάρ με συνεχῶς ἀποπλανώμενον τελειῶσαι τὸν δρόμον.

[12]*Apophth.* Ammonas 4; Jesaias 3. Euagrios. *Mönchspiegel* 81 (Grossmann, *Texte und Untersuchungen* III, 9, H 4 (1913), p. 160): Κυκλευτὴς μοναχὸς μελετήσει ῥήσεις ψευδεῖς, τὸν δὲ ἑαυτοῦ παραλογίσεται πατέρα. Perhaps the designation κυκλευτὴς μοναχὸς is more of a derogatory term than an indication of a way of life. At any rate, this proverb tells us nothing about the organization of the κυκλευταὶ μοναχοί, and the rejection of their way of life seems to be undoubted; against this view, R. Reitzenstein, *Hist. Mon.*, p. 51.

a legendary figure.[13] For all that, real detachment from the world and its pleasures was no less cultivated, together with undisturbed attention to the great ascetic struggle; and here too actual withdrawing from country and acquaintances was held essential as a means to this.

The true monk should be a stranger on the earth—not only in the spiritual sense, but in a quite literal sense he goes into 'the strange land where no one knows him'; and as a technical designation for this requirement there was established the concept of *xeniteia* (ξενιτεία) or *xenia* (ξενία), alienness, with the corresponding verb *xeniteuein* (ξενιτεύειν). This concept should not be taken in the sense of the Syrian ideal of wandering.[14] The emphasis is not placed on the idea of wandering and journeying as such, but, as the literal meaning of the expression brings out, on living and existing in an alien land, as an alien (ξένος), and so on leaving one's own land. In this form the idea of homelessness later on agrees also with the ideal of monastic quiet and stability of place. Only thus is it understandable how, for example, Abbot Jesaias can commend stenochoria (στενοχωρία), confinement to the smallest space,[15] and so the cell, as also *xeniteia*, life in an alien land and as an alien.[16] Finally, the cell itself can be designated as *xenia*,[17] and the often repeated sentence to the effect that silence is the first condition and even a substitute for *xenia*[18] points in the same direction.

The nature and significance of *xenia* is described with especial charm and thoroughness by St. Nilus the Wise, who died about 430 A.D. For him *xenitheia* is the third glorious conflict the monk takes on himself, in ardent faith and in the divine spirit, in order to attain the state of blessedness. It is especially arduous in the case of the anchorite dwelling entirely alone. Then the devil comes to him by night, when he is sick and sad, and points out the consolation, the care, the gratitude, and the joyful admiration awaiting him on his return to his country.

---

[13]Bousset, *ZKG* 42 (1923), pp. 31*ff.* To these legends also belongs Sulp. Sev. *Dial.* I, 17.
[14]Against Bousset, *ZKG* 42 (1923), p. 19, and Reitzenstein, *Hist. Mon.*, p. 48.
[15]*Apophth.* 4.
[16]*Apophth.* 8.
[17]*Hist. Laus.*, Butler, p. 74, 7; 136, 16.
[18]*Apophthegma*: Longinus 1; Thirhoe 2; Pistos; *cf.* also the *Apophthegma* of Andrew A concept allied to the ideal of ξενιτεία is θεύγειν τοὺς ἀνθρώπους : Theodore of Pherme 5; Longinus 1.

Cunningly he adds that most men have attained to virtue not in flight from their own country (φεύγοντες τὴν πατρίδα), but, quite the contrary, in the midst of their own people; and, furthermore, one has to exercise virtue not in a determined place, but only in the right way (οὐκ ἐν τόπῳ, ἀλλ' ἐν τρόπῳ). Such diabolic insinuations must be resisted manfully. After all, we find in the psalms the words: 'Who will give me wings like a dove, and I will fly and be at rest? I have gone far off ... and I abode in the wilderness'. Evagrius Ponticus, the theologian of the Egyptian hermits, is also aware of the value of *xeniteia*: repose (ἡσυχία) is the highest end that he expects from their contemplation, while in one's own country no one can achieve repose. Thus *xeniteia* becomes, along with humility, poverty and silence, a basic demand of the monastic doctrine of virtue. The boundaries separating it from the Syrian ideal of wandering may, on occasion, be somewhat fluid. For example, it may be all part of the ideal of *xeniteia* for monks, even after conversion and without alleging any special reason, to change their residence once or twice, and therefore begin, in a fairly confined area, to 'wander'. They did not wish, even in the desert, to feel at home in any place. But the fantastic and extravagant idea of eternal wandering has given way to a wholly different spirit. No longer is homelessness a purely ascetic sacrifice rewarded with miraculous powers. It has taken on a more noble form as serving the strict, yet delicate, monastic culture of the soul, and, in fact, the entire spiritual training.[19]

We must now consider the cultivation of the ascetic ideal of homelessness in the western, Latin, world. We have already spoken of the Donatist Circumcellions and the later *monachi gyrovagi*. In the first period of enthusiasm *in the west* for the monastic life we find a fairly favourable description by Ambrose of hermits with no fixed abode, and how, 'clothed with shirts of hide and goatskins, poor and necessitous, tortured with want and pain, they wandered about in solitude, among inaccessible rocks and in fearsome caverns and hollow places'. It reminds us at once of the Syrian *wandering ascetics*. But quite apart from the fact that he is here alluding to a biblical text,[20] Ambrose intended, significantly enough, to relegate this ideal as inferior to a

[19]For this conception see also Gelasius of Cyzicus, *Hist. eccl.* III, 9, 8; Löschke-Heinemann, *GCS.* 28, p. 149 ...
[20]Heb. 11.37*f.*

monasticism more connected with the Church and city life; this held the first place in his estimation,[21] It is no accident that we meet the western 'wandering monks' in later times only in the caricatures of their opponents. The more sober spirit of the Latin Church, with its propensity, even in the ascetic sphere, towards discipline and thorough-going organization, was certainly even less favourable than the eastern Church to the development of such a way of life, impossible to regulate. Whenever we hear, later, of wandering monks, it is in most cases, a matter of a temporary aberration of the ordinary stable monasticism, a decline such as happens at all times, rather than an independent and consciously adopted ideal of homelessness. Already Augustine complained of vagabond monks, who, '*nusquam missi, nusquam fixi, nusquam stantes, nusquam sedentes*', without any real function and lacking steadfastness, go from place to place, trading in all kinds of objects;[22] we constantly come across similar instances later. As the medieval author of a rule maliciously asserts, in connection with Benedict of Nursia, they apply themselves 'to their daily wandering evidently more to satisfy gluttony than for the good of their souls.'[23]

On the other hand, the ideal of *xeniteia* as a going out into a distant and strange land did not remain unknown even in the west; it was accepted and followed after, along with monasticism in general. As a rendering of the Greek word *xeniteia* the concept of '*peregrinatio*' and of '*peregrinari*' was adopted, which may equally mean what is alien and being in a foreign land, or the process of travelling itself. Already Paulinus of Nola recognized *peregrinatio* as an ascetic requisite. He also, in his enthusiasm for the ideals of monasticism, 'leaving native land and friends', kept far away from his native Spain for four years, declaring himself convinced that this was the only sure way to peace, which no one could find at home, and urging his friend to imitate him in an adaptation of the words of Paul: *pro gratiae et caritatis augmento*

[21]He was commemorating Bishop Eusebius of Vercelli in the letter 63 *ad eccl. Verc.*, c. 67*f*. In contrast to the original ascetic life as represented by Elijah, Elisha, John, and Elizabeth, Eusebius, even as a monk, remained true to his episcopal calling, and realized the ascetic ideals while living in the city, as Daniel and his companions had done while dwelling in a strange land.

[22]*De opere monach.* 28.

[23]*Regula magistri* c.1. Holst. I, p. 231: '. . . *ut gulae suae magis cotidie peregrinari videantur quam animae*'.

peregrineris a patria, dum adhuc hospes corporis peregrinaris a Christo!
'In order to increase in grace and charity absent yourself from your
native land, since, as long as you dwell in the body, you are absent
from Christ'.[24] It is in accordance with this view that the first to realize
completely in practice the oriental hermit ideal, Martin of Tours,
began his course[25] with a journey in order to set up his cell far from his
native land, first in Milan, then on a small island off the Riviera, and
finally in the neighbourhood of Poitiers.

Above all, we must remember the celebrated journeys undertaken
by Rufinus and the older Melania, Jerome, Cassian, and Germanus,
one after the other, to the east, in order to emulate the great exemplars
of oriental monachism in its own land. For, with them, there was
introduced into the ideal of *xeniteia* a new subsidiary meaning, alien to
the original conception, which obliterated its relationship to the eastern
models and has not received sufficient attention. Along with the
old aim of inner recollection and ascetic deliverance from daily domestic concerns, it acquired, in some degree, an exploratory purpose,
as we can see from Cassian in particular. The idea was to learn about
genuine unadulterated monachism, and to bring back its practices and
aims to one's own country. In his dialogues Sulpicius Severus describes
similar journeys made for the purpose of studying ecclesiastical matters;
they were prompted not only by pious curiosity and the general
fashion, but also by sheer human interest in the events of the journey
and the curiosities of distant countries. From this it is clear how far
xeniteia must have departed from its original seriousness and thoroughness, and it is indicative of this levelling down of the ideal that, for all
the *peregrini* of the west whom we have mentioned—Martin alone
excepted up to a point—the *peregrinatio* signified only a transient phase
of their life, and that the years they spent away from their country
were not characterized by complete seclusion or solitude, and still
less by silence.

Soon, however, there arose yet one more factor to modify considerably the concept of *peregrinatio*. After Egypt, the classical home of the

---

[24]*Ep.* 5 *ad Iesum Seuerum* 14, Hartel *CSEL* 29, p. 34; *ibid.* c. 13, p. 33: *multa sunt, quae
ad nos invitare te et de patria parumper debeant sevocare, prae ceteris amor pacis et zeli fuga,
qui maxime conspectu aut vicinia aemulae conversationis accenditur*; cf. Ep. 1, 10.
[25]Admittedly, it led him first not to a foreign country but to his home in order to
convert his pagan parents: Sulp. Sev., *Vita Mart.* c. 5.

old monasticism, Palestine, which possessed its own monastic heroes, came more and more to gain importance as a place to visit. Jerome especially propagated its merits in glowing terms, and extolled the promised land, held out by God to Abraham as the goal of his wanderings, and watered by dew from heaven, in preference to Egypt, watered from below by the Nile.[26] Palestine is absolutely *the* holy land of the Bible, and so there spontaneously came about an imperceptible transition from the monastic '*peregrinatio a patria*' to the '*peregrinationes ad loca sancta*', which for some decades already had been increasing in popularity. This new connotation was facilitated by the fact that the Latin '*peregrinari*', as opposed to the Greek '*xeniteuein*', could mean not only dwelling in a strange country, but also travelling to distant parts and for a definite purpose. The sacrifice of home and domestic happiness, with its deep interior motivation, became fused with the transient hardship of the pilgrimage, as meriting grace, a pilgrimage the motives for which were already being censured as superstitious and pernicious by such clear-sighted ecclesiastics as Gregory of Nyssa.[27]

Nevertheless, the old meaning of *peregrinatio* was not wholly abandoned even in the west, and in the east ascetic wandering continued in the following centuries. The best known example is that of St. Severinus.[28] Understandably, the Church leaders did not look very favourably on such travels, as is shown, for instance, by an interesting passage attacking them that Claudianus Mamertus inserted into his treatise on the incorporeality of the soul. In it he inveighs sharply against all exterior '*peregrinatio localis*', as he calls it, on the ground that it does not really detach one from the pleasures of the body, which can be effected only in the spirit. 'On that account let us no longer stay as strangers (*peregrinemur*) in Alexandria, but turn away from Egypt to the fatherland of *truth*, sail over the sea of *errors* and cross the deserts of

---

[26]*Ep.* 46, 2 Hilberg *CSEL.* 54, pp. 330f.: ...'*habitet terram repromissionis quae non rigatur ut Aegyptus de deorsum, sed de sursum, nec facit holera languentium cibos, sed temporaneum et serotinum de coelo expectat imbrem. Haec terra montuosa et in sublimi sita, quantum a deliciis saeculi vacat, tantum maiores habet delicias spirituales*'. The same kind of attitude is found in the *Vita Hilarionis*.

[27]*Ep.* 2. *De eunt. Hierosol.*

[28]Eugipp. *Vita Sev., ep. praef.* 9. Severinus did not wish even to let it be known where he came from: *Quid prodest servo Dei significatio sui loci vel generis?* (Mon. Germ. Auct. ant. I, 2, p. 2, 35f.).

ignorance.[29] The geographical designation of the images clearly shows that Claudianus, in this passage, is not attacking the customary pilgrimages to the Holy Land, but has in mind precisely the ascetic peregrinations of a monastic character.

The same adverse view is reflected in the strikingly infrequent use, in the fifth century, of Peregrinus as a proper name, and its use as a literary pseudonym in only two cases, those of the monks, Vincent of Lérins and Bachiarius of Britona. Once again stress came to be laid, as against the exterior ideal of leaving one's country, on the old idea of Christ's life as a unique kind of spiritual wandering, in which the whole world is foreign. Admittedly, the misconception that runs through the work of the historian Gennadius when treating of Bachiarius is significant. He takes literally what Bachiarius meant figuratively, and explains that the latter had resolved, on the model of Abraham, '*vacare deo disponens*', on a peregrinatio—that is a *peregrinatio localis*, to use the expression of Claudianus—and this exposed him to reproaches and calumnies against which he was obliged to defend himself in writing.[30]

With this last piece of evidence we are already on the threshold of a new epoch, and I consider that once we are clear about the meaning of *xeniteia* and *peregrinatio* in the ancient Church as indicated, it is not difficult to go on to the Middle Ages proper—though, strangely enough, this step has never yet been taken by any scholar. In the first place, we must consider the Church in the British Isles and the peregrinations which, particularly with the Irish monks, became an established custom. It is highly probable that the origins of these go back to Christian antiquity. There is evidence of pilgrims from Britain to the east already at the beginning of the fifth century[31], and

---

[29]*De statu animae* I, 22, Engelbrecht *CSEL* 11, p. 80: '. . . *et quoniam sancta anima adfectu casto in deum rapitur, animadverte nec peregrinationem illi localem esse nec patriam . . . in tantum istic peregrinatur, in quantum per voluptatem ac dolores corporis per loca vel tempora, per phantasias et phantasmata a summi boni contemplatione revocatur . . .*'; III, 11, p. 175: '*ac si usquequaque patet animum et corporea non posse videre sine corpore et incorporea cum corpore videre non posse, non diutius Alexandriae peregrinemur, sed ab Egypto redeuntes transmisso errorum mari et emensa ignorantiae eremo veritatis patriam atque ut terram repromissionis intremus non otiosi neque inertes*'.
[30]*De script. eccl.* 24; *cf.* O. F. Frische, '*Uber Bacharius und Peregrinus*', ZKG 17 (1897), pp. 210-215.
[31]Pallad, *Hist. Laus.* 118; Theodoret, *Philoth.* 26 (Haddan-Stubbs I, 14).

towards the end of it—that is with the first certain information we have about the Celtic Church in general—there emerges again the characteristic expression *peregrinatio*.[32] In the following period it occurs so often in biographies of Irish and Anglo-Saxon saints, and its significance is brought out in such detail, that there is no need to cite individual instances.

'For the sake of Christ', 'for the eternal fatherland', 'for the love of God' and 'for the soul's salvation',[33] the Irish monks, when they desire to reach the highest degree of perfection, leave—'like Abraham' again —country, friends, and relations, in order to follow Christ, '*nudum Christum nudi sequentes*'.[34] At the same time, they seek, like the ancient hermits of Egypt, for the 'peace' which the 'desert' should assure for them; only that their '*eremus*' and '*desertum*' must be sought not in Egypt, but in remote islands and far-off lands. We hear of people who embarked as much as three times on long sea voyages in order to discover a really remote place, a 'desert in the uncrossable sea',[35] and the longer the journey the more meritorious it seemed.[36] So it was that two Irish clerics came from Iona into the Gulf Stream—a stream in the ocean 'whose water tastes like warm milk'—and as far as the Shetlands.[37] These religious migrations must be sharply distinguished from the penal exile overseas so often imposed in the Ireland of the time. Exceptional, too, is the ecclesiastical penance, prescribed by the canons and the penitential books, as a motive of *peregrinatio*.[38] Nor-

---

[32]Syn. *Lucus Victoriae* (569) can. 6, Haddan-Stubbs I, 118: *Qui mechatur matris, III, annis, cum peregrinatione perenni.*

[33]Instances of these and other expressions in Dom Louis Gougaud, O.S.B., *Gaelic pioneers of Christianity, the work and influence of Irish monks and saints in continental Europe* (6th-12th cent), Dublin 1923, p. 6, n. 1.

[34]Thus in the later *Vita Mariani Scotti* c. 1, 1 *Act. SS* II, Febr. 364. The motive of *imitatio Christi* increasingly predominated in medieval peregrinations.

[35]Adamn. *Vita Columbae* I, 6.20; II, 42.

[36]Cf. the *Vita* of the younger Columban. *Mon. Germ. SS rer. Mer.* IV, 98, 19f.: '*ob suam peregrinationem augendam*'.

[37]*Imrama Snedgusa ocus Maic Riagla*, H. 2, 16 col. 391-395 (Zimmer, *Über die ältesten Berührungen der Iren mit den Nordgermanen, Sitzungsber. d. preuss. Ak.* I (1891), p. 295).

[38]Adamn. *Vita Columbae* I, 30 is concerned with a penance; likewise II, 39. It is perhaps no accident that whereas the penitential books speak of a limited '*exul paenitere*', doing penance in exile, of an exile of 7 and 10 years, a '*peregrinatio*' originally, as far as we know, was always for a lifetime. '*Dies vitae suae peregrinando perficiat*' (Cap. Jud. III, 1; Poen. Sang. 2.3.), '*cum peregrinatione perenni mundo moriatur*' (Cap. Jud. I, 3;

mally the latter represents an absolutely voluntary ascetic undertaking
of a special character, even when, in the course of time, the recollection
of earlier sins came more to the fore.

All this shows the general acceptance of the ancient equation of
peregrinatio with *xeniteia*. This must have formed the real basis of the
practice, and the usual explanation, adducing the innate wandering
tendency of the Irish, cannot suffice by itself[39]—though certainly the
'sea voyages', *Imrama*, the name given to a whole series of Irish stories
of heroes and adventures, offers the nearest parallel to the descriptions
of our spiritual 'sea voyages'. The express monastic character of the
Irish Church explains why the old monastic custom prevailed in
Ireland longer than in the rest of the west, and even—regardless of the
reaction that arose—continued to develop. Nonetheless, in my
opinion, we can hardly rest satisfied with an ascription to purely
western sources, such as St. Martin[40] or to Jerome, so highly esteemed
in Ireland.[41] The intensity and seriousness with which the ideal was
embraced and practised all through life, the resolution with which
homelessness and alienation as such were once more emphasized without reference to any kind of pious purpose in travelling, and, furthermore, the strong eremetical tendency even to the point—seldom otherwise met with in the west—of *inclusio*, complete confinement to a
cell[42]—all this points decidedly to a direct imitation of the east and its

---

Poen. Cumm. IV, 5), and similar expressions were employed. On the other hand,
even voluntary peregrinations were spoken of figuratively as *'exulari'*; *cf.* Bede,
Hist. eccl. III, 4; V, 10; Bon. *ep.* 30 Tangl. p. 54, 11.

[39]One is constantly referred, in this connection, to Walafrid Strabo (*Vita S. Galli* II,
46), according to whom the *'consuetudo peregrinandi'* of the Irish had become almost
second nature (*iam paene in naturam conversa*), *Mon. Germ. SS rer. Mer.* IV 336, 5).
But the first conclusion to be drawn from this is that the *consuetudo* itself had other,
namely religious, causes. Dunstan says much the same (*Haddan-Stubbs* I, 75): *Quod
aliis bona voluntas in consuetudinem, hos illis consuetudo vertit in naturam.*

[40]*Cf.* Zimmer, 'Über direkte Handelsverbindungen Westgalliens mit Irland im frühen
Mittelalter', *Sitzungsber. d. preuss. Ak.* 1909, I, 572, and similarly Finsterwalder, *'Wege
und Ziele der irischen und angelsächsischen Mission im frankischen Reich,'* ZKG 47 (1928),
p. 206. On the other hand, Schubert rightly warns against too sweeping conclusions
on the dependence of the old Irish Church on the Gallican: see his *Geschichte der
christlichen Kirche im Frühmittelalter*, p. 204, n.1.

[41]*Cf.* Loofs, *De antiqua Britonum Scotorumque ecclesia*, pp. 6of.

[42]See the details given by Gougaud, 'Ermites et reclus. Etudes sur d'anciennes formes de
vie religieuse', Saint-Martin de Ligugé 1928, pp. 57ff., and his *Gaelic Pioneers* pp. 88ff.

xeniteia. Such an influence is all the more probable in that relations between Ireland and Byzantium constantly assert themselves—in theology, liturgy, art, in the remarkable familiarity of the Irish with the Greek language and culture. Consequently, the spread in Ireland of *peregrinatio* presupposes a corresponding connection with the east, however obscure and puzzling we find the mode of this communication.

We will, of course, hardly expect to find in the Irish, with their totally different environment, the precise spirit of Evagrius and of the Scete. There was something barbaric about them, these strange, rough, wandering Irish monks, contemptuous of the world, as they travelled to remote places, with their long staffs and flowing beards, equipped with leather bags and bottles and with writing tablets, their hair blowing about and their eyebrows painted.[43] They lacked the psychological refinement and the spiritual culture of the Greeks, as also, at first, all mysticism and speculative thought. A penitential code of draconian severity, with all the scourgings it prescribed, assisted the process of *mortificatio*. Soon, however, importance came to be attached to a thorough training in the classical sciences, as far as they were then understood. In fact, the historical importance of the Irish *peregrini*, and particularly of their monastic settlements, lies in their reception and propagation of the classical traditions of culture.

What, though not absolutely new,[44] is specifically Irish in its fixed form and wide extent is the *peregrinatio* in larger groups of, as a rule, twelve men, corresponding to Christ and his eleven Apostles. They were the abbot and the first monks of a monastery to be founded in some remote part, which would exist alongside the individual *peregrinationes* or those of two or three persons, not at that time ousting them. The monastery alone constituted in a foreign country a fixed, permanent centre of Irish culture, and, in the case of a pagan country, also a centre of a Christian mission. The stricter coenobitical discipline seems also to have brought in its wake a stricter understanding of the ideal of *peregrinatio*. Already the elder Columba made the taking of a formal monastic vow indispensable for entrance to his monastery on

---

[43]Zimmer, 'Uber die Bedeutung des irischen Elements für die mittelalterliche Kultur', *Preuss. Jahrbücher* LIX (1887), p. 33; cf. Wattenbach, 'Die Kongregation der Schotten-klöster in Deutschland', *Zeitschr. f. christl. Archaeol. u. Kunst* I (1856), p. 23.
[44]Cf. the concept of συνοδία in eastern monasticism: Reitzenstein, *Hist. Mon.*, p. 50.

Iona.[45] In addition, the lifelong element of *peregrinatio* must have been furthered by its adoption in the monastic community. How movingly does the story of the sick Kranich express how this eternal absence from home weighed on the spirit. A storm drove him to Iona, but Columba foresaw 'prophetically' that this stranger would not persevere in *peregrinatio*. And, in fact, the sacred bird was seen three days later flying back to its homeland, 'back to the sweet land of Ireland where it was born'.[46]

Apart from this, there is little about 'love of travel' and 'invincible wanderlust'. For the Irish *peregrini* leaving home and relatives meant, rather, a hard sacrifice, more deeply felt and more meaningful to them than to those belonging to the devitalized cosmopolitan culture of late antiquity. The younger Columban, the first monastic founder in France, made stability of place, '*stabilitas*' or '*unius loci habitatio*', a strict rule for his monks.[47] This was not, either then or later, taken for granted by the Irish, as can be seen by an interesting account we owe to Bede's *Ecclesiastical History*.[48] The Irishman, Colman, had, at the end of the seventh century, founded a monastery in which, besides Irish, a great number of Anglo-Saxons were received. But, after a short time, living together was found impossible. 'For the Irish (Scotti) abandoned the cloister in the summer time, when the corn had to be harvested, and roved in all directions through the neighbourhood, so familiar to them. In winter, however, they came back and wanted to share with the English the enjoyment of what their work had produced'. Even if we leave out of account this piece of impertinence, which evidently made Bede indignant, there still always remained the strange fact of the '*monachi dispersi vagantes*', which, as far as the Irish are concerned, had nothing to do with the customary *peregrinatio* (since the monastery was in Ireland). It does, however, recall in a striking fashion the *monachi gyrovagi*, already mentioned, and also the wandering ascetics of the east.

[45]Adamn. *Vita Columbae* I, 32.
[46]Adamn. *Vita Columbae* I, 49. The love for '*dulce solum natalis patriae . . . et viridas terras*' (Vita B. Mariani *Ratisponensis* I,6, *Act*. SS. II. Febr. 366) is brought out also by Gougaud, *Gaelic Pioneers*, pp. XIIf.
[47]Ordo III, *ZKG* 14 (1894) p. 87; Regula, *ibid*. 15 (1895) pp. 382f.
[48]Bede, *Hist. eccl*. IV, 4.

There is no longer, it seems to me, any need to spend time on refuting the old and not yet quite defunct idea that the Irish—apart from their wanderlust—were moved by missionary zeal in their travels to foreign lands. It was convincingly refuted nearly fifty years ago by Loofs, who brings out clearly the fundamental ascetic character of the monastic *peregrinationes*,[49] though he was not aware of the antiquity of the practice. Certainly, the Irish monk was accustomed from the outset to pastoral activity, nor did he give it up when a *peregrinus*.[50] If his wanderings brought him to a pagan district—which was not usually the case—he might become a successful preacher of Christianity, but he was not, for all that, essentially a missionary. The idea of missionary work first emerges definitely with the younger Columba,[51] but even he did not manage to pursue it to any great extent. His own ideal remained that of the '*patres perfecti*', the perfect fathers of monasticism, 'to sit in the desert'. We cannot altogether deny to the Irish living in Germany in the seventh and eighth centuries a certain missionary intention, but at best it was only additional to their original and dominant motive of ascetic perfection. This explains the lack of real impact, the sporadic and uncertain character of the Irish missionary undertakings in Germany. The 'mission' was practised more for the sake of the missionary than of the people to be converted. It is significant that the only person before Willibrord and Boniface, of whom this cannot be said, Pirmin of Reichenau, the apostle of the Alemanni, was, as we now know, not an Irishman but a Goth.[52]

No less significant of the real meaning of the Irish *peregrinationes* is the fact that, even in the subsequent period, when the work of conversion had ended, they by no means ceased in Germany. They filled the various 'Scottish monasteries' with a stream of new wanderers, and led certain of the Irish, especially those who were prized as calligraphers, even to Poland, Kiev, and Bulgaria.[53] It was only with the

[49]Friedr. Loofs, *De antiqua Britonum Scotorumqeue cclesia, Lipsiae* 1882, esp. pp. 114*ff.*
[50]Finsterwalder, *ZKG* 47 (1928) p. 209.
[51]Columb. *ep.* 3, Mon. Germ. *ep.* III, p. 167, 37*f.*: *mei voti fuit gentes visitare et evangelium eis a nobis praedicari, sed . . .*
[52]*Cf.* Jecker, *Die Heimat des heil. Pirmin, des Apostels der Alamannen* (1927).
[53]On the other hand, the islands, in part, had so much to suffer from the Norman pirates that they became deserted (Dicuil, *Demens orbis terrae* 7, 15 on the Faroes: *causa latronum Normannorum vacuae anachoretis*): Zimmer, *Sitzungsber. d. preuss. Ak.*

conquest of Ireland by the English that the influx of Irish *peregrini* began notably to fall off, and, towards the end of the Middle Ages, we hear from the Scottish Congregations the usual complaints of loose living and general decline.[54] Many monks resolved on a wandering life for reasons quite other than the old ideal, not, that is, on grounds of asceticism, but only '*propter abundantiam et propter liberam voluntatem vivendi*',[55] for love of idleness and good living. Finally, the Scots successfully contested with the Irish the ownership of their German possessions, and Leo X, misled by the similarity of names, handed over, in 1515, the ancient mother-abbey of the Irish, St. James, in Ratisbon, to these inheritors of the name of the ancient 'Scotti', who only then were beginning to disappear from Germany.[56]

We will now turn back again to the early Middle Ages, and, by way of conclusion, see what form the old ideal of abandoning one's country eventually took with the Anglo-Saxons. The young Anglo-Saxon Church was, indeed, practically the daughter-Church of the Irish, and even the practice of *peregrinari* was taken over from the Irish by the English monks, despite their Benedictine organization. Often enough it was carried on in quite the same way as before. At the same time, however, the idea, which now spread widely even among the laity, took on a more and more comprehensive meaning, which whittled down its fundamental connotation and threatened to deprive it of any precise sense. Certainly the *peregrinatio* remained, as before, something of religious value, an ascetic practice—but how variously it could turn out in fact! Not only the monk in his solitude or in the remote

---

1891, I, 289*f.* It recalls the ἐρήμωσις of Skete! On all this see Bousset, *Apophtheg-mata—Studien zur Geschichte des ältesten Mönchtums*, 1923, p. 64.

[54]Yet the decline of the Scottish monasteries was not really worse than elsewhere, as is shown by an examination of the main sources concerning Vienna by P. J. Barry, *Die Zustände im Wiener Schottenkloster vor der Reform des Jahres 1418*, Aichach 1927.

[55]Oefele, *Script. rer. Boic.* p. 1343.

[56]Later, the Scots also became homeless wanderers 'on account of the faith', being, as Protestants, driven out in the 16th century, and remained such even in the subsequent period for the sake of gain; *cf.* Riemann, *Zeitschr. f. preuss. Geschichte*, III (1866) pp. 597*f.* Not only in England but even in eastern Europe the traders and pedlars of the 16th and 17th centuries were Scotsmen, and were only supplanted by the Jews in the 18th century—these also a people whose religion destined them to homelessness, wandering, and trade. *Cf.* W. Eckert, *Kurland unter dem Einfluss des Merkantilismus* (1926) pp. 239*f.*

monastery to which he had fled, but also the serious student wishing to study the Church and theology of Ireland on the spot, the cleric dwelling for a long period for similar motives in a Gallic monastery, and, above all, the constant stream of pious pilgrims who, year in year out, journeyed to Rome, the 'dwelling-place of Saints Peter and Paul', and from there, in many cases, on to Palestine—all these had taken the decision for the *peregrinatio*, '*pro Christo peregrinam ducere vitam*'. This latter, in particular, the most favoured form of wandering —to Rome, that is—was an innovation soon seen to be momentous. It was equally practised by monks, clerics, and laymen. We hear of no fewer than four kings who freely chose this way, abdicating their sovereignty;[57] women, too, by no means held back. As a rule, indeed, abandonment of country was intended for life, '*propter adquirendam quietem et contemplationem Dei*', for the sake of peace and pious contemplation, and, more and more frequently, also '*propter delenda peccamina*', to expiate sins. But it was also the case that to the fixed holy aim of the journey were conjoined certain extraneous superstitious expectations which a single journey was able to satisfy; nor were there wanting among the pilgrims elements of a less serious nature.

One consequence, as Boniface complains, of Roman pilgrimages is that everywhere in 'Lombardy, Gaul and France' he comes across Anglo-Saxon prostitutes.[58] It was, in fact, a kind of mass migration on the spiritual plane, and it was in vain that the Irish set themselves against this development: 'Going to Rome means great toil and brings little profit. The (heavenly) king whom thou dost miss at home, thou wilt not find there if thou dost not bear him with you. Great is the folly, great the madness, great the senselessness, great the lunacy. For it is surely entering upon death to draw on oneself the anger of the Son of Mary'.[59] The Irish did indeed recognize the veneration of saints and relics, but belief in the religious significance of particular places played little part in their piety, and entered not at all into their idea of *pere-*

---

[57]*Cf.* Zwölfer, *Sankt Peter, Apostelfürst und Himmelspförtner, seine Verehrung bei den Angelsachsen und Franken* (1929), pp. 24*ff.* Zwölfer, however, failed to see the relationships with the Irish *peregrinatio*, and this resulted in certain misconceptions on his part. Sporadically there were also Irish pilgrimages to Rome already; *cf.* Loofs, *De antiqua Britonum Scotorumque ecclesia*, p. 115. Gougaud, *Gaelic Pioneers*, pp. 31*f.*
[58]*Ep.* 78, Tangl. p. 169, 22.
[59]Irish verses in the *Codex Boernerianus*.

grinatio. Thus, in the fusion of the Irish ideal of pilgrimage with that of the west in general, we see repeated the process already noticed as regards the east and the west in the fourth and fifth centuries. The role then allotted to the Holy Land and Jerusalem is now, in its essentials, taken over by Rome, whose influence on the development in England is everywhere palpable.

There was, however, another way in which the Irish idea of *peregrinatio* underwent transformation, and this was of far greater significance. The Anglo-Saxons, in fact, exhibited something which must be denied to the Irish *peregrini* on the whole, and that is the conscious, indeed enthusiastic will to missionize, so combined with the ascetic ideal of homelessness as often to constitute the real driving force and decisive motive of the departure. Bede's *English Church History*, itself in its spirit really a missionary history, affords numerous and evident examples of this. Not in vain was a seventy-year struggle, with so many alternations, carried on for the conversion of his people; it was on that account that there now prevailed in the Anglo-Saxons a sense of missionary responsibility hardly to be found elsewhere at this time. We may leave aside the question how far Roman influence, especially the example of Pope Gregory the Great, was of parallel significance. More important was the consciousness, abundantly evidenced in this connection, of a blood-relationship with the heathens across the Channel. It was this that impelled the Anglo-Saxons, precisely as such, to go and convert their 'brothers of the same flesh and blood' and to 'snatch them from Satan'.[60] The ecclesiastical form available for these missionary designs was, at first, no other than that of the customary Irish *peregrinatio*—the ascetical journey to a distant land for Christ and the soul's sanctification. The transition was very gradual. Egbert, the first to aim at the conversion of the Frisians, had long been a *peregrinus* for his personal salvation, before deciding to be of use to others by preaching, *pluribus prodesse.*[61] The same may be supposed of the other Anglo-Saxon missionaries, who are soon after to be found scattered among the Frisians[62] and Saxons—where both the 'white' and the 'black' Ewald met their martyrdom[63]—among the Brukterns[64]

---

[60]Bede, *Hist. eccl.* V, 9; Bonif. 2 p. 46, Tangl. pp. 276, 25.
[61]Bede, *Hist. eccl.* V, 9. [62]*Ibid.* V, 9 (Wictberct).
[63]*Ibid.* V, 10; *cf.* Alcuin, *De sanctis Eubor. eccl.* 1071*ff.*
[64]*Ibid.* V, 11 (Suidberct).

and the Thuringians.[65] Of course, this definite aim of conversion does not necessarily exclude any motive of individual advantage; the two may be conjoined by the idea, so often expressed, that the intercession of souls won over to Christianity by one's own efforts is of weight in the next world. Later, national pride in the results achieved by the English Church clearly played a part, as we see from the letters of Boniface.

The difference from the Irish form of *peregrinatio* is at once clear, and the more pronounced the Anglo-Saxon missionary attitude became, the more conspicuous must have appeared the defects of the previous form of *peregrinatio* as a means to the desired end. At first, even the mission of the Anglo-Saxon *peregrini* was lacking in order and plan, in coherence and consistency, and they remained scattered, just like the Irish apostles, and liable, without regular oversight, to decadence and indiscipline. For that reason, Willibrord, who went out with his eleven companions to win over Friesland, adopted a form of monastic settlement; in fact, in the interests of his work he made the first tentative approach to what the Irish always eschewed, collaboration with the Frankish State and the Roman Church. But his disciple, Boniface, was the first to make this a definite policy and to create, in his grandiose yet careful work, the firm organized framework within which the German mission could be conducted with renewed vigour. The particular dangers attaching to his system, for the most part unintended by him, yet historically inevitable, we need not dilate upon here.

But even for Boniface the *peregrinatio* was the point from which his work took its beginning. It is certainly misleading on the part of his biographer to try and describe the first departure from his homeland in the customary terms, as the peak of devout world-renunciation, without the least mention of his firm resolve on missionary work.[66] Yet Boniface himself speaks over and over again in his letters of the laborious '*peregrinatio*' he carried out on German soil, and his fellow-workers were nearly all '*peregrini*',[67] that is, as we may venture to interpret, not merely Anglo-Saxon '*foreigners*', but also '*peregrinantes*' in the specific sense, which always implies an ascetic overtone. The im-

[65]*Vita Bonif. auct. Willibaldo* c. 6, Levison, p. 33 (Torchtwine, Berehthere, Eanbercht, Hunraed); cf. Boehmer, *Zeitschr. f. hess. Gesch.* N.F. 40 (1917) p. 192, n. 4.
[66]*Vita Bonif. auct.* Willibaldo c. 4, Levison, p. 15.
[67]*Ep.* 93 Tangl. pp. 213, 11.

portance of Boniface as a missionary is due not least to the skill and tact by which he was able, in contrast to the excessive zeal of the Popes for hierarchical organization, to make fruitful for missionary work the homeless way of life and the particular spirit of his British monks. On the other hand, it is interesting to see how Boniface was always reserved and sceptical about *peregrinatio* when practised in the hitherto unregulated fashion as an ascetical end in itself, and equally so about journeys to Rome. When asked for advice, in the early part of his career, he only gave his approval with much hesitation to the plan of an acquaintance to perform a pious *peregrinatio*, that is a permanent remove to Rome.[68] Later he directed to the Archbishop of Canterbury a formal injunction to check such *peregrinationes* by women, for the reasons we have already mentioned, through a categorical prohibition of the king.[69] Boniface's attitude to his most distinguished disciple, Lullus, was in line with this. The latter had gone on pilgrimage to Rome with his relatives, and Boniface sought to gain him for the work in Germany.[70] Lullus—evidently referring to his time at Rome— later commended his master for teaching him to despise that idleness so harmful to the soul that he had formerly loved as a '*vagabundus*'.[71]

So it came about that the old Irish and Anglo-Saxon ideal of *peregrinatio* no longer found any scope in Germany itself, despite close contacts with that country, and finally vanished with the consolidation of the Church there and the departure of the foreign missionaries. The line of development breaks off at this point, having after centuries once again approached its point of departure, the early Christian travelling apostolate of pastoral care and evangelization. Admittedly, the difference is not to be ignored. The purity of the motive of gratitude to God and love for the brethren still remained sullied by the

---

[68]*Ep.* 27 Tangl. pp. 48, 6*f.*: *iter peregrinum nec interdicere per me nec audenter suadere praesumo.*

[69]*Ep.* 78 Tangl. p. 169.

[70]For the view that Lullus first came to know Boniface in Rome see Tangl. '*Studien zur Neuausgabe der Bonifatiusbriefe*', *Neus Arch. f. ält, deutsche Geschichtsk.* XLI (1919), p. 14, n. 1.

[71]*Ep.* 103 Tangl. pp. 227, 24*f.*:

> Otia dum vagabundus amabam dulcia credens,
> Quae constat cunctis animabus noxia semper.

The Council of Châlon-sur-Saône (813) can. 45 demanded of Charlemagne measures against the evildoers who took the road as pilgrims to Tours or Rome: *Mon. Germ. Con..* II, 1, pp. 282, 23*f.*

secondary one of ascetical self-interest, and, instead of a living community of faith, we have—crudely expressed—the struggle for the
establishment of a Church imposing obligations of a legal and magical
nature. Certainly, this does not conclude the history of ascetic journeying and abandonment of home. These also played their part in the
high Middle Ages, when they became still more widespread and
arduous, being reanimated by certain sects and Orders, and by fresh
influences from the East. At the same time, a certain stage is concluded
with Boniface. The details we have given do not claim to exhaust the
question; their intention is simply to bring out explicitly the connection, hardly noticed before, which, in the history of this ideal,
subsists between East and West and between antiquity and the Middle
Ages.

Admittedly, the historical connection is not enough to account completely for this strange phenomenon, which, indeed, is by no means
peculiar to Christianity. Ascetic abandonment of one's homeland is
more than an accidental phenomenon, appearing at one moment and
then vanishing, a curiosity arbitrarily dug up from the infinite reper-
toire of monastic and religious self-chastisement. In the ultimate
analysis it reflects a law of religious psychology, valid in all ages. It is
the crudest expression of the painful and strenuous effort to cut loose
from the accustomed way of life, domestic and traditional, an effort
everyone must carry through if God is to be for him, as for the ancient
monks, a real personal experience, so that it destroys the dulling inner
attachment to house and country, to what is inherited and personal
and therefore loved. 'The man whom God seeks is without a
country.' He alone who is ready to abandon his last possession, his
own self, can be given anew by God the incomparable good of the
fatherland and every other earthly good—in fact, we believe, receive
it in truth for the first time, and only so follow out to the end the way
entered upon by the monastic *xeniteuontes* and *peregrini*. But this final
sacrifice is beyond the reach of the man who abandons country for
ascetic reasons. For there is only one genuine way of absolute abandonment of self, which is direct personal service of others and this way
cannot be found by one who flees to a strange land and to the desert.
Like any other ascetic ideal, that of abandonment of country has its
nobility, but, fundamentally, it is a demonic and despairing distortion
of the Christian reality.

Books referred to in the text which are available in English

Karl Barth: *Church Dogmatics* Vol. IV 2 (1958) trans. G. W Bromiley, T. & T. Clark, Edinburgh; Alec R. Allenson, Inc, Naperville, Ill. (U.S. distributors).

Dietrich Bonhoeffer: *The Cost of Discipleship* (revd. ed. 1959) trans. R. H. Fuller, SCM Press, London and Macmillan, New York.

Günther Bornkamm: *Jesus of Nazareth* (1960) trans. I. & F. McLuskey, Hodder & Stoughton, London and Harper & Bros, New York.

Rudolf Bultmann: *Theology of the New Testament* (1951-1955: 2 vols.) trans. Kendrick Grobel, SCM Press, London and Scribner's, New York.
Primitive Christianity in its contemporary setting (1956) trans. R. H. Fuller, Thames & Hudson, London and Meridian, New York. Also issued in Fontana Library (1960).
The History of the Synoptic Tradition (1963) trans. John Marsh, Blackwell, Oxford and Harper & Row, New York.

Hans Conzelmann: *The Theology of St Luke* (1960) trans. G. Buswell, Faber, London and Harper & Bros, New York.

Oscar Cullmann: *Early Christian Worship* (1953) trans. A. Stewart Todd and James B. Torrance, SCM Press, London and Regnery, Chicago.
Peter: Disciple, Apostle, Martyr (revd. ed. 1962) trans. Floyd V. Filson, SCM Press, London and Westminster Press, Philadelphia.

Martin Dibelius: *From Tradition to Gospel* (1934) trans. (in collaboration with author) B. L. Woolf, Nicholson & Watson, London and Scribner's, New York.
Studies in the Acts of the Apostles (1956) trans. Mary Ling, SCM Press, London and Scribner's, New York.

Erich Frank: *Philosophical Understanding and Religious Truth* (new ed. 1967) trans. Prof & Mrs Ludwitz Edelstein, Oxford, New York.

*Adolf von Harnack: *History of Dogma* (1903-07: 7 vols.) trans. Neil Buchanan, based on the 3rd German edition, Little, Brown & Co, Boston.
Expansion of Christianity in the First Three Centuries (1904-05) trans. and ed. James Moffatt, Putnam, New York.

Werner Georg Kümmel: *Man in the New Testament* (revd. ed. 1963) trans. John J. Vincent, Epworth, London and Westminster Press, Philadelphia.

*These also appear in paperback: the first in Dover Books (Constable), London and the second in Harper Torchbooks, New York.

Ernst Lohmeyer: *The Lord's Prayer* (1965) trans. John Bowden, Collins, London and Harper & Row, New York.

André Parrot: *Golgotha and the Church of the Holy Sepulchre* (1957) trans. E. Hudson, SCM Press, London and Philosophical Library, New York.

John A. T. Robinson: *The Body:* A Study in Pauline Theology (1952) SCM Press, London; U.S. distributors, Alec R. Allenson.

James M. Robinson: *The Problem of History in Mark* (1957) SCM Press, London; U.S. distributors, Alec R. Allenson.